D0734680

Philosophy of Physical Education

BROWN

PHYSICAL EDUCATION SERIES

Edited by

Aileene Lockhart
University of Southern California
Los Angeles, California

Philosophy of Physical Education

Randolph W. Webster, Ph.D.
Professor of Health, Physical Education and Recreation

Michigan State University
East Lansing, Michigan

WM. C. BROWN COMPANY PUBLISHERS
135 SOUTH LOCUST STREET • DUBUQUE, IOWA 52003

Library of Congress Catalog Number: 65-20895

Manufactured by WM. C. BROWN CO. INC., Dubuque, Iowa
Printed in U. S. A.

To My Wife

Leona C. Webster

Preface

Successful understanding of any profession depends mainly upon knowledge of the origin, nature, meaning, aims, and objectives of that profession. Finding the underlying truths and making interpretations is a function of philosophy. It is extremely important for students preparing to teach and for teachers already on the job to know and to understand the purpose and fundamental bases of their profession. The success of their teaching, the motivation they give to their students, the examples they set for others to follow all reflect their philosophy of life and the philosophy underlying their specific area of teaching.

This book is written with the hope that it will contribute to a better understanding of physical education and aid both prospective and experienced teachers in formulating a philosophy of life and of physical education and/or re-evaluating it in terms of new information.

This book is divided into four parts. In Part I the antecedents of physical education are discussed. This section includes consideration of the meaning and significance of physical education; the historical background of basic philosophy; some classical contemporary philosophies of education; and the historical background of physical education from primitive societies up to the present time. This background provides the reader with fundamental knowledge and information with which he may formulate his own personal philosophy.

In Part II a way of building a personal philosophy of physical education is described. The discussion begins with a consideration of the meaning of physical education and its relation to other phases of the profession such as health education, recreation, varsity athletics, intramural sports, safety education, school camping, and outdoor education. This leads to a presentation of some factors influencing philosophy of physical education such as biological, economic, historical, political, psychological, religious, and sociological. It further discusses a philosophic procedure for constructing a philosophy, giving definitions and examples of the elements of a philosophy of physical education and a method of analyzing facts and, finally, synthesizing them into a formal belief.

It is essential to know and to understand the historical background and philosophic tenets of one's profession and to be able to formulate one's belief from them, but this alone would be of little value if it were not possible to apply this to life in general and to one's teaching field in particular. In Part III, therefore, philosophy in action relative to some basic issues in physical education is considered. The thought here is that if philosophy really is important and if it is to help in the understanding of one's profession, to assist in solving problems and to make better teachers, then it must be practical and it must be used to understand the basic issues of the profession. A few important basic issues are selected for study; these include administration and curriculum construction in physical education.

Part IV is devoted to a discussion of establishing a system of values as the culminating aspect of philosophizing and of formulating one's philosophy.

To assist in this study and discussion, questions for review and a bibliography and supplementary references are placed at the end of each chapter.

This publication is designed as a text for professional upper-class and graduate students in physical education, and should serve as a source book for experienced teachers, administrators, and supervisors of physical education.

The writing of this book has been a distinct joy and a source of much pleasure to the author. It has entailed a great amount of research, study, travel and interviewing, writing and editing. It is hoped that the reader will be rewarded for his efforts in reading and studying this text by gaining some helpful knowledge about philosophy and perhaps, more important, by being stimulated to search further about the ultimate nature, meaning, and interpretation of philosophy.

The writer wishes to acknowledge the assistance, the inspiration and patience of his wife, Leona, during the laborious and painstaking endeavor of writing this book. He wishes to thank the many professional leaders who gave him information, criticisms, and suggestions. He greatly appreciates the many helpful suggestions, comments, and constructive criticism received from the professional editor, Dr. Aileene Lockhart, in preparing this book for publication. He further wishes to acknowledge the useful comments and friendly understanding of his colleagues at Michigan State University.

Michigan State University
East Lansing, Michigan

Randolph W. Webster

Contents

PART I

Antecedents of Physical Education

PART II

Building a Personal Philosophy of Physical Education

PART III

Philosophy in Action

PART IV

Establishing a System of Values

Part I

Antecedents of Physical Education

Meaning and Significance of Philosophy

1

The understanding and application of basic principles of engineering and designing are necessary in order to build a strong, durable and useful building. Similarly, understanding the application of historical antecedents and basic principles of older philosophic structures is necessary in order to build an effective, practical and dynamic philosophy of physical education. It is for this reason that basic philosophy and its fields of study are discussed first in this chapter; this is followed by a consideration of personal philosophy of life, educational philosophy, and the meaning of physical education.

BASIC PHILOSOPHY

The word "basic" carries the connotation of something fundamental like "at the bottom," a cornerstone, or a foundation for something. Everything rests upon a foundation. The theories of the early Greeks and Christians are the cornerstones of our present Western philosophy. For further clarification of the subject of basic philosophy, let us consider the meaning of the word "philosophy."

The word philosophy is derived from both the Latin and Greek languages and fundamentally means "love of truth" and/or "love of wisdom." Love of wisdom means the desire to search for the real facts and values in life and in the universe, and to evaluate and to interpret these with an unbiased and unprejudiced mind. Philosophy is concerned with questions of right and wrong, justice, freedom, and discretion. Though there is a distinction between philosophy and science, philosophy can be said to be a science since it organizes knowledge about man and the universe for the purpose of evaluation and comprehension. As Durant says, "Every science begins as philosophy and ends as art; it arises in hypothesis and flows into achievement." (3:2) Philosophy criticizes, evaluates the worth of things, and synthesizes facts; while science describes, discovers and analyzes facts. For the welfare of humanity and for the advancement of knowledge and its proper use, every scientist should be a philosopher and every philosopher should be a scientist. Scientists discovered atomic energy; they know how it works and how to use it, but only philosophers deliberate about where and for what purpose it should be used. Both processes are essential.

Originally philosophy included all of the physical and social sciences. As knowledge in each increased, however, many splintered off and became special disciplines, the first being astronomy, chemistry, physics and others of the physical science group. Later economics, psychology and others of the social science group developed to the point that they too became separate disciplines. This left meaning, value, appreciation, interpretation and evaluation as the subject matter of current philosophy.

Philosophy is comprised of several basic fields of study, namely aesthetics, ethics, logic, metaphysics, epistemology, and politics. Aesthetics is the study of the nature of beauty, as in the arts: painting, sculpture, music, drama, dance, and others. Ethics is the study of the nature of good and ideal conduct; from this is built a moral philosophy, a knowledge of right and wrong, a standard of right by which to live. Logic is the study of the theory and practice of investigating the truth through methods of thought and reasoning such as induction and deduction, major and minor premises and conclusion. Metaphysics is the study of the ultimate nature of all things concerning man and the universe; it seeks to explain what is real, what really exists. Epistemology is the study of the theory of knowledge: its origin, limits, and nature. Politics is a study of the various forms of government or social organizations such as anarchism, aristocracy, communism, democracy, monarchy, and socialism.

These are the fields of inquiry, then, from which one seeks answers to the problems of beauty, of right and wrong, of reasoning, of what is real, of how we know what is real, and of government. These basic concepts are considered in all philosophies. One may philosophize about all aspects of life but only that deemed pertinent to the subject of this book will be discussed here — historical and personal, and applied as to subject matter — education and physical education.

HISTORICAL

One of the ways of obtaining an understanding of philosophy in general is to study the thought of great men of the past. This information is very useful in helping to formulate one's own philosophy of life and that of special teaching subjects. Only a few examples have been selected, but these should provide the reader with a brief historic account of philosophy and give him a frame of reference for considering the other philosophies discussed in this text.

Greek Philosophy

The Greeks, among the earliest known philosophers, advanced many theories in an attempt to explain the nature and composition of the universe. Some said the earth was made of one or several elements such as water, atoms, and air. Thales, who lived in Miletus about 600 B.C., declared that everything in the world was made of water. This idea was developed from the observation that water turns into steam and air when heated, and into a solid piece of ice when frozen (4:2). Democritus, one of the ancient cosmologists, thought the universe was made up of atoms, small particles of different shapes and sizes which moved according to natural law. He thought that the human body also was composed of atoms: body atoms and soul atoms. This theory later became known as "atomism" and is related to "materialism" and "determinism." (5:22-23)

Anaximines, another philosopher who lived in Miletus, suggested that everything in the universe was made of air. He reasoned that since men and animals were animate bodies and needed air to live, air must be transformed into bones, flesh, and blood as well as into clouds, wind, earth, and water.

Heraclitus, on the other hand, criticized the idea that the world could be reduced to elements such as water, air and atoms. He believed that since fire was never the same and was always changing things, that since everything in the universe was forever changing, and since change is a fundamental characteristic of the world, fire must be what the world is made of. This idea of "everything always changing" is similar to that concept of "transient processes" used today in physics. Anaxagoras thought the explanation of order and arrangement of the world and its composition could be found in the "nous-mind," or reason. Pythagoras tried to explain reality through number or quantitative terms.

Many other of these early philosophers had similar ideas about the nature of the universe. As study and exploration continued, however, doubt of and dissatisfaction with these theories began to appear. How does change take place? Is there really a change? How does one know? These and other questions were asked. The Sophists were responsible for starting this new kind of inquiry and turned attention from cosmology to human affairs. Socrates did not believe in cosmology either, but unlike the Sophists, he believed that knowledge of self was the only knowledge obtainable. He believed that goodness was based on knowledge and evil on ignorance. Socrates, a moral philosopher, tried to teach the young men of his time the principles of righteous living. He was interested mainly in man as a total unit in a social environment. In this respect his view was similar to that of the modern behaviorists. The early behaviorists were more interested, however, in physical environments. (5:28)

Plato, who was Socrates' pupil, explained for the first time in a systematic way the difference between mind and matter. He was an idealist and formulated the doctrine of ideas. He believed that the ideas of the mind which are revealed by reason are more real than those revealed by the senses; to him the conception of the world obtained through our senses provides only copies of ideas in the ideal world. The tree or flower that one sees passes away, but the general idea of the tree or flower is always the same. This doctrine of ideas, to a large extent, is a source of dualism. Aristotle, the last of the great philosophers of ancient Greece and a pupil of Plato, believed also that ideas existed, but in addition he believed that matter and form existed. Further, he thought they existed eternally together in some manner of continuity. This idea of continuity in a somewhat different concept is employed in psychology today.

There were other philosophies proposed by many other men. Two rival schools of thought which were particularly prominent during the last centuries of ancient Greece were held by the Stoics and the Epicureans. The Stoics believed knowledge helped one find his place in Nature, that Nature was perfect and anything which happened must be accepted cheerfully and calmly. Without this point of view a person could not be a true Stoic. This was a belief in suppression of desires by the mind in the interest of goodness. Epicureans believed that pleasure was the source of all good but, contrary to popular belief, this value was best obtained from simplicity and moderate living.

Philosophy of the Early Christians

The philosophy in the early Christian period was influenced by that of Plato and the Neo-Platonists. The Christian leaders thought there was change and imperfection in the universe, as some of the Greek philosophers believed, but they felt also that God was perfect and unchanging. Men who tried to harmonize these two views were called Apologists. St. Augustine was foremost in formulating this theory. In the Middle Ages, however, philosophers turned more to the theory of Aristotle: " . . . that forms existed in things, but were distinct from matter." (4:20) This attempt to harmonize the beliefs of the Christian leaders in the medieval period and the philosophy of Aristotle and other Greeks was called Scholasticism. One of the greatest and best known of these "Schoolmen," as they were called, was St. Thomas Aquinas. Others were Anselm, Peter Abelard, Duns Scotus, and William of Occam.

It will be noted by the reader that there were many philosophies. More have since been formulated but are mostly borrowed and expanded from these early ideas. Hence, many theories today stem from some of these beginnings, viz., naturalism, idealism, realism, and pragmatism. These four have been selected for review, study, and discussion in the following chapters because they seem particularly pertinent to the field of education and physical education.

SIGNIFICANCE OF PERSONAL PHILOSOPHY OF LIFE

Accumulation, interpretation and application of beliefs, principles, laws and knowledge about man, the universe, and reality of life give purpose, meaning and direction to life. From these it is possible for each individual to form his own life objectives and use them as directional posts and achievement points to guide his steps and shape his destiny. Each person has his own personal philosophy whether or not he realizes it. The way one thinks and talks, what one does and says, the manner in which words are spoken, one's reactions to people, their reactions to you, all indicate a certain philosophy of life. One's personal philosophy of life may be very difficult to write out on paper. This task is highly recommended, however, for it clarifies what one actually thinks and believes and lives. It may come as a shock to some to discover what they are actually doing, what their life objectives are, and the direction in which they are going. Sometimes it may seem easier to have someone else describe our personal philosophy. This may be done through observation of another's actions and speech and his reactions to the many daily situations and problems of life. However, to wrestle with oneself, to evaluate, to modify and thus to evolve one's own philosophy is much more beneficial.

The question is not whether one has a personal philosophy, but what it is. The compelling inward and outward drives which propel one may be weak or strong, good or bad. It may be that the source of power is weak though the objectives which are sought are worthy. It may be that the source of power is strong but the objectives unworthy. Or a third and better possibility, it may be that the source of power is strong and the objectives worthy. One's success in life, therefore, depends to a great extent upon the strength of his drives and upon the worthiness of his objectives. Without a philosophy of life one would be like a ship without a rudder drifting over the sea of life aimlessly, going no place in particular, doing little good if any, with danger always imminent and shipwreck a possibility. Life cannot be satisfying, happy and successful without a good personal philosophy of life. Happiness and success, however, are relative terms. Some people have more of these qualities than others. The degree to which these are attained depends upon the kind of objectives set up and the force expended for their accomplishment.

Positive Personal Philosophies

What are some examples of precepts or maxims by which people live? Some live by an acceptable or positive philosophy, while others prefer to live by an unacceptable or negative philosophy. On the positive side we find that some say they live by the golden rule: the precept that one should behave toward others as he would wish they would behave toward him. (Matt. 7:12) Others say that uppermost in their minds is keeping the "Ten Commandments." (Exodus 20:3-17) Theodore Roosevelt advised people to, "Do the best you can, wherever you are with what you have, all the time." Dr. Albert Schweitzer, the great philosopher and physician, directs his daily activities by the philosophy "Reverence for Life." (6:621) During the last world war an Army chaplain was credited with having originated the following prayer to help the sick, wounded, and mentally distressed soldiers to recuperate: "God grant me the serenity to accept the things I cannot change, the courage to change the things I can and the wisdom to know the difference."

Other positive thoughts on how to live come from Thoreau who said that to become a philosopher is not only to possess a keen intellect and to make certain accomplishments ". . . but to so love wisdom as to live, according to its dictates, a life of simplicity, independence, magnanimity and trust." (3:2) The Master in His teaching expressed His views upon the good life when He said, "Ye shall know the truth and the truth shall make you free." (St. John 8:32) In this statement it is significant to note that wealth, position, influence, distinction or prestige were not mentioned as the things which can make us free; only truth was mentioned.

"Live and help live" is another maxim exemplifying a positive and righteous way of thinking and living. This carries the idea of "What's mine is yours and I will share it with you." The type of individual who lives by such a philosophy is needed in our society, in all our organizations and professions. Willing workers, doers and leaders are needed who will help and share with others. Reflected here is the idea of service which illustrates a great precept of life: to give is better than to receive and, by giving, many good things will be received. This could be considered a law of all life. Animals, birds, plants, forests, oceans, lakes, and rivers also give as well as receive something in their existence.

Negative Philosophies of Life

Unfortunately, the lives of all people are not guided or directed by a positive philosophy of goodness and service. Rather, many are guided by a negative philosophy of plunder, selfishness, greed and pleasure. The philosophy of some is epitomized by the slogans, "Might makes right" or "What's mine is mine if I can take it." The individual who subscribes to such beliefs demands things without working for them. He gives nothing, produces nothing, but takes everything. Another negative kind of philosophy is characterized by the individual who says, "What's mine is mine if I can keep it." This is a form of selfishness and greed which contributes little or nothing toward improving the well-being of humanity. Embodied in this is the idea "As long as you don't bother me, I won't bother you," an unwholesome maxim by which to live. There are other persons whose sole motive is to extract as much pleasure and satisfaction out of life as they can regardless of how it may affect anyone else. They take their pleasures where they find them and "live it up" today because tomorrow may not come. The emphasis is on material things and gratification of desires. These people try to get what they want and do what they please with little or no regard for law, order, custom, or truth. These are the "gimme" people of today, who want security with little or no effort on their part, who wish to live with little discipline or restraint. Surely these are not the kind of people who can be depended upon to give new life, new ideas, integrity, thriftiness, industriousness, leadership and wisdom to the world.

Many other examples of personal philosophy might be cited for each person has one, and it is demonstrated by his thoughts, actions and deeds. Unfortunately, some persons may have a double philosophy, one that they profess and one they actually live by. It may be possible for a person to have a double philosophy and not know it. It is more difficult to see inconsistency in one's self than in someone else. Of course it is conceivable that some people may live this way by choice.

The success and happiness of one's life depend upon the philosophy chosen. The important questions each person must ask of himself are: What philosophy have I chosen? Will it work for the good of humanity as well as for myself? Do I actually know what my philosophy is?

Important Questions Concerning One's Philosophy

Discussion of several questions may help in identifying and understanding some of the situations which influence the formation of one's philosophy.

What are some factors which influence one's philosophy? There are many which have a bearing on its kind and quality. They can be classified mainly under hereditary and environmental factors, particularly the latter. The type of physical constitution, mental traits and characteristics inherited affect one's personal view. Are they good or bad, weak or strong, susceptible to malfunction and weakness or superior in quality? This is not to say that a physically handicapped person necessarily has a negative philosophy. Rather, because of it he might develop a very fine philosophy. Similarly, neither does it follow that a person who has no mental or physical defects necessarily has a good philosophy. He would have more reason to, but there are factors, environmental ones, which influence his thinking. One way or another, however, and to a relative degree, the type and kind of physical and mental qualities inherited do have some influence upon one's point of view. Environmental factors have more influence and these will be discussed at length later. Suffice it to say here that the customs and traditions of one's community, the social and economic status of one's family, the amount and quality of education obtained and the political and religious views held have a very profound effect upon one's personal philosophy.

Another question for consideration is: Does one's philosophy change? There are two aspects involved here, one denoting a voluntary desire for change and the other suggesting the occurrence of a gradual subconscious change. In either case a change of viewpoint does take place. Whether this belief is for better or for worse depends upon the amount and quality of knowledge obtained and upon the influence of environmental factors. All experiences affect one's life one way or another. The more one learns, the more people one meets, the more likely one's philosophy will be changed. Therefore, one should be careful to select the kind of knowledge and the type of friends which are conducive to constructive living.

Still another question for reflection is: What effect do one's personal beliefs have upon one's philosophy of education? The answer to this question can be given by citing an example. It is very difficult, for instance, to teach under the theory of naturalism if one believes in strict discipline and authority, for it is difficult to separate personal views from methods of teaching. Personal qualities and characteristics, such as friendliness, initiative, integrity, dependability, loyalty, adaptability, and love for people, or the negative opposites of these, most certainly will carry over and thus influence one's philosophy of teaching.

SIGNIFICANCE OF PHILOSOPHY OF EDUCATION

For clarity and understanding it seems appropriate to begin with a discussion of meaning and purpose of education and then continue by considering the relationship of philosophy of education to one's personal philosophy and to that of physical education.

Meaning and Purpose

Education has been defined by many writers and has had about as many definitions as there are authors, for education means different things to different people.

John Locke believed that education should, through a study of the most frequently used and most important daily activities, prepare a person physically and mentally *for* living. John Dewey, on the other hand, emphasized the present, not the future, saying that education *is* life, not preparation for life. He contended that education is obtained through the process of continuous experience which helps an individual to grow and be better able to make adjustments in light of new experience. His method of education was one of problem solving and pupil-teacher planning. The teacher's role, according to Dewey, was to stimulate, to assist and to interpret. (2:315)

Johann Friedrich Herbart, on the other hand, thought the purpose of education was the moral development of the individual. Goodness, he felt, could be learned and therefore must be taught. He believed that knowledge already attained would help a person to interpret new knowledge. This is called the doctrine of apperception, a doctrine which he originated. His method of teaching included five formal steps: (a) preparation – the process of recalling to mind ideas from past experiences which help assimilate and interpret the new; (b) presentation – stating and explaining the new experience to be used; (c) association – actual assimilation of new experience by combining it with the old; (d) generalization – formulation of definitions, general rules or principles from the analyzed experiences; (e) application – evaluation of the generalized idea through testing its ability to solve assigned problems. (2:249)

The aim of education, according to Horace Mann, was to educate people for social efficiency, civic virtue and character. Education should be free, universal and nonsectarian. Mann was one of the founders of the free public schools of the United States. (1:226)

All outstanding educators have definite views on education. Johann Heinrich Pestalozzi thought that education should develop the whole child morally, mentally and physically, be based on observation and reasoning, must organize and direct sense impressions and stimulate self-activity. Education, he felt, should be well-organized and graded according to the natural development of the child's instincts and his mental and physical capacities. Discipline to him was freedom with control, and learning proceeded mainly from doing. (1:348) Herbert Spencer viewed education as a process to prepare one for complete living and felt that a knowledge of science should be applied to all subjects. (1:470)

Education may be viewed as a process or a product. As a process, it may generally be said to be the instructional means which produce desirable changes in the individual, making him the most useful citizen. Instructional processes include all aspects of learning through self-help, experience, informal and formal teaching in schools. The desirable changes are concerned with forms of behavior, forming habits and skills of body and mind, acquiring knowledge and developing abilities.

Views and Concepts of Education

From the foregoing discussion and from other sources several prominent views on education can be stated very briefly.

Education as a continuous reconstruction of experience. According to this point of view opportunity should be provided for continuous growth and development through daily experiences, and experiences of the past combined with the new help one to understand present situations.

Education as adjustment. The growth and change which occur in the individual help him make adjustments. Through analysis of experience he is better able to solve perplexing problems. Ability to adjust enhances his chance for happiness and success.

EDUCATION AS GROWTH. This is the concept that education is a process of growth which is evaluated in terms of the potential for further growth.

EDUCATION AS DISCIPLINE. A specific study designed to develop knowledge and efficiency in a given branch of learning is sometimes referred to as "a discipline." Generally speaking, all kinds of studies and branches of learning are forms of discipline applied either by outside authority and/or by the individual. A person may or may not really want to work for a college education, but he knows that if he submits himself to all the requirements of a particular curriculum and graduates he is more likely to be successful in life. Another viewpoint is that discipline involves the study of a difficult subject not so much for its own sake but for the self-discipline and training it provides.

EDUCATION AS CULTURE. Culture is acquired in many ways. A wide range of experiences is one major source of culture. The study of history is another source. Customs, traditions, folkways, and institutions of mankind are other sources of culture. It is helpful to know the happenings, events, and experiences of the past in order to understand what education has been, what it is and how it might be better formulated and directed in the future. Knowledge of the problems of the past help solve those of the present and future.

WHAT IS PHILOSOPHY OF EDUCATION?

Basic philosophy is composed of both speculative and practical philosophy. Speculative philosophy is concerned with the theories of the nature of reality and the nature of knowledge as in metaphysics and epistemology. Practical philosophy is concerned with the study of the nature of ideal conduct and creation and appreciation of beauty as in ethics and aesthetics. Philosophy of education is the application of the principles of these areas to education. Philosophy of education is concerned about the accomplishment of objectives that have been established for education, about their meaning, value, nature and interpretation. It is not as concerned about the tools and techniques necessary to obtain these objectives. This is the task of science. However, philosophy of education is related to science just as philosophy in general is related to science. All science began as a philosophy and many philosophers were once scientists, e.g., Kant (physics and geography), Descartes and Leibnitz (mathematics) and Laplace (astronomy). Though philosophy of education is related to science it differs particularly in its methods of obtaining information. Philosophy is interested in the experiences of man, nature, value and worth. Science obtains knowledge through controlled experimentation, scientific measurement, verification, organization, classification, analysis and comparison.

Why a Philosophy of Education

Philosophy of education is needed in order to give purpose and direction to educational thinking and action. One's philosophy of life cannot help but permeate and filter through to one's philosophy of education. Principles and objectives of education by means of which knowledge is understood, evaluated and interpreted, come from philosophy of education. A sound philosophy is essential for intelligent and successful teaching.

Meaning and Purpose of Physical Education

Physical education may be described by considering its characteristics. It is a phase of general education, that is, it is a part of the whole instructional process. It is education through the physical, not of the physical. For this purpose, it employs motor activities which involve both small and large muscle groups. It affords experiences in many related areas, such as health and recreation, and it provides opportunity for the development of honesty, fair play, cooperation and sociability in connection with all kinds of play activities and games. Physical education, then, is a phase of general education which specifically employs motor activities and related mental, moral, and social experiences for the purpose of developing an integrated individual and useful citizen.

Relationship of Physical Education to Philosophy of Life

Included in an adequate philosophy of life is a high regard for health and safety, for self and for others. The treatment accorded the body and mind is related to physical and mental health. An individual has only one body, one mind and one soul; they cannot be traded in or exchanged for new or different ones. It is paramount that they be used properly, treated carefully and cared for wisely for the most rewarding results to self and mankind. Daily thoughts and actions not only exemplify one's philosophy but also most certainly influence the philosophy of teaching physical education or coaching athletic sports.

Relationship of Physical Education to Philosophy of Education

Knowing the meaning and purpose of physical education, education, and philosophy itself helps one to see the interrelationships among these three areas and to understand where and how philosophy of physical education is related to that of education. Considerations in the former two are given to the same basic elements: principles, aims, objectives, standards, criteria, subject matter and methods of instruction. The ultimate objective is the same – that of producing the most useful citizen – but the approach by which the objective is reached and the area of study emphasized are different. In physical education the approach is mainly through the physical; in other aspects of education the approach is mainly through the mental. Both are involved always, however, for the whole individual goes to school and should be instructed according to his total needs and interests. One's philosophy of physical education therefore should not differ from his philosophy of education.

Why a Philosophy of Physical Education

A philosophy of physical education is necessary for the same reasons that a philosophy of life and a philosophy of education are necessary. How else can one's professional course of thought and action be charted progressively and intelligently? How can one know what is important to teach? How can one know the value of what is taught and whether or not the results obtained are desirable and beneficial? These and other questions should be raised in an endeavor to form a workable, consistent and useful philosophy.

SUMMARY

In the foregoing pages four areas have been discussed: basic philosophy, significance of personal philosophy, significance of philosophy of education and the meaning and purpose of physical education. Consideration has been given to these topics because they give introductory and basic information upon which the remainder of this book is predicated. It has been seen that everyone has a philosophy of life and that it influences his philosophy of education and physical education.

In the next chapter consideration will be given to selected basic philosophies which have distinctive implications for education and physical education.

QUESTIONS FOR REVIEW AND DISCUSSION

1. What is the basic meaning of the word "philosophy"? With what fundamental questions is philosophy concerned?
2. Originally, philosophy included what sciences? Discuss how the various sciences splintered off and left the subject matter we call philosophy today.

3. Name and discuss the basic fields which comprise philosophy.
4. Name and discuss three early Greek philosophers who tried to explain the nature of the universe and its composition. What contribution did they make to philosophy?
5. Who were the Sophists? What contribution did they make to philosophy?
6. What philosopher thought the universe was made up of atoms? Do you think this early idea may have helped in the discovery of atomic energy?
7. Who were the Apologists? What were their views?
8. Discuss the significance of a personal philosophy of life. Explain your personal philosophy.
9. Discuss the views of the following educators: John Locke, Johann Herbart, Johann Pestalozzi, and Herbert Spencer.
10. What is philosophy of education? Define. Explain.
11. What is the meaning and purpose of physical education?
12. Discuss the relationship of physical education to philosophy of life.
13. Discuss the relationship of physical education to philosophy of education.
14. Discuss the importance of having a philosophy of physical education.

Bibliography

1. CUBBERLY, ELLWOOD, P. *Public Education in the United States.* New York: Houghton Mifflin Co., 1934.
2. DUGGAN, STEPHEN. *A Student's Textbook in the History of Education.* New York: A. Appleton-Century Co., 1936.
3. DURANT, WILL. *The Story of Philosophy.* New York: Garden City Publishing Co., Inc., 1938.
4. FROST, JR., S. E. *Basic Teachings of the Great Philosophers.* New York: Barnes and Noble, Inc., 1957.
5. HEIDBREDER, EDNA F. *Seven Psychologies.* New York: D. Appleton-Century Co., 1933.
6. SELDES, GEORGE. *The Great Quotations.* New York: Lyle Stuart, 1960.

2

Naturalism

We have learned something about the origin, the early development and meaning of philosophy. We have discussed the meaning of education and the reasons for a philosophy of education. In the following discussion the historical approach will be employed in considering the development, modification and application of philosophies of education because of the interest, meaning, purpose, and use this method should bring to the physical education student.

Throughout the history of man interest has been focused on some form of education. Primitive man's attention and activities were centered mainly around supplying basic needs of food, shelter, clothing, protection against wild beasts and the elements of nature. The system of education consequently was simple. The children learned the necessary activities of life from their parents and other members of the family. They learned to hunt, to fish, to fight; in general, they learned to survive in their environment. Survival was the main aim of education.

Life in subsequent societies was not quite so simple. Certain ways of doing things developed into customs and traditions. The purpose of education, therefore, was to perpetuate the culture. Gradually, the simple method of education by parents was insufficient to teach children all that was required of them. It became necessary for group leaders and older men to instruct youth at certain times, for example at puberty, an occasion for initiation and celebration. Youth were instructed in the ritual and procedure and if they passed all the tests, they were accepted into the adult group with all its rights and privileges. Instructors thus were used for a definite purpose.

As societies became more complex group leaders devoted more and more of their time to instructing youth in ritualistic work, custom, tradition, and folklore. Since much of this involved their gods and centered about religion, the instruction was given in the worship places. Thus, it was natural for education to have a religious flavor.

In later societies, as more emphasis was placed upon education, the group leaders of the earlier periods became the teachers and philosophers. These thinkers began to be concerned about methods of teaching and the aims and objectives of education. Every philosopher has had something to say about education. Since views differed and social, economic and political conditions changed, philosophers found it difficult to agree on the kind of education youth should have and the method by which it should be taught.

Many formal philosophies have developed over the years but there are four which are most distinctive and have had major influences on education: naturalism, idealism, realism, and pragmatism. Naturalism will be discussed first since it is the oldest of the organized philosophies of the western world.

MEANING OF NATURALISM

The meaning of naturalism becomes clear when one understands that the word "Nature" in philosophy has a wide perspective. It is concerned not only with nature in the sense of land, forests, rivers, and wild life but also with astronomy, chemistry, physics, man and his culture and the continual interdependence of these on one another. It is thought of as a physical world or universe and as a region of regularity. (4:39) Naturalism from the standpoint of metaphysics is the theory that all reality is Nature. Nothing exists beyond, above, or apart from it. There is no God, no soul other than that which is found in Nature. If one thinks of Nature as did some of the ancient philosophers, such as Thales, Anaximenes, Anaximander and others who tried to describe the composition of the world as one inert substance moving in space, this naturalistic view is called "materialism." If one thinks of Nature as did Spencer, who contended the world was made out of energy, it is called "energism." Though Spencer agreed with others that the world was composed of one substance, he did not believe it was solid matter, but energy.

Naturalism developed through the various stages of atomism of the ancient philosophers, through the early simple forms of materialism to the period of modern scientific investigations of exact science. When naturalism began to employ the sciences to explain reality objectively, it became the parent of realism. (1:83) There is also some relationship between modern naturalism and pragmatism because both consider the sciences the only source of knowledge. They differ, however, in other respects. Pragmatism depends more upon human society and less upon the physical universe for its meaning and concepts, while in naturalism the reverse is true. Naturalism from an educational point of view stresses that the aim of education is the development of that which is natural in man.

HISTORICAL ASPECTS OF NATURALISM

Historical aspects of naturalism will be discussed under the names of some of the various philosophers who were largely responsible for initiating this theory and extending it through the ages.

Ancient Philosophers

Some of the men responsible for initiating the idea of naturalism were Thales, Anaximander, Anaximenes, Leucippus, Democritus, Epicurus and Lucretius. Thales believed that the world was made of one thing: water. Anaximander tried to explain reality in terms of an anonymous fundamental matter. Anaximenes explained reality in terms of air. All three lived in the same century and had two things in common: they tried to explain reality in terms of one substance, although in each case the substance was different, and they did not try to identify this one substance beyond the realm of nature.

Naturalism had its roots more firmly established by the theory of atomism proposed by Leucippus and Democritus who lived in Abdera, Thrace (about 500 B.C.), by Epicurus (341-270 B.C.), and by Lucretius (96-55 B.C.). (1:52) Leucippus and Democritus were the ones who first tried to explain reality from the atomistic view. They thought the world or Nature could be reduced to two things: empty space and atoms. Empty space, they thought, contained no substance. However, they did think that the vacuum contained small indivisible units called atoms. These atoms were of all shapes, sizes and weights, and were free to move about in this empty space. If, when moving about, these atoms came together and formed clusters, "things" came into existence. When these atoms moved apart, "things" were dissolved. These thinkers believed that the mind and soul were composed of atoms, specially fine, smooth, round ones which were very mobile. According to this theory the whole of Nature was formed and developed by the movement of the atoms: animals, plants, minerals, man, customs, traditions, education and related experiences.

Epicurus accepted the philosophical ideas of Democritus and admired the practical, simple and pleasant life he lived in harmony with Nature. Epicurus considered pain and fear as evil and peace and enjoyment as enduring good. His fondness for a simple life of pleasure and contentment does not mean, however, as is often believed, that he was an unrestrained or licentious person. His views of the atomic theory were about the same as those of Democritus in that he reasoned that if everything were made of atoms, including the mind and soul, some way must be found to explain how the mind perceives impressions from objects in the Universe. This process was carried out, he thought, by a film of atoms given off by objects. The film was conveyed through the senses to the mind where it formed a photographic image of the object. Lucretius, the last of these early atomists, lived several centuries after Epicurus. He did not improve or change the atomic theory of Epicurus, but tried to promote it and identified himself with it.

Early Modern and Modern Philosophers

Some of the greater philosophers who accepted the idea of the early naturalists and developed the naturalistic theory were Hobbes and Rousseau. Thomas Hobbes, (1588-1679), an Englishman, was famous for his work in political theory as well as in philosophy. He wrote extensively on social development and conduct and did some work in physiology, psychology, and physics. Hobbes' views were undoubtedly influenced by some of the events of his time, particularly the civil wars in France and England. These disturbances apparently created in him an interest in studying government. He believed that political organization was necessary for the good of man and that the ruler had the right to decide the type of education his subjects should have because this could strengthen the state. A strong state could preserve peace and end the strife and competition of man against man. Everyone was to be trained to serve the state. This is an example of education controlled by the ruler purportedly for the good of the state. (3:245) Great strides in science were made during his time and he himself was a student and writer in this field. His study of the laws of Nature influenced his philosophy. Although he was not an atomist, he did believe, like the early naturalists, that Nature was an arrangement of bodies moving in space. His natural philosophy therefore was concerned with the property of bodies. (1:61)

Jean Jacques Rousseau (1712-1778) was a great French writer and educator. *Social Contract,* a book on political philosophy, is considered one of his greatest works. In it he advocated the doctrine of democracy, of freedom and equality for the people. He challenged the prevalent idea that the monarch's right to rule was given by God. Instead he claimed that the right to rule was given the monarch by the people, and if he ruled badly the people could rescind that right.

Rousseau was an outstanding writer in other fields also; an exceptional piece of writing was *Émile.* This book was about the education of a boy who was permitted to grow and develop naturally in his own way without interference from society. Rousseau felt that the schools of that day confined boys too much and warped their natural growth, and that society destroyed their inner nature. He proposed that boys' education be organized into five periods. (7:205) From infancy to four years, emphasis was placed on physical development. During this time boys were to run and play and develop physically according to the dictates of their own nature. Boys five to twelve years of age were to develop their senses through life in a world of nature. They were to have a greater variety of, and progressively more, difficult physical activities, plays, games, and sports. They were to observe things in nature, sharpen their senses, and become hardened physically. The sense experiences thus obtained were to supply information and data for future thought processes. Twelve to fifteen was the period for the initiation of a more formal type of education, but only those studies in which youth were interested and could use immediately. This was the period in which the mental powers of the youth were awakened and therefore was the proper time to begin formal instruction. During this period also, youth were to learn something about agricultural activities, manual arts and related subjects so they could learn a trade and support themselves. These activities were also to keep them physically fit.

Fifteen to twenty was the period where the boys received their training in moral, religious, and social learnings. Rousseau felt that the youth had developed sufficiently by this time in powers of reason and judgment to cope with these problems. As they came in contact with people, they would learn about good and evil, how to cooperate, how to make adjustments to changing situations, and how to be of service to man. The fifth and last period was that of matrimony. Here Rousseau had Émile marry an ideal girl named Sophia. Curiously enough she did not have the same naturalistic training as that given to Émile. Rather, she received the conventional type of that time. Rousseau thought that girls should be educated to make men happy and to help them in their work.

Rousseau felt, as did others of his time, that life involved too many restraints. He believed in more freedom — freedom from the restraints of the church as well as from society. He was a naturalist but not from his metaphysical belief, because he was a deist. He believed that God created the Universe but existed apart from it and without any interest in it. Religion was a natural "one" without creeds and dogmas, with the real meaning of human living coming from Nature, not God. He was a naturalist because he enjoyed the simple and quiet life afforded in Nature and because he exalted Nature and prompted naturalistic ideas in his writings and discussions on politics and education. He felt that Nature was good, dependable, orderly and peaceful, but society was bad, irresponsible, restraining and autocratic.

Rousseau had many followers in the field of education. Noteworthy among them were Johann Bernhard Basedow (1723-1790), Johann Heinrich Pestalozzi (1746-1827), Johann Friedrich Guts Muths (1759-1839), Phillipp Emenuel Von Fellenberg (1771-1844), Friedrich Ludwig Jahn (1778-1852) and Friedrich Wilhelm August Froebel (1782-1852). While these educational philosophers did not agree with all of Rousseau's naturalistic ideas they tried to apply many of them to actual teaching.

Basedow, a German student of education, was greatly influenced by Rousseau's ideas. He not only published his views in books but tried to apply them in teaching. He opened a school at Dessau in 1774, the Philanthropinum, where he tried to apply his naturalistic ideas. He believed that instruction should be "child centered" and begin with the materials and things most interesting to the child. (2:216-218)

Pestalozzi, a Swiss, was the greatest of the educators to be influenced by Rousseau. Proper education, he believed, started by first trying to understand the nature of children and then by assisting them to develop their mental, physical and moral powers and capacities in a natural and harmonious way much like the growth and development of a plant in Nature. He believed that education should be centered around the child instead of being focused on the subject matter. He stressed the study of human nature and training of the senses. He taught that the discovery of facts through the study of nature, familiar objects and daily experiences, was more important than the teaching of facts from books. He believed in strict but understanding discipline. The teacher's role was to encourage self-activity and observation and to give wise and sympathetic guidance. He believed that physical exercises, sports and games were beneficial from both a health and recreational standpoint. He insisted at his school at Yverdun (1807) these activities be included in the educational program of children and be given one hour per day. (6:90) Because of his new ideas of study and teaching he was considered a great reformer and the founder of a modern pedagogy.

His outstanding works were *Leonard and Gertrude* and *How Gertrude Teaches Her Children.*

Guts Muths was an outstanding German instructor in physical education at the Schnepfenthal Educational Institute which was established by Christian Salzmann in 1785. This Institute was patterned after the Philanthropinum and was the most prominent of all the naturalistic schools of the eighteenth century. Guts Muths, because of his long and commendable service at this school, became known ". . . as the real founder of modern physical education and 'grandfather' of German gymnastics." (6:84) He based his program on the scientific knowledge of physiology and medicine and encouraged improvement by keeping individual records of the students' progress. Exercises were always held outdoors when the weather was suitable. They were planned to be beneficial for the whole body and mind and to be pleasant and enjoyable as well as strengthening. He believed, like Rousseau, that children should be permitted to grow and develop according to nature. He thought that girls should participate in games and gymnastics, but the activities for girls should not be as vigorous as those for the boys. Guts Muths taught French, geography and technology as well as physical education. Because of his respected position he had great influence not only on the growth and development of physical education but in other educational fields as well. He made many written contributions to physical education. His greatest works were *Gymnastics for the Young* and *Games.* The former was concerned with the fundamental background of physical education and the latter with the natural classification of games according to development of skills.

Fellenberg, a Swiss and a follower of Pestalozzi's theories, established a famous school at Hofwyl about 1806. At this school he attempted to educate the children of the poor and rich together in order to bring about a greater understanding between them. Another purpose of this school was to train teachers, particularly for the schools in the country. Students engaged in such activities as gardening, shop work and various kinds of manual labor activities. He also encouraged the students to take part in physical training which was given daily and was composed of play and physical exercises. He felt that systematic exercise and play activities were very important in the general education of the individual and did not believe that manual labor should be substituted for it. His idea of industrial education spread to the United States and many manual labor schools were founded between 1825 and 1850. (2:236-237)

The ideas of naturalism spread to Germany and were promoted by Jahn. Although Jahn's interest in physical education came from patriotic motives, his methods of teaching and love for nature and the outdoors stamped him as a naturalist. He was the great champion of liberation of Prussia from France. With this objective in mind he preached and worked for unity of the independent German States. He felt that freedom rested in the youth of the country and that physical exercise would develop strong, healthy and patriotic citizens capable of unifying Germany and defeating her enemy. His program of physical exercise stressed the use of outdoor activities such as jumping, running, wrestling and games on the Hasenheide, which was a hilly and woody play area. In time, other events and equipment were added to the program. There were ladders, horizontal bars, vertical ropes, balance beams, a running track, pole vaulting and high jumping standards and other similar apparatus. At first he did not arrange a definite program, but permitted the boys to choose activities they wished to do. Later, however, he became more systematic and wrote down the names, description and methods of performance of the exercises. Through his program of games and exercises he tried to develop individual initiative, freedom of thought and action, cooperation and understanding among people, and strong healthy bodies. Jahn also encouraged schoolboys to take part in games and gymnastics.

Later, as his program continued to gain in popularity, men beyond school age became interested and Turner Clubs were formed where both boys and men could perform. Jahn's program did aid substantially in unifying the German States and in finally winning the war from France. However, because his games and exercises and his liberal ideas of respect, worth and freedom of the individual tended to break down class distinction, the German kings opposed him. He was finally arrested, jailed, and then freed after many years in prison. The Turner movement was suppressed for a few years but later revived. Jahn's most famous work in physical education was *German Gymnastics.* Other books written by him were *German Nationality* and the *Promotion of Patriotism in Prussia.* Because of his initial and extended work in gymnastic exercises he was called the "father of German gymnastics and the Turner Clubs." Jahn's ideas influenced physical education in the schools of Germany and many other countries including the United States. Before Jahn's system of gymnastics came to the United States, however, some of the naturalistic character had changed because of the formalistic influence of Adolph Spiess (1810-1858), an educator who organized gymnastics for the schools and was instrumental in having them adopted into the educational curriculum. Because of this accomplishment he was called the "father of school gymnastics."

Froebel was a German educator born in Oberweissbach in Thuringia. (5:279) He, too, was a promoter of many of Rousseau's naturalistic ideas. These ideas coupled with his own unhappy childhood experiences undoubtedly motivated him to establish a kindergarten (child garden) in 1836 at Blankenburg. Here he did for other children the things that he had missed in his own childhood. He believed that children should be permitted to grow naturally through self-expression, social participation and all kinds of activity under the guidance of a friendly teacher. The teacher was thought of as a gardener who helped plants to grow. The teacher and parents were to cooperate with nature in guiding children through the periods of mental, physical and moral growth. Froebel accepted Rousseau's idea that the child should be permitted to grow naturally as an individual, but went beyond this insisting that the child should at the same time be a member of a group. While he believed the natural growth of the individual should not be interfered with, he also believed that society influenced the total education of the individual. Since the individual must live in society, he should not be protected from it, but help to adjust to it. Froebel tried to harmonize two different theories of education, one with emphasis on the individual, the other upon the group. He practiced these two ideas in actual teaching. He began the day's activities in the kindergarten by having the children form a circle and join hands. This was to remind them that they were all members of a group. Breaking the circle they participated in other activities the remainder of the day, in smaller groups or alone. At the end of the day's program he had them form a circle again so they would realize that while they were still individuals they must recognize their responsibility to the group. These theories have other applications. In totalitarian countries education is controlled by the state and the individual is educated to serve the state. In countries with a democratic form of government the individual is encouraged to grow in his own natural way according to his needs, wants and desires. Although natural development results in many deviations from the group, it does make certain contributions to group improvement. Froebel, like Pestalozzi, influenced modern pedagogy. His works were *The Education of Man, Education by Development,* and *Mother Play and Nursery Songs.*

Herbert Spencer (1820-1903) was an English philosopher and writer. He became famous for trying to work out a fundamental theory for determining reality which could be applied to all sciences. In his *Synthetic Philosophy* he described this theory as the process of evolution and dissolution. Force, he said, supplied the energy for this process to take place. (5:7641-7642) Force, to him, was inexplainable. He thought it was the Supreme Being, always present, persistent and continuing in Nature. This was his idea of reality. Nature, because of the forces of evolution and dissolution, was always in constant change. The forces of evolution in Nature changed forms of life from the simple to the complex. For example, a full grown dog was once a single fertilized cell, but through growth and development became an animal with a complex system of organs, bones, muscles, nerves, and blood vessels. As the dog aged and finally died, his body disintegrated and returned to the materials of the physical world from which he had come. This process which broke things down to simpler forms, he called dissolution, just the reverse of evolution.

Because of his use of this idea of force or energy in explaining reality, he was called an energist. (1:73) Spencer applied these principles of evolution and dissolution to other fields such as politics, sociology, psychology and education. In education he merely restated some of the concepts of Pestalozzi: that education should be interesting, arranged according to degree of difficulty, and proceed from the particular to the general. (2:277) On the subject of moral education Spencer accepted Rousseau's idea that it should be based on the theory of natural punishment. He believed in health and physical education. He thought individuals needed a proper amount of rest, exercise, diet and recreation in order to develop strong, healthy bodies and minds. His writings were *Essays: Scientific, Political and Speculative*, and *The Inadequacy of Natural Selection.*

NATURALISM IN EDUCATION

The central aim of naturalism in education is to learn about the pupil and to free him from all bondage. Education is focused on the pupil. He is given a life-centered curriculum, highly competitive and in accordance with his natural developmental stages, needs and interests and level of readiness. Education should encourage self-activity, be pleasurable, and add to one's store of knowledge. Education should encourage not only self-activity but independent discoveries and observations and collection of facts, in other words, teaching by the inductive method. Education should encourage self-discipline, development of moral character, individual differences and physical health.

NATURALISM IN PHYSICAL EDUCATION

Rousseau believed, as did Spencer and many other naturalists of the modern era, that there is an interrelationship between body and mind; that the activities of one influenced the working of the other. Rousseau thought that recreation was essential to free youngsters from the restraints of their environment and counteract some of the evils of society. Basedow's school program at the Philanthropinum was based on the philosophy of naturalism, and it was there that the first modern program in physical education was started. Guts Muths contended that the fundamental objective of education was health, not knowledge, and objected to the inactivity of the school program which was being forced upon children. He divided the activities for instruction into three classes: manual labor, gymnastic exercises and social games. (7:207) Many physical educators hold to some of the tenets of naturalism, with certain modifications. Naturalism can be interpreted and applied to physical education in the following ways:

Aim

The aim of naturalism as applied to physical education is to develop and to perfect naturally inherent human abilities through participation in motor activities and related experiences.

Objectives

The major objectives of naturalism are to determine the interests and needs and to encourage self-expression. Self-control is also a worthy objective but is considered more incidental and less positive than interests, needs and self-expression.

Program

The school program is organized around the interests, needs, desires and feelings of students. A large variety of physical activities are offered for exploratory purposes and for the development of natural ability, freedom and self-expression. Cooperation is emphasized, self-improvement encouraged, but highly competitive performance between individuals is discouraged.

Method of Teaching

The method of teaching is informal and moderately democratic. It is the kind of method which permits students to develop naturally at their own speed and according to their needs and urges, with little interference from outside such as parents and teachers.

Discipline

The naturalist believes that inexorable laws of nature govern the development of human nature and that the nature of the child is inherently good, not bad. The teacher should know and understand these laws and assist, not interfere, with their operation. What the child does is right because he is expressing some natural and basic urge. Therefore, since the child has developed in an environment of freedom and friendly guidance with opportunities for self-selection and self-expression, his discipline must be that of self-restraint. If the child does not obey the laws of nature he brings on his own punishment.

The Teacher

The job of the teacher is to know and to understand the laws of nature and to help the child to develop according to these laws. The key to this understanding is to study child psychology and to discover what are the natural instincts that give rise to expression. These indicate the needs of the individual. The teacher's job is to help the child in every way possible to satisfy these needs. The teacher is a friend and a helper, not a director.

The Administrator

The role of the administrator is to provide and maintain an environment which is conducive to the flourishment of naturalistic philosophy, to establish policies concerning this philosophy, and to see that these policies are executed. The administrator is very likely to employ the functional type of organization to conduct the administrative affairs of the school.

Evaluation

The emphasis of evaluation is placed upon the individual's norm and how much he deviates from his previous performances. More importance is placed upon competition against an individual's own performance and less upon that of the opponent. Evaluation goes on continuously and is concerned with the progress an individual makes in satisfying all the aspects of human nature: needs, interests, wants, desires, urges and other forces arising from human instincts.

SUMMARY

We have seen in this chapter how education was initiated by the desire of ancient people to perpetuate their culture and to instruct their youth in ritualistic function and in their customs, traditions and folklore.

Naturalism was discussed first because it precedes other philosophies. Theories of ancient philosophers were examined and this was followed by a chronological presentation of the ideas of some of the more prominent philosophers of the early modern and modern periods. It was pointed out that, historically, the central aim of naturalism in education was to learn about the individual pupil, to free him from all bondage, and to have him grow and develop according to his own nature. The aim of physical education in naturalistic philosophy was to make children healthy, strong, physically, mentally and morally fit, and happy.

QUESTIONS FOR REVIEW AND DISCUSSION

1. Discuss the philosophy of naturalism.
2. What other philosophies are related to naturalism? Describe them.
3. Name three or four prominent ancient philosophers from whose theories naturalism evolved.
4. Name and discuss the theories of Thomas Hobbes and Jean Rousseau.
5. Which one had the greater influence on physical education? Why?
6. Rousseau's philosophy influenced the ideas of the following men. Discuss their theories of education. How did these views affect ideas about physical education?
   Johann Basedow
   Johann Pestalozzi
   Johann Guts Muths
   Phillipp Von Fellenberg
   Friedrich Jahn
   Friedrich Froebel
7. Who was Spencer? What were his views on reality and on education?
8. Explain naturalism in education and in physical education. What is the aim in both?
9. Explain how naturalism can be interpreted and how it might influence physical education in the following ways: aim, objectives, program, method of teaching, discipline, the teacher, the administrator and evaluation.

Bibliography

1. Butler, J. Donald. *Four Philosophies and Their Practice in Education and Religion.* New York: Harper and Brothers, 1951.
2. Duggan, Stephen. *A Student's Textbook in the History of Education.* New York: A. Appleton-Century Co., 1936.
3. Frost, Jr., S. E. *Basic Teachings of the Great Philosophers.* New York: Barnes and Noble, Inc., 1957.
4. Hocking, William Ernest. *Types of Philosophy.* New York: Charles Scribner's Sons, 1939.

5. JONES, J. MORRIS. *The World Book Encyclopedia*. Chicago: The Quarrie Corporation, 1947.
6. RICE, EMMETT A., JOHN L. HUTCHINSON AND MABEL LEE. *A Brief History of Physical Education*. New York: The Ronald Press Co., 1958.
7. VAN DALEN, DEOBOLD B., ELMER D. MITCHELL AND BRUCE L. BENNETT. *A World History of Physical Education*. New York: Prentice-Hall, Inc., 1953.

3

Idealism

Idealism, like naturalism, has been found commonly in the philosophical and educational realms of the past and is still quite prominent today. The history of idealism extends from the period of Plato to the present. Basically it is a doctrine in which ultimate reality is interpreted in terms of mind or self or spirit. Through an historical study of the views and contributions of philosophers it is possible to obtain a fuller understanding of this theory, its meaning, value and significance in education and physical education.

MEANING OF IDEALISM

Idealism can be approached from two viewpoints: the popular concept and the philosophical. The popular view may have many meanings. One is an idealist in the nonphilosophical sense, for example, if he envisions some lofty social or political reforms; such views are seldom based upon practical consideration. One is an idealist, in the popular sense, if he lives by exceedingly high moral standards, those almost impossible to reach. Such views are based on the word "ideal" meaning something visionary, as in the first example, or meaning a perfect standard, as in the second.

From the philosophical viewpoint, however, idealism conveys a different meaning. According to Hocking idealism should suggest ideas not ideals, therefore, "idea-ism" is perhaps a better term. He states that "Idealism is the philosophy which holds that reality is of the nature of the mind." (5:247) Metaphysically, reality of the world is mind, self, ideas and/or spirit. Idealists believe in Nature but interpret it in terms of Mind,

Spirit, Idea. Objective science may describe life processes as long as everything in the world is not categorized as matter, according to philosophical idealism.

HISTORICAL ASPECTS

To chart the inception and development of idealism let us turn to a description of individual beliefs of a few of its outstanding proponents. Since occidental idealism originated with Socrates and Plato their views will be discussed first.

ANCIENT PHILOSOPHERS

Socrates (469-399 B.C.) was a great teacher, chiefly of young men, who worked industriously at his profession all his life, but he did not leave any known writings of his own. Knowledge of his philosophy comes to us only from the works of Plato. "Socrates' guiding rule was 'Know thyself.' He believed that goodness was based on knowledge and wickedness was based on ignorance." (6:7539)

Plato, the pupil of Socrates, was born about 427 B.C. and died in 347 B.C. His philosophical ideas have influenced the thought and life of philosophers in every generation since his time. His writings are in the form of a dialogue, with Socrates acting as the main interrogator. Plato's most outstanding work is the *Republic;* others are *Charmides, Laws, Phaedrus, Symposium,* and *Timaeus.* His doctrine of ideas assures his relationship with idealism. To him ideas of the mind were more real and lasting than the ideas represented in physical forms. Ideas of the mind were the only real things in the Universe. These were the perfect ideas and were impressed upon matter to form the physical objects of the world. Physical objects were only imperfect copies of the real or perfect ideas. Plato believed that truth was to be discovered through the process of thought and reason, by asking and answering questions, by gathering and evaluating data, and by considering and reconsidering possible solutions. Plato's belief that ideas are the basis of real life and his description of the process of thought and reason have continued to exist through the ages.

EARLY MODERN AND MODERN PHILOSOPHERS

René Descartes (1596-1650), a French philosopher, has been called the "father of modern philosophy." (6:1959) The fact that he was a mathematician and was familiar with exact methods of thinking probably led him to explain things in a mechanical fashion. He believed that substance of two kinds was the basis of the Universe: mind and body. Each was a separate entity but dependent upon one absolute substance which was God. There were no ideas, forms, or empty spaces in the Universe, according to this concept, but there were bodies which filled all space and were capable of being divided endlessly into smaller bodies. This property of bodies, that of occupying space, is called extension. Through some modification of this process Descartes believed that bodies combined to make different kinds of matter. Moreover, bodies moved from place to place by motion which was originally supplied by God and was always constant. Thus, bodies moved about according to fixed mechanical laws of motion. (4:31-32)

The important ideas of Descartes which are related to idealism are these: the prime reality is self, and self's ability to originate an idea of a perfect being proves the existence of God. Descartes believed that all knowledge is uncertain and the way to find truth is to begin by doubting everything, the only undoubtful thing being one's ability to doubt. This ability he reasoned, makes man a thinker. Thinking has to be done by someone. Since he was doing the thinking he was someone. Hence, he drew the inference, "'I think, therefore I am' (Cogito, ergo, sum)" (3:166) This was his belief regarding the prime reality of self. Using a similar approach he determined the existence of God. He reasoned that an imperfect being cannot originate a perfect idea. He was an imperfect being because he doubted. Therefore, he could not initiate a perfect idea. This perfect idea had to come from some place. Since it could not come from him and it could not come from nothingness, it must have come from some perfect Being. If this be true, a perfect Being, God, exists. (2:129) This was Descartes method of doubt which became the basis of modern philosophy. His philosophy may be classified as mechanistic from the standpoint of the laws of motion, and dualistic from the viewpoint of his belief that mind and body exist independently of each other. He wrote *Discourses on the Method of Reasoning* and *Principles of Philosophy and Geometry.*

Baruch Spinoza (1632-1677) was born in Amsterdam of Spanish and Jewish parents. Because of the influence of the ideas of Van den Ende, a Dutch scholar, upon him he was known as a Dutch-Jewish philosopher. He also studied the philosophy of Descartes and was influenced by it. Spinoza believed that God and the Universe are one and that mind and matter are the only two parts of the Universe. He described mind and matter as thought and extension and believed they were the only characteristic forms of God. He believed that these form one substance which is ultimate, infinite, unchanging, and underlies all things. This substance is more lasting than matter. This idea thus differs from Descartes' dualism of spirit and matter. Spinoza's theory is called "psycho-physical parallelism" – mind and matter or thought and extension are attributes of the same substance and are always parallel. (4:35) He maintained that mind and matter are independent of each other, but exist together and both are dependent upon God. According to Spinoza ideas of the mind have their counterparts in the physical forms of matter and all forms in matter have corresponding ideas in the mind. (6:7652)

The main part of Spinozan philosophy which concerns idealism is his treatment of thought. Existence, he reasoned, is a substance or being which thinks and thought is a feature of God. God is a thinking being and expresses Himself in many forms in Nature. Viewed introspectively, He is Mind. Man, as are the many other physical objects of Nature, is a form or part of God. Man also is a thinking being. Man's duty is to try to understand God and the Universe and to seek His love. This belief that God is the Universe is called pantheism. (2:132) Spinoza's writings include *Treatise on Theology and Politics* and *The Ethics.*

Gottfried Wilhelm Von Leibniz (1646-1716) was a German scholar and philosopher of the seventeenth century. His metaphysical theory of the Universe is based on units of force, called atoms of force or "monads"; hence, his philosophy is called monadology. Monads of the Universe are indestructible, unchangeable from external causes, everlasting and of several different kinds. All Nature is mental or psychical according to this belief, and is composed of living units. This is called panpsychism. (2:133) The lowest order of monads includes inorganic things like stones and organic things like plants. The next higher order of monads forms animals. While the body of the animal is composed of simple monads there are also more complex monads which have powers of perception and retention, these providing the soul or psyche of the animal. A still higher and more complicated order of monads forms man complete with "spirit." The spirit possesses all the capabilities of the other lower orders but adds the ability to think. It is this ability to think, to obtain knowledge and wisdom, to understand self and to know God that differentiates men from animals. The highest and most supreme order of all monads is the one which is infinite, limitless – the Supreme Monad, God. (4:40)

Leibniz explains rather clearly the mind-body relationship in his philosophy. Each monad, from its very beginning, is a complete Universe within itself. It has no "windows" so cannot be changed by exterior causes. Any change that occurs must come from inner causes. A monad cannot affect another monad. Yet, since God created monads, they work together in harmony with one another in a kind of body and mind parallelism. (2:135) The activities of the body always correspond to the activities of the mind. The important idealistic items in this philosophy are the interpretation of the monads of men as spirit, and the Supreme monad or Spirit, God who is infinite. Leibniz's philosophy is a living, dynamic philosophy rather than mechanical and revives the older atomistic theory of Democritus of the ancient Greeks. He did not leave any writings about his philosophy other than articles in journals and personal letters to friends.

George Berkeley (1685-1753) was born in Kilkenny, Ireland. He objected to the popular theory of the early eighteenth century that matter in the Universe is controlled by mathematical laws, such as Newton's law of gravity. He disagreed with Spinoza, Descartes, and Locke in their belief that matter is the fundamental element of the Universe. He declared that it cannot be proven there is a universe of material objects. There is nothing real, he said, but ideas. Ideas come from God and the sensations and impressions which cause the ideas come from God. Knowledge is obtained from the Universe through our senses. Unless material things of the world are perceived through these senses they do not exist and then they are not real. They are really only ideas of the mind. If there were not any mind to perceive them, they would not exist. Berkeley can be identified as an idealist because of two characteristic beliefs: the only source of knowledge of the objective Universe is God or Infinite Mind, and the existence of things in the world depends upon perception. In his own words he said, "To be is to be perceived." (8:191) This type of idealism is called subjectivism. Berkeley wrote many papers on philosophy, the most important being *The Principles of Human Knowledge.*

Immanuel Kant (1724-1804), born in Königsberg, Prussia, ranks as one of the greatest thinkers who ever lived. He was particularly noteworthy in his explanation of the process of knowledge, answering the questions: How can we know, and what can we know? He explained that we know only by experience. We obtain experience when our minds receive sensations which are related in time and space and then convert these into ideas. There are the impressions we get of the world through our minds, but it is impossible for us to really know what the physical world is like by this method. By reason, however, we can build an idea of the world and find out how things are related to each other. In this kind of world time and space are infinite, freedom is present; the soul is immortal and a Supreme Being exists who is the Creator of all things. We do not obtain knowledge of this kind of world from experience, but by reason. By reason we can imagine that this world exists and is real. Belief in such a world encourages man to be moral and to strive for good objectives. In the universe of reason there are universal, moral laws by which men live. Kant believed that no man would participate in an act if it could not be engaged in by everyone. To do so might jeopardize society. Man would not commit any such acts because of a sense of duty which comes to him through reason. Kant called this a "categorical imperative." (2:145) It is mainly his theory of process of knowledge which identifies him with the philosophy of idealism. Kant influenced many philosophers by his concept of moral law and his process of knowledge. Because of this he is known as the father of modern idealism. His most famous book is the *Critique of Pure Reason.*

Georg Wilhelm Friedrich Hegel (1770-1831) was a German philosopher whose thought had considerable influence upon the promotion and development of idealism. Like Fichte and Schelling, Hegel was a pantheist but with a slightly different version. He believed that the Universe and God are one; that there is a continuous and gradual evolutionary process of mind or idea from nature or the physical world up the scale to Mind, Infinite Idea or God. He believed that the Universe is a whole, that the mind pervades everything and that there is an unfolding from within, an evolutionary development taking place. This developmental process is called the principle of contradiction which proceeds by the dialetic method. This method of reasoning is based upon the following stages of thinking: thesis, antithesis, and synthesis. Hegel believed that an idea or fact (thesis) working against another idea (antithesis) produced a new idea (synthesis). The new idea (synthesis) then became the thesis and the whole process was repeated as before. (2:152) By his idealistic theory of thought Hegel explained all progress and development in the world as in politics, religion, culture, and social organization. His dialectic form of thought became the basis of Karl Marx's dialectic materialism and of the national socialism of Adolph Hitler. Hegel's method of reasoning was used by other philosophers to strengthen the evolutionary theories of Charles Darwin. Other people Hegel influenced were such conservative philosophers as Francis Bradley of England and Josiah Royce of America. (6:3362) His philosophy thus had wide impact. His writings include *The History of Philosophy, Logic, The History of Art,* and *The Philosophy of Religion.*

Other Philosophers of Europe and of Great Britain

Because of the strong expression and deep feeling for idealism of the outstanding philosophers discussed, other leaders of thought in Europe and in Great Britain were influenced and many became exponents of some phases of this philosophy. It has already been mentioned that Karl Marx (1818-1883) of Germany accepted Hegel's dialectic system of thought, though not his idealistic views. Marx, together with Friedrich Engels (1820-1895) also of Germany, promoted the philosophy of dialectic materialism. The Communist government of Soviet Russia and of several other countries were organized, in part, on the theories of Marx.

The outstanding idealistic philosophers of Italy were Giovanni Gentile and Benedetto Croce, and in France it was Henri Bergson (1859-1941). In England idealism received its greatest impetus from the writings of James Hutchison Stirling (1820-1909). Other prominent English idealists were Benjamin Jowett (1817-1893); John Caird (1820-1898), formulator of a philosophy of religion based on idealism; Edward Caird (1835-1908), John's brother, writer and interpreter of Kant's and Hegel's philosophy. Other contributions which served to break the ground for idealism in England were made by the poetry of Samuel Taylor Coleridge (1772-1834) and the literature of Thomas Carlyle (1795-1881). (2:155-156)

Idealist Philosophers in the United States

Idealism came to the United States through the writings of Coleridge and Carlyle of England, through the study of Americans abroad, and through the importation of professors from Europe, particularly from Germany. Ralph Waldo Emerson's (1803-1882) literature also helped to break the ground for idealism in the United States, but the seeds of idealism were already planted by German immigrant teachers. Charles Follen (1796-1840) was one of these teachers who came to America and joined the faculty at Harvard University as its first professor of German. Soon afterward he also began teaching German gymnastics at Harvard and in the first Boston gymnasium. He had learned gymnastics from Jahn in Germany. Subsequently he discontinued the teaching of gymnastics and concentrated his efforts on history, ethics, and German. (7:208-209) Another of these German immigrants was Francis Lieber (1800-1872) who was a friend of Jahn in Germany and succeeded Follen as a teacher of gymnastics at the Boston gymnasium. Later he became a teacher of history and political science at Columbia College in New York City. (2:158) He was considered as the "first academic political philosopher" of America. He wrote *Political Ethics, Civil Liberty and Government.* (7:209) It was through the efforts of Follen and Lieber and subsequent German immigrants that the system of German gymnastics was established in the public schools of many important cities in the United States including Milwaukee, Chicago, Kansas City,

Davenport, Cleveland, St. Louis, Denver, Dayton, and Cincinnati. It was this German influence that helped place physical education as a subject in the public school curriculum.

The most important man to accept idealism and promote it in the United States was William T. Harris (1835-1909). He was influenced by a German immigrant by the name of Henry C. Brokmeyer. Harris was the founder and editor of the *Journal of Speculative Philosophy* (1867), the first journal of its kind in the United States; he was an outstanding lecturer and a prominent leader in the field of education. The aforementioned men and others like Josiah Royce (1855-1916), William E. Hocking of Harvard, and the late Herman H. Horne of New York University have been instrumental in teaching and promoting their own versions of idealism in the United States.

TYPES OF IDEALISM

In the earlier part of this book mention was made concerning the large number of philosophies which have been formulated and held by various men; too many in number to be discussed in one volume; too varied in theory to be organized into one simple system or classification. In a similar way, but to a somewhat lesser degree, the same problem exists in attempting to discuss all the different types of idealism. Titus simplifies this problem by suggesting three main types of idealism: subjectivism, objectivism, and personalism. He calls attention to two other types: phenomenalism, which occupies a midway position between the two domains of subjectivism and objectivism; and panpsychism, which occupies a position between objectivism and personalism. (8:238-244) For a general understanding of these types of idealism a brief discussion is given.

Subjective Idealism

Subjective idealism is a theory that knowledge is obtained only from one's own mental awareness and personal experience. Ideas or perceptions are the only things that exist or are real, so the world is a mental or spiritual world. The objects that we see are not material or real things; they are only perceptions of the mind. There would not be any objects unless there were someone to perceive them. Since this theory deals only with the mind it is referred to by some as mentalism. This philosophy, however, does not rule out the existence of the material world; rather it is concerned with how existence is interpreted.

The outstanding exponent of this type of idealism was George Berkeley who based his philosophy upon the thesis that nothing was real except minds and ideas. Objects that we see are only perceptions of the mind. He did not believe in a separate order and existence of the material world, but thought that it was due to an active Spirit (God) who determined the continuity and sequence of our ideas. Existence of the real (material) world was interpreted only by the individual mind (self) that perceived it.

Objective Idealism

Objective idealism is a theory that the external world is real, is organized in an impersonal, rational order and is identified with the activity of Mind or Spirit.

There are many different views on what objective idealism is but two important views are those of Plato and Hegel.

Plato "believed in the objective reality of our ideals and values." He thought the world consists of two regions: first, there is the temporal and expendable region of sense perception which is not real but only appears real. Second, there is the region of ideas and concepts which is above and beyond the region of sense perception. (8:241)

Hegel believed that "Thought is the essence of the Universe, and Nature is the whole of mind objectified," and that "Nature is the Absolute Reason expressing itself in outward form." (8:241-242)

Thus, objective idealism embraces objective reality, the principle of order and reason in nature, and the existence of the identifying or underlying Mind or Spirit.

Personal Idealism

Personal idealism is a theory based upon a person as a controlling self and upon the awareness of the qualities, sensations, feelings and thoughts of being a person. Titus states that "personalists emphasize the reality and worth of individual persons, of moral values, and of human freedom." (8:243) The theory of personal idealism also embraces the belief in God, especially a personal God, who is inherent in the Universe yet is capable of rising above experience and knowledge of the world. Personalists place great importance upon the development of personality, freedom, and self control and believe that society should be organized to provide everyone a full and abundant life. (8:244)

IDEALISM IN EDUCATION

Idealism, as it relates to education, is concerned chiefly with the explanation of the Universe and things in the Universe in terms of ideas, mind (self), and spirit. Knowledge obtained from this process must be searched for or sought after; it is not self-evident. The individual is a unitary self as well as a spiritual being. He learns and develops his body and mind through self-activity. The learning process is initiated within the self and proceeds outward. In a way he is self-taught. While the teacher plays an important guiding role in the education of the pupil and sets up the environment in which the educative process takes place, the pupil still determines, to a great extent, his own environment through the selection of things in which he is interested and finds useful, and in which he can show his own creativeness. Learning proceeds through the realization that the true things in life are ideas. Brubacher states that: "Truth has always been true; it does not become true." (1:312)

The idealistic teacher does not confine himself to one method of presenting his information. He selects the method which he feels will produce the best result at a particular time. Various methods from which he may select include: (1) the dialectic, or the question and answer method; (2) the lecture method; and (3) the project method. (2:245-247) Idealism may embrace the principles of essentialism or those of progressivism. The principles of essentialism, however, are more prominent and dominant and outweigh those of progressivism.

IDEALISM IN PHYSICAL EDUCATION

We have seen that idealism has made contribution to education and has influenced considerably its theory and practice. Likewise, idealism has left its impact upon the field of physical education, its leaders, its educational thought, practices and methods of teaching. Early Athenian physical education was based upon concepts of beauty, harmony, excellence, virtue, and development of the whole self, mind and body. In physical education, recreational and athletic programs today, great emphasis is placed upon the principles of honesty, fair play, sportsmanship, effort, interest, self-discipline, initiative, and courage. A conception of physical education held by many people today can be traced to idealistic beliefs . . . that physical education does not rank as high in the realm of values as intellectual studies. A basis for his belief is found in many Christian philosophies which teach that the body is controlled by mind or spirit. Things of the mind therefore are held higher in esteem than things of the body.

Brubacher, in discussing ideas of the cosmos and education, arrives at the same opinion by another approach. He indicates that if a child lives in an environment of fixed ideas, these become an essential part of his education and form a background for the educational program.

Education of the senses, and especially those related to physical education and vocational education, are a phase of this program. But they probably will not rate high in any ranking system of educational values. "Formal intellectual studies and methods will rank highest." (1:310)

Can these attitudes toward physical education be changed? Can physical education become a genuine discipline? Shermis thinks that affirmative answers to these questions can be made if certain conditions are met. He points out that if we can accept the premise that disciplines are not fixed branches of knowledge, but become intellectual by studying questions which are of great importance to man, then it is possible to agree that the marginal intellectual disciplines may become real ones ". . . by developing the tools to deal with their subject matter — just as now the established disciplines are developing theirs." (9:86) It would seem then that physical educators could change the present view of physical education. This could be accomplished, partially at least, by engaging in respected basic and applied research, by using accurate and appropriate equipment and devices in experimentation, by employing adequate statistical procedures, by using logical and conceptual cognition and scientific procedures in order to arrive at the solution and interpretation of problems. A general interpretation of idealism which may aid the physical educator follows.

Aim

The aim of idealism is to explain the Universe in terms of ideas which are perfect and unchanging. Ideas are the only real things of the world and are impressed upon matter to form the physical objects of the Universe. Beauty, truth, and harmony are examples of these ideas.

Objectives

The objectives of idealism are to search for knowledge in the world and to develop one's body, mind and soul to the greatest fulfillment.

Program

The program is a traditional one based upon discovered truths, knowledge of the Universe and fixed ideas. Thus, the educational program can be prepared by the teacher in advance for it is a fixed, formal program.

Method

The method of teaching and presenting information may vary depending upon the nature of the students, the subject matter, and the results to be attained. Some methods may involve the principles of essentialism as the question-answer and the lecture method; others may involve the principles of progressivism as the project method. The idealistic teacher may also accept the scientific method in order that he can learn more about the world and God and, therefore, be better able to transmit this knowledge to students.

Discipline

The type of discipline resulting from idealistic philosophy is likely to be paternalistic, firm and rather formal. This does not mean that the teacher will be a domineering or an autocratic individual, but he is likely to be a very orderly and efficient person who insists upon accuracy, reliability, promptness, and organization. His real purpose is to pass on true and basic knowledge and to inspire students to attain the highest human goals. He expects students to develop and to use self-restraint.

The Teacher

The idealist teacher plays an important role in the learning process and is its central figure. Through his guidance he helps students to search for the truth and understand it. He helps students to understand themselves and to develop such personal qualities as self-initiative, self-responsibility, self-decision, and self-restraint. He is interested in assisting students to mature to the highest possible degree.

The Administrator

The idealist administrator is likely to be a friendly and understanding person yet firm in maintaining his own convictions. He is apt to be a person who is willing to discuss professional problems and policies with his staff members. He is likely to be a person who accepts the responsibility for maintaining a school environment favorable to the established idealistic policy. He is very likely to employ a line type organization to conduct the administrative affairs of his school.

Evaluation

The idealist teacher in physical education uses both objective and subjective evaluation techniques, but he is concerned more with the subjective. He is not so much interested in highly competitive performances and in establishing records as he is in what these performances and activities do to the student. He wants to know if these activities are helping the student to develop his personality, his mind, his body, his character, and his behavior. He may use records to set up the student's own learning curve or norm in order to note deviations and to chart improvement. He may also compare student performances with established norms for diagnostic and prognostic purposes. The idealist teacher gives examinations, but he also encourages the student to examine himself.

SUMMARY

In the foregoing pages consideration has been given to several aspects of idealism. The meaning of idealism was discussed from two viewpoints: the popular and the philosophical. The development of idealism was traced through a brief review of individual beliefs of representative philosophers in the ancient, early modern, modern, and contemporary periods. To aid in the understanding and the clarification of idealism selected types were discussed: subjectivism, objectivism, and personalism. Finally, the influence of idealism on education and physical education was discussed.

QUESTIONS FOR REVIEW AND DISCUSSION

1. Distinguish between the popular and philosophical viewpoints of idealism.
2. Describe the idealistic views of Socrates and Plato.
3. What early modern philosopher was called the father of modern philosophy? Describe his idealistic beliefs.
4. What part of Spinoza's and Leibniz's philosophy leans particularly toward idealism?
5. What is subjective idealism? What philosopher(s) is associated with this point of view?
6. What is Kant's "categorical imperative"? Explain. What effect may this have upon society?
7. Explain the principle of contradiction. What philosopher proposed it?
8. What is dialectic materialism? What two famed leaders used this form of thought? What relationship does it have to the principle of contradiction?
9. Name some philosophers of Great Britain who were exponents of idealism. How did they promote idealism?
10. Name some philosophers of the United States who were exponents of idealism. How did they promote idealism?

11. What is objective idealism? Explain. Name some proponents of this type of idealism.
12. What is personal idealism? Explain. Name some proponents of this theory.
13. Discuss idealism as it relates to education, physical education.
14. What idealistic principles do programs in physical education, recreation and athletic emphasize?
15. What is the source of the view held by some people that physical education does not rank as high in the realm of values as intellectual studies? Discuss.
16. How can the profession of physical education be improved? How can a better academic and professional attitude be attained?

Bibliography

1. Brubacher, John S. *Modern Philosophies of Education.* New York: McGraw-Hill Book Company, Inc., 1950.
2. Butler, J. Donald. *Four Philosophies and Their Practice in Education and Religion.* New York: Harper and Brothers, 1951.
3. Durant, Will. *The Story of Philosophy.* New York: Garden City Publishing Co., Inc., 1938.
4. Frost, Jr., S. E. *Basic Teachings of Great Philosophers.* New York: Barnes and Noble, Inc., 1957.
5. Hocking, William Ernest. *Types of Philosophy.* New York: Charles Scribner's Sons, 1939.
6. Jones, J. Morris. *The World Book Encyclopedia.* Chicago: The Quarrie Corporation, 1947.
7. Rice, Emmett A., John L. Hutchinson, and Mabel Lee. *A Brief History of Physical Education.* New York: The Ronald Press Co., 1958.
8. Titus, Harold H. *Living Issues in Philosophy.* New York: American Book Company, 1946.
9. Shermis, Sherwin S. "On Becoming An Intellectual Discipline," *Phi Delta Kappan,* 44:86; November, 1962.

Realism

4

Realism as a formal philosophy is not as old as naturalism or idealism; however, traces of realistic thinking can be identified in the works of early philosophers such as Plato, Aristotle and Democritus. These philosophers were not realists by present day standards, but some of their ideas conveyed realistic meanings and prepared the way for twentieth century realism, a philosophy which began as a revolt against idealism. The term realism encompasses a number of philosophic doctrines all of which believe that objects have an independent existence from the knower. The history and development of this philosophy is an interesting one.

MEANING OF REALISM

As an ordinary term, realism is a combination of the word real, meaning factual or true, and the suffix ism, meaning theory or doctrine – hence, the theory of existing facts or practical existence. As a philosophical term, realism has a technical meaning: the theory that material objects exist in and of themselves, without being dependent upon being perceived, as believed by the idealists. To one who accepts this point of view, things are as they appear through our senses. The philosophy emphasizes things which are objective, not ideas which are subjective; the use of exact methods and procedures of scientific investigation, not the employment of mediative, theoretical or speculative instruments. Reason and sense experience are the important things. Hocking says that "Realism as a general temper of mind is a disposition to keep ourselves and our preferences out of our judgment of things, letting the objects speak for themselves." (4:383)

HISTORICAL ASPECTS

Though realism as an organized philosophy is relatively contemporary, ideas of some early philosophers conveyed meanings of realism. These early roots sprouted into different varieties of realism during the modern and contemporary periods.

Ancient Philosophers

While Plato is definitely identified with idealism, one of his concepts opened an avenue to realism. This was his belief that universals (or ideas) are more actual than particulars (or single things), and are not dependent upon infinite mind. This concept brings together idealism and realism. Titus refers to this as Platonic realism and says it is closer to "modern idealism than to modern realism." (7:273) Plato's doctrine of ideas, however, marks the embryonic beginning of realism.

Aristotle (384-322 B.C.), a student of Plato, was more systematic in his methods of gathering and analyzing knowledge and was more inclined to accept the material world as part of reality than was Plato. He believed that matter and form (or ideas) not only exist but that they exist eternally together in some manner of continuity. Both act as one and are experienced together through our senses. He was more interested in particulars than he was in universals. He was more fascinated by the causes which created the natural world than in the probability of its existence. He did not think of the world as merely mechanical but as material as well, where matter has purpose and seeks to become something. His was a teleological world, a world with a purpose or a goal. (3:12)

These are some of Aristotle's beliefs which, together with his doctrine of form, point in the direction of realism. Aristotle wrote prolifically, including the books *Sophistical Refutations, Physics, Metaphysics, Politics* and *Poetics.*

Early Modern Philosophers

Saint Thomas Aquinas (1227-1274 A.D.) was born near Naples. He was a noted philosopher and theologian of the Roman Catholic Church who, with others, attempted to reconcile the theories of the early Greek philosophers, particularly Plato and Aristotle, with the religious faith of the Church, an integration known as the philosophy of Scholasticism. While not actually an advocator of realism, some of Saint Thomas' ideas have realistic leanings, particularly those concerning the reality of matter. Saint Thomas believed that the world, made by God, is a combination of matter and universals. He used the word "universals" in the same sense that Plato used "ideas" and Aristotle used "forms." In explaining Saint Thomas' philosophy, Frost states that "God is continually creating the world as he brings universals and matter together to produce new objects." (3:22)

The Scholastics emphasized the intellectual discipline of theology, and, generally speaking, the intellectual objectives of scholasticism are exact and narrow. Because of the theological belief held by these schoolmen, that the body should be subjected to the mind, there was little interest in that which we call health or physical education. Saint Thomas' greatest work is *Summa Theologica* which discusses the theological system of the Catholic Church.

Modern Philosophers

John Amos Comenius (1592-1670) was born at Nivnitz, Moravia, and was a religious and educational leader of his time. He was a Protestant pastor and subsequently bishop of the Moravian Church, and encountered great difficulties both personally and professionally during the religious conflict of the Thirty Years' War. (2:408) Persecuted and forced to wander in exile, he sought unceasingly to bring religious and educational reforms to his people. He was more of a student of educational methods and theology than of philosophy. His ideas of teaching, however, are characteristic of the philosophy of realism. In his book, *The Great Didactic,* Comenius discussed two basic ideas relating to education of children. The first idea was that instruction must be arranged in progressive natural steps. The second idea was that knowledge must be attractively and regularly presented through sense perception according to the level of comprehension of the child. (2:409-410)

These ideas not only clearly identify Comenius with the general philosophy of realism but classify him specifically with sense realism. This philosophy is concerned with the belief that knowledge and understanding come through the senses and can be developed by sensory training. He held other beliefs which were unusual for his time; for example, he believed that play contributes to the natural education of children and that physical exercise is essential for the harmonious development of minds and bodies.

Like many philosophers, all of René Descartes' (1596-1650) views are not aligned with one distinct school of philosophy. He used a logical system of doubting to prove the existence of self as the prime reality. Similarly he proved the existence of God. These ideas support the doctrine of idealism.

It was in his belief in the reality of the physical world that Descartes showed realistic tendencies. According to this idea the basis of the world was substance and was composed of two kinds, mind and body (matter). Each was independent but dependent upon one absolute substance which was God. Both mind and matter are found in man, the former being spiritual and the latter being mechanical. God is spirit. Matter is physical, and it operated by mechanical laws. "René Descartes held that everything in nature must be explained mechanically and anything spiritual must be reconciled with this." (3:68) All this indicates that while God originally established the physical world and supplied its motion, God and Nature are independent of each other and distinctly different.

Baruch Spinoza's (1632-1677) philosophy has in it elements of both idealism and realism. Some of his beliefs are accepted by both idealists and realists, for example, his theory of substance which is infinite, unchanging and underlying all things. While all realists would not agree with Spinoza that there is only one substance, or that God and the Universe are one, some would accept his attributes of the one substance, thought and extension, as the basis of their dualistic belief of mind and matter.

The phases of Spinoza's philosophy which are more definitely associated with realism are the theories of extension and determinism. Extension, as one of the attributes of substance or God, exists forever and appears in precise ways or forms, in time and space. Titus states that: "Nature extended is matter; nature thinking is mind." (7:158) Butler adds that: "There is no thought without extension in time and space, according to Spinoza." (1:285) Extension is basic to reality and affords fundamental knowledge with which our experiences can be understood and interpreted. Determinism is a theory that everything in the Universe is conducted by natural law. That a plant grows is caused by certain factors, and these are caused by other factors and this procedure continues on in an unbroken and efficient chain of causes. There is no chance or freedom of will in the Universe; everything is organized and dependable. Even human behavior is conditioned and guided by natural laws. This theory does not mean that everything in the Universe is predetermined. It does mean, however, that everything is conducted by unavoidable laws. (7:160)

Deterministic philosophers are favorably influenced by work in science because of the emphasis there on analysis of causes and effects; in fact, the progress of scientific investigation depends upon the principle of determinism.

John Locke (1632-1704) influenced many thinkers of his time and, in fact, some of the philosophical and psychological theories of the modern era are based on his ideas. He brought forth such doctrines as the "disciplinary theory of education," "mind devoid of ideas at birth" and "the reasoning process, an association of ideas." Locke was also a prolific thinker in the fields of politics, religion and health. He held strong beliefs regarding individual freedom in thought, speech, religion and politics. He was opposed to the doctrine of the divine right of kings and the authority of church. (6:170) He believed that education should develop soundness of both mind and body, and agreed with Comenius that education should provide opportunities for relaxation, recreation and fun. Rousseau was probably one of the foremost of the many thinkers influenced by Locke and was the one who helped carry forward the theories which shaped, in part, the philosophy of modern education. (2:403)

The ideas of Locke which point toward realism are those which concern the origin of ideas, and substance as the composition of the world. The mind, Locke said, is not filled with ideas at birth, but is devoid of ideas. "There are no innate ideas in the mind." (1:291) The mind is like a blank photographic sheet of paper upon which the impressions of the world are registered. Impressions or experiences come to us through sensations and the process of reasoning about sensations which results in the association of ideas. People who hold this belief that all knowledge comes from experience, are known as empiricists.

The world, according to Locke, is composed of two kinds of substances, bodies and souls. Bodies have certain material qualities. They must be capable of being moved, of filling space and being solid. Souls have immaterial qualities. These are of the spirit. There is an interaction of bodies, souls and minds upon each other. What affects one may affect the other. Bodies may act upon the mind, for example, in such a way that sensation of sound, smell or color may be produced. The idea of an apple which fills space and is solid is not of the same substance or quality as the idea of red, the color of the apple. There is some power present in the body that acts upon the mind to produce the red color. These substances are capable of producing ideas in the individual through sensations. Sensations and the associative thinking about sensations convey to us impressions of the world and form our experiences. Experiences of the physical world therefore are the source and basis of all knowledge. Some of Locke's theories are somewhat contradictory. While he believed in the interaction of body and mind, he held a dualistic idea about the Universe. He believed the universe is composed of two substances, bodies and minds. Bodies and minds are not made of the same substances. (3:36) Locke's most famous works include *Some Thoughts Concerning Education* and *Essay Concerning*

Human Understanding. His philosophy is known as representative realism. (7:274)

Some of Immanuel Kant's (1724-1804) beliefs on idealism are close to those held by the critical realists. One concerns the theory of knowledge. Kant explained that we know only by experience, and we obtain this experience from the sensations our minds receive from the external world. Our minds convert them into ideas, but these are representative impressions of the physical world for it is impossible to know the real world by this method. By reason, however, we can get ideas of the world and discover the relationship of things. The critical realists hold similar views. They believe that we know the external world indirectly; that certain media convey knowledge to our minds; and that through perception and thinking we construct ideas about the world. Runes states it this way: "The mind knows the objective world not directly (epistemological monism) but by means of a vehicle through which we perceive and think (epistemological dualism)." (6:71) Another aspect of Kant's philosophy which leans toward realism is his theory of the "thing-in-itself." We know things from experience, the way things appear by a priori reasoning. (6:159) We cannot know "the thing-in-itself," which some philosophers call the soul or will. (3:189) It cannot be defined. Frost states: "Although experience reveals only phenomena, an appearance must always be the appearance of something. There is a reality which causes the appearance." This kind of reality is what Kant called the "thing-in-itself." (3:47)

Johann Friedrich Herbart (1776-1841) was a distinguished German educator and psychologist who, in his early years of study, was influenced by Johann Fichte, his teacher and an advocate of idealism. Soon, however, Herbart turned to the theories of Immanuel Kant and then evolved his own ideas. Because of his early and extensive work in methods of instruction based upon psychology he became known as the "father" of scientific pedagogy. (6:125) Part of his psychology, "the doctrine of reals," is considered as philosophy. It is in this connection that he is associated with realism. In his day psychology and philosophy were grouped together as one science. In explaining the Universe Herbart contended that it is composed of fixed laws or substances called "reals." The Universe is governed by these reals and is operated like a machine. "In the world of reals there is no change, no growth: it is static." (3:46) He reasoned that if the Universe is composed and governed by these unchangeable laws or reals, man's body which is a component of nature is also so ruled. Even each soul is considered a real. (3:46) Each real competes against other reals and strives to preserve itself. Each acts differently in the presence of others. Man combines and rearranges these reals to create his universe of experience. Under this theory the Universe is real and this philosophy is classified as realism. (3:47)

From this theory of reals Herbart formulated his doctrine of apperception. Ideas, he explained, come from the conflict between reals as they inhibit, interact and affect one another in striving to rise in consciousness. This process goes on according to certain mathematical laws. There are ideas already in consciousness, the residues from past experiences which are called the apperceptive mass. These are the interpreting ideas. There are new ideas just appearing in consciousness; these are ideas to be interpreted. Apperception is the process by which new experience is interpreted and assimilated in terms of past experiences and formulated into new knowledge.

William James (1842-1910) was a famous American psychologist and philosopher whose works influenced the content and characteristics of both of these fields of knowledge. He had a wealth of training and experience in many subjects. His first interest was in art. He studied in Paris and did some painting for a short while. Soon he turned to the field of science, studying biology, anatomy and physiology. He received his degree in medicine at Harvard University and taught anatomy there for a few years. Later, he became immersed in psychology and finally philosophy. He wrote and lectured extensively in both of these fields. His most famous writing is *Principles of Psychology.* Some of his other works are *The Will to Believe, The Meaning of Truth,* and *Pragmatism – A New Name for Some Old Ways of Thinking.* He is credited with helping to initiate and to develop the philosophies of realism and pragmatism in America. Only his thoughts on realism will be discussed here; those on pragmatism will be considered in the next chapter.

The elements of his thinking which identify him with realism are several. He contended that consciousness is not a substance and has no reality; instead, it is a characteristic action of experience. "Consciousness," James said, "is merely 'a witness of happenings in time.'" (1:296) He held "that when objects are experienced in consciousness, they are directly presented in consciousness, not represented; and that the universe is many, not one." (1:295) Further, he believed that "Knowing is a simple relation with presented objects in experience." (1:296) Experience is not confined to personal experiences of self, but includes all human experience. The world of human experience is the real world. He held, also, that experience like consciousness is not a substance. Nor did he believe that all experiences have some common being or power, rather "There are all kinds of qualities, substances, or essences which exist in time and space. There is not one common substance." (1:297)

James' theories of consciousness attracted much attention and had considerable impact upon the studies of psychology and philosophy. The excitement that his theories created among philosophers in America no doubt gave impetus to the formation in 1910 of a group known as the neorealists whose purposes were to refute idealism, to explain and to support the new realism, and to emphasize the scientific characteristics of the new movement. This new group consisted of "Ralph Barton Perry and Edwin B. Holt of Harvard; Walter T. Marvin and Edward Gleason Spaulding of Princeton; and Walter B. Pitkin and William Pepperell Montague of Columbia." (1:297) This group was not without its opponents. In 1916, a group of philosophers formally objected to the theory of the nature of knowledge, as proposed by the neorealist, that the perception of objects in consciousness is direct. Rather, they said the objects were represented in consciousness. Because they criticized both the idealist and the neorealists they were called the critical realists. This group consisted of men from several different educational institutions: C. A. Strong of Columbia, George Santayana, a retiree from Harvard, Arthur O. Lovejoy of Johns Hopkins, Roy W. Sellars of Michigan, James B. Pratt of Williams, and Arthur K. Rogers of Yale. (1:298)

REALISM IN EDUCATION

Realism arose, in part, as a protest against idealism which insisted that the Universe and things in the Universe could be explained in terms of ideas, mind and spirit, and in part because of certain changes taking place in the world. The nature of thinking had been changing gradually for many centuries. It was affected by the cultural, political, economic and religious forces of the Middle Ages. It was influenced by the general intellectual awakening of the Renaissance with its new spirit of inquiry and its emphasis upon things human rather than divine. Educationally speaking, realism was also a reaction against the classical humanists who were more interested in the beauty and style of the classical literature than they were in the realities of life. There were three stages of development of realism in education – humanistic realism, social realism and sense realism.

Humanistic Realism

The humanistic realists had some points in agreement with the classical humanists. They both agreed that the Bible and the old classics provided all the knowledge that was necessary in order for man to be educated. They disagreed, however, regarding the aim of education. The classical humanists emphasized the form and style of the classics and were interested mainly in reviving an intellectual culture. The humanistic realists, on the other hand, proposed to study classical literature for the purpose of obtaining ideas and meaning that would be beneficial to people in living better lives in this world.

A few of the noteworthy and representative exponents of this philosophy were Desiderius Erasmus (1466-1536), François Rabelais (1483-1553) and John Milton (1608-1674). Erasmus was born in Holland and was one of the great leaders of the Renaissance. He was one of the first to emphasize the importance of content and meaning of the ancient classics in advancing mankind. He taught that that which was learned about the realities of life was more useful than the mastery of the vocabulary, form and style of the classics. He printed a book called *Colloquia* in 1519 which was a compilation of religious, social and educational dialogues. Other books which followed were mainly on the subject of religion.

Rabelais was a Frenchman of many accomplishments — a monk, a physician, a scholar and a writer. He conveyed his realistic thoughts through humorous and satirical writings. These are especially set forth in his two works, *Life of Gargantua* and *The Heroic Deeds of Pantagruel.* He opposed the formalism and the inadequacy of the old scholastic learning and advocated the study of the old classics for the education and promotion of a more realistic life, unfettered by the strict and unmeaningful principles adhered to by the classical humanists.

Milton, the great English poet, expounded his theories of realism in many writings, particularly in his *Tractate on Education.* His theories influenced the educational thought not only in England during the rise of the academies but, to some extent, years later in America. He not only believed that understanding the meaning of the classics is more important than their style and form, but thought that the body should be developed as well as the mind. Education, he contended, should not be limited to intellectual achievements alone. He felt that all knowledge should be useful and should prepare one for earning a living and serving people. (2:397-400)

Social Realism

The social realists were more adamant than the humanistic realists in their demands that education be useful and practical. They thought that education should meet the needs of a functional life. The lives and works of two men, Michel de Montaigne (1533-1592) and John Locke

(1632-1704), give some clues to purposes and objectives. Montaigne was a French scholar and writer, a member of the nobility. He was well-educated, loved sports and games and was an excellent swordsman. Locke was an English philosopher whose theories were discussed earlier in this chapter. These men represented a small group of people who were powerful because of their wealth and social position. Their educational aim was to prepare the young men of their day for the practical life of gentlemen. They were firm in their belief that young men be educated by tutors rather than in schools. They urged that the tutors emphasize characteristics of dynamic living: meaning, understanding, good judgment, proper manners and functional living. The aim of education was a useful, happy, efficient and active life, not scholastic appreciation and achievements. Locke's ideas on the disciplinary theory of education and representative philosophy of realism had influence on subsequent education, and some of his ideas influenced the thinking and writings of Rousseau. (2:401-403)

Sense Realism

Sense realism was the culmination of that movement of realistic philosophy which emphasized the importance of scientific knowledge. Many scholars contributed to this reservoir of knowledge: Descartes with his work of analytical geometry, Copernicus with his heliocentric theory of the solar system, Galileo with his discoveries of celestial bodies and laws of falling objects, Harvey with his discovery of the circulation of the blood, Vesalius with his drawings of the dissected human body, and many others. Men became dissatisfied with the ways of doing things suggested by the ancient classics and old literature. They began to doubt; more and more men began to think for themselves and occasionally to discover, either by accident or as a result of new and efficient methods, new things about the Universe and new solutions to problems. They sought answers to the problems of life by studying laws of the Universe and by trying to understand the forces of nature. No longer were they satisfied just to study the classics for their meaning and useful ideas as the social realists had done, or for form and style as the humanist realists had advocated. The sense realists were instrumental in initiating the scientific method of thinking which was to influence all fields of study including education and physical education. (8:182-183)

Many philosophers supported the movement of sense realism. Brief description will be made, however, of only a few outstanding representatives of this philosophy who either were involved in starting the movement or giving it strong support. They were Richard Mulcaster

(1531-1611), Francis Bacon (1561-1626), Wolfgang Ratke (1571-1635) and John Amos Comenius (1592-1671). (2:405-412) Mulcaster, a renowned schoolmaster of the Latin grammar schools in London, is considered by some authorities to have been the forerunner of the sense realists, paving the way for its incorporation in education and physical education. He wrote two books, *Elementarie* and *Positions,* in which he gave evidence of his interest in both education and in physical education; he also strongly recommended the study of the English language and its use in class instruction. He thought that education should be useful in a practical sense and be based upon the child rather than upon content.

Bacon was a famous English philosopher and writer. Because of his organizing ability, to him is due much of the growth of sense realism. In his book, *Advancement of Learning,* he urged that the new scientific knowledge be used in class instruction, that a better curriculum be formulated and adequate equipment and facilities be provided. He was not a teacher, but his writings influenced others who promoted his ideas. He formulated the inductive method of reasoning, based upon facts observed and discovered and moving from the particular to the general. He had designed that method particularly for the sciences. Ratke, a German student of Bacon, later attempted to apply many of Bacon's ideas to education but with little success. He did, however, break the ground, preparing it for more influential educators and philosophers. Comenius was one of these; in fact, he is considered the greatest exponent of sense realism prior to the latter period of the eighteenth century. (2:408) Some of his ideas which were oriented toward realism were his insistence that subject matter be graded from simple to complex and that it follow the order and course of nature; that learning is accomplished by observing through the senses; that learning be based on doing useful things and relating new knowledge to old. "Comenius was the first to formulate a practicable school method, working along the new lines marked out by Bacon." (2:410) Since Comenius was a very religious man, he logically believed the main aim of education to be belief and happiness in God, but he felt individuals should be educated because they are human beings rather than just for their own salvation as Luther and other religious enthusiasts had contended. (2:410)

Some of the chief aims and contributions of the sense realists may be summarized briefly as:

1. Application of the inductive method to education.
2. Instruction given in the vernacular rather than in Latin.

3. Presentation of useful subject matter based on the sciences.
4. Utilization of sense-perception in the gathering and understanding of knowledge.
5. Instruction based on the order and course of nature, proceeding from the simple to the complex.

REALISM IN PHYSICAL EDUCATION

Changes produced in education by the philosophy of realism are reflected in all subject matter areas including physical education. The philosophers of the three stages of realism previously discussed held definite views relating to physical education.

Humanistic Realism

Erasmus believed that education about the realities of life is important. These realities for him included physical education; he felt physical exercise is important in conditioning the body for intellectual achievements. He was not interested in developing athletes, however, nor in physical education for its own sake, but for its use in the development of scholars. (8:143) Rabelais too believed that the whole man should be developed – the physical as well as the mental, moral and religious – in order to be able to perform well the duties and functions of life. He was cognizant of the importance of daily health habits, good food and recreational exercise in keeping the individual fit to perform well his duties in society. As was the case with Erasmus, Rabelais' interest in physical education was secondary. His primary objective was to prepare gentlemen for the pursuit of war. (8:175-176) Milton also agreed that the body should be developed as well as the mind. He, like Rabelais, would use physical exercise as a conditioning measure for war and a relaxing and rehabilitating procedure between periods of labor. His primary aim, also, was preparing gentlemen for the arts of war.

On the whole, the humanistic realists drew attention to the fact that there is more than a visionary or idealistic world. There is a physical world, a real world, a world of bodies, objects and things. In this world man has a body and it needs development as well as the mind. While the humanistic realists believed in training and exercising the body, the main objective for this emphasis was for military purposes. They did not recognize physical education, with its program of sports, games and exercise, for its social and recreational value. They thought of physical exercise only for its training of skill, courage and agility for military purpose. They did, however, revive an interest in the physical.

Social Realism

The social realists demanded that education be useful in the functional life in society. Education was aimed particularly at the sons of gentlemen. It was aimed at the whole man: body, mind and spirit. Montaigne felt that all these components of an indvidual should be developed in order to make a well-balanced and integrated personality. He believed that the proper development of the body contributes greatly not only to the development of the physical but to the mental, moral and spiritual aspects of the individual because of the close interrelationship and interdependence between them. Both Montaigne and Locke viewed physical exercises as necessary to condition and toughen the body. Both men formulated their system of education expressly for the higher class of people. Since they had little faith in the schools, they recommended that tutors do the teaching. The tutorial method of teaching made it impossible to hold group games or physical contests. (5:75) This isolation from others more than likely was a major reason why the social realist did not recognize the aesthetic and recreational value of games and physical activity. Their main aim was to prepare youth for the practical life of a gentleman. However, since they believed in developing the whole man and advocated a broad curriculum with which to accomplish this, physical education and health were included as part of this education. This inclusion in the curriculum was an innovation in the instructional practices of that period. (8:181)

Sense Realism

The increase of scientific knowledge brought about by the reflective thinking and the critical and inquisitive attitude of pioneer scientists encouraged men to think for themselves and look for truth by studying and observing nature rather than by accepting the authoritarian doctrines of the past. The sense realists relied upon the sciences and the scientific method of obtaining knowledge more than any of the other classes of realists. This scientific inquiry affected all areas of education including physical education. Since man was to get his information from nature it was logical to think that knowledge must come through and by means of the senses. Great emphasis therefore must be placed upon sensory training. This stress, in turn, drew greater attention to the study of the body. It was a natural consequence, then, that more concern was given to physical education. Mulcaster was one who realized the importance of physical education and felt that proper equipment and adequate facilities for exercise under favorable conditions of fresh air, sunshine and sanitary environment should be provided for youngsters.

He believed that education should be useful and designed especially for the child. The child, not the content, should be the center of attention.

Bacon contributed some information on physical education in his writings. He saw relationship between the body and mind, and thought there was a possibility of preventing disease by some form of exercise; he believed that physical skill should be developed only for the practical use of the individual, not for financial or professional gain. (8:185) Bacon was known mainly for his organizing ability and for his method of inductive teaching. His method of thinking opened up new avenues of teaching. He emphasized searching for the truth through investigation, observation and critical thinking; general principles could then be established on objective bases.

Comenius was by far the greatest exponent of sense realism. His idea that instruction should follow the regular order of nature could be applied well to play activities and physical exercise of children since there is nothing more natural than their desire for and active participation in plays and games. He believed that many forms of activities should be encouraged: jumping, running, gymnastics, wrestling and games. He insisted upon regular habits of eight hours for work, eight hours for sleep, and eights hours for relaxation, physical exercise and eating. (5:77) He believed, also, in discipline, but felt that it should be mild and gentle rather than brutal as was the case in his day. (2:410) Comenius held that education should include opportunities for recreation, relaxation and fun; that play contributes to the natural education of children; and that physical exercise is necessary for the proper development of mind and body. Because of his firm belief in natural exercise and play activities for children, that a playground was a necessary part of every educational facility, and the fact that Comenius was a great educator and philosopher, it would not be too presumptuous to infer that his thinking influenced subsequent educators and helped in laying the groundwork for the playground movement which began the latter part of the nineteenth century.

The sense realists, because of their reliance upon the sciences as the basic source of knowledge, upon method which followed the order and course of nature and upon the use of sense perception in gathering and understanding knowledge, formed a primary foundation for physical education; this coupled with succeeding events and movements added to the philosophy of the new physical education of the early part of the twentieth century. Factors contributing to the evolution of this philosophy were the contributions made in the natural sciences by John

Dalton, Charles Darwin and others; educational developmentalism by G. Stanley Hall, William James, Edward L. Thorndike and others; and social education by John Dewey, William Kilpatrick, Thomas Briggs and others. These together with men and events helped to evolve the new physical education pioneered by Thomas Wood, Rosalind Cassidy, and Clark Hetherington, which was later strengthened and enlarged by Jesse F. Williams and Jay B. Nash.

From the various views gleaned from the three stages of realism just discussed, certain statements can be made which are relevant to physical education.

Aim

The aim of realism is to prepare a person for a functional and happy life in society in which things of the world are accepted as they really are and as they appear through the senses.

Objectives

The objectives of realism are: (1) to obtain knowledge of the world through the senses; (2) to emphasize sensory training and study of the body; (3) to work out a harmonious relationship between body and mind; (4) to prepare for a useful and happy life in society; and (5) to emphasize the value of objective facts and scientific thinking.

Program

The program derived from a realistic point of view is both traditional and naturalistic in character. It is traditional because the most important knowledge of the past is accepted and is organized in a definite way such as the formal Swedish and German Gymnastic Systems. It is naturalistic because new knowledge is obtained through the senses, is aided by scientific investigation and is arranged in natural progressive steps for presentation. The program thus is not only a combination of old and new knowledge but a relationship between the two.

Method

Method may have many aspects. It may be traditional sometimes, when the time tested techniques are used such as the lecture, recitation and assigned work. It may be naturalistic when the method of instruction is based on the order and course of nature, proceeding from the simple to the complex. It may even be pragmatic in character when the project method is used. It may also be inductive, based upon facts observed and discovered and moving from the particular to the general.

Discipline

The type of discipline varies with the method of teaching. The use of the traditional method is more likely to dictate the employment of firm discipline because the teacher has data well-organized in lesson plans and drills and expects students to be diligent and attentive in their work. The use of the project and the inductive method is more likely to result in the employment of a gentle and informal discipline because the teacher wishes to encourage students to observe and to discover facts by themselves.

The Teacher

Since the teacher may use different methods or combination of methods in presenting materials to students he must have certain personality characteristics. He should be methodical, orderly and systematic in his teaching and because of this and his interests in objective things, he may appear rather impersonal at times. However, he is equally friendly, enthusiastic, and considerate in his relations with students as he encourages them through projects and demonstrations to find out for themselves new objective knowledge and to relate this new knowledge to the old.

The Administrator

The realist-administrator is likely to be a fact-minded person, interested in all kinds of school records, organized curriculums, definite teaching units and lesson plans. He is more likely to be interested in exact scores, in grades, and in measurement than in evaluation. He is likely to be a person who sees that definite school policies are formulated and are executed with promptness, justice, and firmness. He is likely to be interested in scientific research and make adequate provision for research and other such operations in his school. He is likely to employ the line and staff type of administrative procedure.

Evaluation

The realist-teacher in physical education may use both objective and subjective evaluation techniques, but he is more concerned with objective. He is more interested in records, grades, and scores of performances, something that he can treat statistically, than he is in anecdotal statements and chronological happenings. He also prefers to devise and to give objective rather than subjective type tests, and he may at times encourage students to do self-testing.

SUMMARY

The philosophy of realism has been discussed through a presentation of the views of a limited number of philosophers. These are representative of many others who lived in the various periods of history during which realism developed: ancient, early modern, and modern. Realism developed not only as a protest to idealism but as a result of many cultural, political, economic and ideological changes which took place; these, in turn, affected the nature of thinking and created new ideas. Many of these new ideas were applied to education by philosophers who were identified according to their beliefs as humanistic realists, social realists and sense realists.

The humanistic realists were found to be more concerned about useful and meaningful education and the realities of life than they were about reading the classics in order to study the form and style. The social realists placed still more emphasis upon a useful, happy and efficient life, particularly as it was applied to the sons of gentlemen, the higher class of people. The sense realists pulled farther away from the older knowledge obtained from the classics, and relied more upon the basic sciences and the employment of sense perception for their source of knowledge. Many of these philosophers had ideas on physical education. In general, the humanistic realists and the social realists thought that the whole man should be developed – physically, mentally and morally; the former more for the art of war, the latter more for the preparation of life in society. Neither group recognized a social or recreational objective of physical education. The sense realists were seen to be more deeply concerned with education through the senses; thus, the body and its care was brought into focus. Physical exercise, play and recreation were considered a valuable part of education. The center of attention was directed toward the child and less attention was paid to the content of subject matter.

QUESTIONS FOR REVIEW AND DISCUSSION

1. Discuss the meaning of realism.
2. What contributions did Plato and Aristotle make to realism?
3. Discuss the ideas of St. Thomas Aquinas which have realistic meaning. What implications do these ideas have for physical education?
4. Who was Comenius? What were his ideas which link him to realism? How do they apply to education, physical education?
5. What part of Descartes belief can be classified as realism?

6. What are Spinoza's views on realism? Discuss extension and determinism.
7. Who was Locke? What doctrines did he advocate? What were his ideas about realism, education and physical education?
8. Who are the empiricists? Discuss their idea of knowledge.
9. Explain the part of Kant's philosophic belief that supports realism.
10. Why was Herbart known as the father of scientific pedogogy? What part of his philosophy is connected with realism? What is his doctrine of apperception?
11. What is William James' theory of realism?
12. There were three stages of development of realism in education: humanistic realism, social realism, sense realism. Discuss each stage, naming some of the important exponents and discussing their views on education and physical education.
13. How would the realist be likely to interpret physical education? Discuss in terms of aim, objectives, program, method, evaluation, discipline, the teacher, the administrator.

Bibliography

1. Butler, J. Donald. *Four Philosophies and Their Practice in Education.* New York: McGraw-Hill Book Company, Inc., 1950.
2. Cubberly, Ellwood P. *The History of Education.* Boston: Houghton-Mifflin Company, 1920.
3. Frost, Jr., S. E. *Basic Teachings of Great Philosophers.* New York: Barnes and Noble, Inc., 1957.
4. Hocking, William Ernest. *Types of Philosophy.* New York: Charles Scribner's Sons, 1939.
5. Rice, Emmett A., John L. Hutchinson, and Mabel Lee. *A Brief History of Physical Education.* New York: The Ronald Press, 1958.
6. Runes, Dagobert D. *Dictionary of Philosophy.* Paterson, New Jersey: Littlefield, Adams & Company, 1962.
7. Titus, Harold H. *Living Issues in Philosophy.* New York: American Book Company, 1946.
8. Van Dalen, Deobald B., Elmer D. Mitchell, and Bruce L. Bennett. *A World History of Physical Education.* New York: Prentice-Hall, Inc., 1953.

5

Pragmatism

As a fully formulated philosophy, pragmatism is of more recent vintage than the other three philosophies discussed and is, in fact, the only one of the three which can be said to have been formulated not only in recent times but mainly by Americans. It therefore can be classified as a modern American philosophy; however, it had its beginning in other times and involved philosophers in other countries. Before tracing the early developments of pragmatism and noting its relation to education and to physical education, the general meaning of this philosophy will be discussed. In brief, pragmatism is a philosophical doctrine which holds that the meaning of anything derives from its consequences, in other words that the test of truth is action.

MEANING OF PRAGMATISM

There is probably no other philosophy which has proceeded farther from its original concept or has been so misunderstood and erroneously interpreted as pragmatism. Time, study and usage, however, are bringing greater stability, less differences in meaning, a clearer understanding and a higher respectability to the philosophical position labelled pragmatism.

Charles S. Peirce (1839-1914) is credited with inventing the term "pragmatism" but the word "pragmatic" was actually used earlier by Kant to mean "counsels of prudence." (4:245) Others used this term, but gave it a much different meaning. William James changed and extended its meaning in connection with his theory which expounded the "will to believe" or the "essence of free will." (1:415) John Dewey deviated still further and developed his theory around instrumentalism and experimentalism. Dewey's conception of pragmatism is almost identical with the objectivity of the scientific method.

Pragmatism, unlike the other philosophies studied, has its roots deeper in the epistemological than in the metaphysical realm. It is based more upon a theory of knowledge than upon a theory of reality. It interpretes ideas in terms of consequences. It is not concerned with what exists outside of experience, only with experiences: their origin, growth, and effect upon other experiences. It attempts to reconcile the position taken by the religious philosophers on the one hand and the scientific philosophers on the other. The religious philosophers contend that, on the whole, the Universe is friendly to man and that a good life on earth will be rewarded in heaven. The scientific philosophers contend that the Universe is controlled by fixed and dependable laws which themselves are not concerned with good or bad effects upon man. For the individual pragmatist, human experience with its consistencies and inconsistencies *is* the Universe and he interprets the Universe in terms of his experiences. He believes that, "Man's experience is the measure of the Universe, the only possible measure which we can have, for no man can get outside of his experience." (2:84) Further, the pragmatist is not concerned with facts alone, but with the essence of knowledge. Experience to him is the proving ground for all things. He is concerned with both knowledge and practice and interprets experience in terms of its practical consequences. He emphasizes the process of acting more than the process of knowing. "He concentrates his attention upon experience, which he finds is ever becoming, changing, being enriched." (2:53)

Some concepts of pragmatism are these: (1) theory of knowledge is more important than theory of reality – depending, of course, upon the meaning of reality. "Reality, in the thinking of Dewey, is growing, changing, developing according to laws which are laws of human experience"; (2:84) (2) experience is basic to knowledge; (3) knowledge must be sought, for it is not a mere collection of facts; (4) experiences are ever changing and developing; (5) meaning is derived from the practical consequences of experience; (6) action is the proving ground of truth; (7) experiences influence other experiences; and (8) the process of acting is emphasized more than the process of knowing. With these concepts in mind let us now turn our attention to a brief consideration of the historical development of these pragmatic beliefs.

HISTORICAL ASPECTS

Ancient Philosophers

One of the important characteristics of pragmatism and one which has been a common factor throughout the history of this philosophy, is the concept of change. The process of change was noted by the early Greek philosophers and this observation is the connecting link between some of the ancient philosophers and modern pragmatism. Many of the early Greek philosophers such as Thales, Anaximines, Pythagoras and Heraclitus were extremely interested in the nature of the Universe and proposed elements of which they thought it was composed, for example, water, atoms, air and/or fire. In all of their observations and study they noted the process of change. Water changed into steam or ice, night changed into day. Gradually some philosophers began to recognize that change itself was a problem which needed to be considered.

Heraclitus seemed to be more concerned about this problem than any one else of his time. He believed that fire was the essential element of the Universe because fire was always changing and changing things in the Universe. Everything in the Universe was always changing. Nothing was stable. For Heraclitus there was not anything so permanent or real as change, e.g., like the flowing waters of a stream which are never the same. (2:4-5) This was the doctrine of change advocated by Heraclitus. According to this philosophy reality is not a substance, rather it is a state of continuous movement – a constant change. This ancient theory of change is a basic part of modern pragmatism.

Another feature in the theory of the ancient philosophers which is similar to that of modern pragmatism is the tendency toward skepticism. The Sophists, Protagoras, Gorias, and others in the fifth century B.C., traveled around the country teaching in an easy, persuasive but sometimes confusing way. Because of their oratorical cleverness and the fact that they accepted fees for their services they were not always held in good repute. In those days it was thought unethical for philosophers to accept fees. However, the Sophists probably did some good by stimulating other teachers to re-examine their thinking about knowledge. The Sophists questioned not only the meaning of knowledge but also the very existence of knowledge itself. For Protagoras, sense perception was the nearest approach to knowledge. He said, "man is the measure of all things." (1:399) In Dewey's brand of pragmatism, however, the tested hypothesis is the nearest approach to knowledge. He believed that "the social mind, by virtue of its ability to experiment, is the measure of all things." (1:400) The former considered man as a single person, the latter as a complete society of men.

Modern Philosophers

Francis Bacon (1561-1626) was an English writer, statesman and philosopher. His most famous works are *Novum Organum*, *Advancement of Learning* and the *New Atlantis*. He was the father of two ideas which have influenced modern pragmatism: the idea of inductive reasoning and the idea of society working cooperatively in science toward a common objective. (1:404) The inductive method of reasoning employs the process of observation, is interested in the particulars and in conditions of things as they are. It proceeds from the particulars to the general; from many facts to a generalization, a law or principle. It is a method of finding new ideas, facts and knowledge by observation and investigation. The inductive method is just the opposite of the deductive method formulated centuries before by Aristotle, a method which was based upon abstract reasoning and syllogism. Deduction is more concerned with general propositions, formal logic and accepted ideas; it is not as conducive to free thought or as productive of new knowledge as inductive reasoning. The important contribution of inductive reasoning to pragmatism and the greatest connection between them is the concept of particulars. While pragmatism gives an important place to the inductive method of reasoning, it is especially interested in particulars because, through the study of particulars by means of observation and experimentation, new knowledge may be obtained. Thus a shift of emphasis is made from the formal logic of the mind to the study of the external world.

Bacon's other pragmatic contribution, that of science being conducted and maintained cooperatively by society for a common purpose, was later accepted by Dewey. There are many problems on which individuals and groups of individuals work independently, endeavoring to find solutions through scientific research. According to Dewey's variety of pragmatism, the study of the sciences and the application of scientific procedures to social problems is a concern of the group working cooperatively together for the common good. If the common good of man is to be achieved, social and moral progress must keep pace with the discoveries in sciences. Each segment of society may work on the same problem, each making its contribution to the solution of the whole. Each would share in the knowledge revealed; in this way a process of checks and balances would exist. The sciences give us knowledge and technique, but philosophy tells us when and for what purpose this knowledge should be used. Atomic energy, for example, is the product of the sciences. This energy may, however, be used for the benefit or detriment of society. Cooperation of science and philosophy working together on social problems is necessary for the improvement and good of society.

Immanuel Kant contributed ideas which supported and anticipated more than one philosophy: idealism (Chapter III), realism (Chapter IV) and now pragmatism. As noted, Kant used the term pragmatic "to apply to rules and standards based on experience as distinct from those he thought were above or beyond experience." (5:253) According to Kant's reasoning, the nature of the Universe is known by experience and by reason. In the Universe there are universal laws by which man, by nature, feels compelled to live. Man would not commit acts which would jeopardize society because of his sense of duty to the moral law or the "categorical imperative." However, this law cannot operate unless there is freedom of the will. This moral law, together with the belief in the reality of God and the immortality of souls, compose the basis of Kant's "principle of the primacy of practical reason." (4:159) This phase of Kant's philosophy contributed in a way to the development of certain aspects of the philosophy of pragmatism.

Auguste Comte (1798-1857) was a French philosopher and a student of the sciences, particularly mathematics and sociology. He was the first to describe and name the field of sociology. He opposed the theories of nature and society of his time which were concerned mainly with the origin and development of the nature of reality. He thought that the only real knowledge came from those things which had objective and interrelated existence: the observable facts. This theory was called positivism and was an outgrowth of the persistent stress on empiricism and the scientific method of the nineteenth century. (5:203)

Comte thought that the history of man and man's thought could be divided into three stages: the theological, the metaphysical and the positive or scientific. In the theological, the first stage, thought was influenced by supernatural beliefs. Reality was interpreted largely in prejudicial and superstitious ways. In the metaphysical, which was the second and the next higher stage, abstract reason and comprehension were employed to explain reality, but without the support of facts. This type of reasoning used some powers or substances as the basis of reality which were not considered supernatural in character. In the second phase then, an attempt was made to substitute abstract thought for supernatural belief. This was a stage of gradual transition between the first and third stages; it prepared the way for the last and highest stage, the positive. In the positive stage, factual knowledge began to be substituted for beliefs based upon abstract thought. This period was also called the scientific stage because it considered the laws and the observable facts of exact sciences as the basis and source of knowledge. Reality was thus founded on facts and laws of the sciences, not on the supernatural, spiritual, metaphysical or substance.

It is Comte's last stage of thought, positivism, which has had some influence upon modern pragmatism. Butler states that at least two positions in Comte's positive philosophy contributed to the formulation of modern pragmatism. "They are the positivistic treatment of metaphysics and an intense interest in social relations." (1:408)

The connecting point between Comte's positivism and modern pragmatism is the disbelief of both in substance as the essence of existence. Both positivism and pragmatism give a great deal of attention to the social sciences and are interested in the social life and education of people. Comte's main work and that from which his theories come is *Course of Positive Philosophy.*

Philosophers of Pragmatism in the United States

We have seen certain phases in the philosophies of ancient and relatively modern thinkers which anticipated a new kind of philosophy. These phases included the belief in reality as a state of continuous movement as proposed by Heraclitus, the tendency toward skepticism of knowledge as seen in the Sophists, the study of particulars by observation and experimentation and the conduction and maintenance of science by society for a common purpose as advocated by Bacon, and the principle of practical reason proposed by Kant. This new philosophy was called pragmatism. The men largely responsible for its modern formulation and development were Charles S. Peirce, William James and John Dewey. Since its chief development was made in the United States by Americans it reflects many characteristics of American society and can be called an American philosophy. Let us look now to the contribution of each of these three Americans.

Charles S. Peirce (1839-1914) was a physicist, mathematician and philosopher. He was the originator of the idea from which modern pragmatism has developed, and together with William James was responsible for initiating this thought and developing it into a movement. Peirce had been influenced in his thinking by Kant's works in which Kant had used the term pragmatic and had discussed the "principle of primacy of practical reason." Peirce then originated the term pragmatism to describe his theory of thought that, "The meaning of a proposition is its logical (or physical) consequences." (4:245) Later when William James used this term but with a different meaning Peirce changed the name to pragmaticism. (3:6168) For James, pragmatism meant "that the end of man is action" but Peirce intercepted it as "a theory of logical analysis or true definition." (4:245) Actually, Peirce was a realist, not a pragmatist, because of his objective views of the world. His training, experience and interest were in physics, mathematics and other sciences. He was familiar with scientific investigations. It was natural for him to think in terms of objective realities of the Universe. His relation and contribution to pragmatism was mainly that of originating the term for his theory and formulating "a criterion for determining the meanings of ideas." (1:411) While Peirce was not a well-known philosopher of his time, he was considered an original thinker. He gave many lectures, wrote many essays and papers but completed only one work, *The Grand Logic,* which was published after his death.

William James (1842-1910) was an eminent American psychologist and philosopher, a very popular and an inspiring teacher, lecturer and writer. Some of his famous works are *The Principles of Psychology; The Will to Believe; Pragmatism – A New Name for Some Old Ways of Thinking; A Pluralistic Universe,* and *Essays in Radical Empiricism.* His linkage to pragmatism was through his theory of radical empiricism and the will to believe. In his theory of radical empiricism he held that all ideas come from sensations and experience in a continuous state of consciousness and serve as a standard by which the reality of knowledge is determined. He believed that things are accepted as they exist, fragmentary and partly connected, and that the relations among these things are as much a part of experience as "the things themselves." (4:90) He held that consciousness proceeds from both the will and the senses and exhibits interest and attention, but it is the will which determines the method and subject of thought. Through a process of selection and rejection of existing things by one's consciousness, the individual to a great extent determines his own world. Ideas operate much the same way as sense perceptions. One selects and attends to those things which are most appealing and most interesting and which bring the most satisfaction, and rejects the others. (5:254-255) James' "doctrine of the will to believe" recognizes that life is composed of more than formal thought and theory. It includes characteristic values of life which are revealed when severe experiences are faced. There are many situations in life in which men must make decisions with insufficient data because adequate data are simply not available. "This is where their will to believe may enter and create new truth or new value simply through the will to believe." (5:256)

Further, many times man feels the presence of something greater or higher than himself, something spiritual or divine. Man learns to accept and depend on this spiritual essence because it reveals to him the Truth and brings to him comfort and peace. This spiritual essence, religiously speaking, is described as God. But James did not think of God as an infinite and absolute being. He held that God did not create the world but is part of it; that reality is not monistic but pluralistic, and that the world is composed of neither completely good nor wholly evil possibilities. Furthermore, when God is a finite being he and man have more mutual relationships and can work together in trying to improve the world. This belief is known as the doctrine of meliorism. (5:256)

John Dewey (1859-1952) was one of the greatest American philosophers, psychologists and educators. His influence in these fields extended far and wide, not only in the United States but also in many foreign countries. He was a prolific writer and a prominent lecturer. Some of his important books are *School and Society, How We Think, Influence of Darwin on Philosophy, Democracy and Education, Reconstruction in Philosophy,* and *Human Nature and Conduct.* We have seen that American pragmatism had its roots in Kant's "practical reason," that Peirce coined the term "pragmatism," that James was responsible for its rapid rise, but Dewey was the one responsible for its great growth and development. In the formative years of his philosophy Dewey was influenced by several men, chief of whom were George S. Morris (1840-1889), an idealist, and G. Stanley Hall (1844-1924), an experimental psychologist. His associations with Morris grounded him in some of the conceptions of idealism, particularly those of ethics and theology. His study with Hall imbued him with an interest in psychology which was later to form an important part of his philosophy: experimentalism.

In a latter period of the formulation of his philosophy, Dewey shifted from the metaphysics or the nature of reality of idealism toward the empirical variety of idealism in which many of the idealistic concepts continued to exist, with the exception of the reality of the Supreme Being. Other important steps in his swing away from idealism were his final rejection of theism and the doctrine of a Universal Self. He began to turn his attention more and more toward the influence of social institutions and cultural environment upon the formation of habits of thought, attitudes and beliefs of men. (1:417-420) He was interested in the particular things of experience, but not just mere collection of facts. Facts must be organized, but not for the production of a Universal

Truth or the formulation of a principle by inductive process of reasoning. "Instead, the pattern for organizing facts, which constitutes the core of knowledge, is a hypothesis which works successfully." (1:425)

There are many other characteristics of Dewey's philosophy. He believed that the mind was capable of inventing tools or instruments like ideas, attitudes, techniques and methods with which to solve a given problem. This takes place in the environment of experience through the employment of experimental inquiry. This is called his theory of instrumentalism. While he thought it impossible to know ultimate reality, reality to him meant that all things were in a continuous state of flux, always changing, always developing. It was only with this concept of reality that things could be studied and made to work and current values could be realized. Dewey also believed that the scientific method should be applied to the field of social thought and that the problems of society should be worked out cooperatively for greatest benefit of man. He maintained that the meaning of an idea could not be determined unless it was put into use and the consequences of this action noted. Learning takes place through knowing and doing, especially if the activities are of interest to the individual and the end results are satisfying.

PRAGMATISM IN EDUCATION

There are many fine aspects in the philosophy of pragmatism which are related to logic, social thought, psychology, religion and education. There seems to be a natural affinity between education and pragmatism. These have blended together extremely well and have produced an outstanding theory of education. No other philosophy in recent times has influenced and exalted education and strengthened its foundations as much as pragmatism. John Dewey was the person largely responsible for promoting and developing this modern philosophy and applying it to education. His emphasis on a new and dynamic approach to learning stimulated and augmented the growth of the Progressive Education Movement. He was not, however, the originator of this movement as many people have thought. The movement was not initiated by any particular person or developed and sponsored by any distinct branch of philosophy. It arose rather as an outgrowth of protests, both in Europe and in the United States, against formalized learning and traditional teaching methods. (1:466) The movement officially began in the United States in 1918 when the Progessive Education Association was founded. In 1944 the name was changed to the one by which it is known today, the American Education Fellowship. (3:2210)

Pragmatism brought many new ideas to the field of education. As would be expected, the basic concept of its approach is through experience. The individual learns through actually experiencing, doing meaningful things, inquiring, observing, and participating in life activities. Under this theory, the wise teacher would begin with the present experience of students and, through the introduction of new experiences, would reconstruct newer ideas so that learning would become, according to Dewey, a "continuous process of reconstruction of experience in line of new experiences."

Education influenced by pragmatism does not concentrate on facts, on rote memory or repetitive exercises. It encourages continuous doing, acting, thinking and learning by dynamic living. The general educational objective of this philosophy is social efficiency; that is, the degree of adjustment of the individual to his environment, the satisfactory solutions of problems, the ability to adapt to new and changing conditions, and the willingness to share and cooperate in working out problems of society. This method emphasizes the study of the child, not subject matter. The school therefore is child-centered. It recognizes the doctrine of individual differences; consequently, each child is treated differently and is permitted to progress at his own natural speed. It stresses that the whole child goes to school. Both body and mind therefore must be taken care of so that a socially, morally, physically and mentally integrated individual can be developed. The important thing is growth and development in these categories.

There are other concepts of this philosophy. Learning must be purposeful and creative. To accomplish this, activities must be based on needs, interests, and desires of the individual. The activities most beneficial, according to this point of view, are those which are self-chosen and which bring satisfactory results or consequences. This type of learning emphasizes individual initiative, individual and group thinking, the value of interdisciplinary study, constructive project and the experimental or the pragmatic method of knowledge. The experimental method as described by pragmatism is composed of "five steps: activity, problem, observation of data, formulation of hypotheses, and the testing of the hypotheses." (1:429-439)

PRAGMATISM IN PHYSICAL EDUCATION

Several movements occurring in the United States in the latter part of the twentieth century helped to prepare the way and to create a fertile soil so that pragmatism flourished. The scientific movement led by John Dalton in chemistry, Michael Faraday in physics, James Cattell in anthropometry, and others emphasized the use of scientific procedures in solving educational problems and directed attention in general toward the employment of precise measurements and the development of effective methods. The movement of educational developmentalism initiated by G. Stanley Hall and supported by Edward L. Thorndike, William James and others focused attention upon the study of the child and his needs and interests rather than upon the subject matter. The pragmatic movement was closely associated with the field of psychology. The social education movement led by Lester Ward, John Dewey, William Kilpatrick and others concentrated its efforts toward developing social consciousness, democracy and cooperation in societal living. The shift of emphasis was from the individual to the group. This movement was closely related to the field of sociology. (6:359) The germ-idea of pragmatism had been transplanted from Europe from such philosophers as Bacon, Comte, and Kant, but it was planted in the American soil by Peirce, nursed by James and developed by Dewey and others.

From about the middle of the nineteenth century to the turn of the twentieth century formal gymnastic physical education systems were brought to the United States by Charles Follen, Charles Beck and Francis Lieber of Germany and by Hartvig Nissen and Baron Nils Posse of Sweden. These systems emphasized drill, effort, formal commands, content, required exercises and training of the physical body. Gradually these formal systems were accepted in many American public schools and flourished there for some time. Eventually, however, in the early part of the twentieth century, because of the influence of the several movements mentioned and particularly because of educational developmentalism and social education, dissatisfaction developed regarding the formal gymnastic systems. There was a demand for a shift from exercises based on effort to those that were based on the interests, needs, and desires of the individual; for a change from obediently following commands to the development of individual initiative; for a swing from all required activities to self-selected activities, and for a shift from a formal to an informal program. Physical education leaders began to think of physical education as an essential part of general education and not as a separate entity; consequently, education in physical education was considered to proceed *through* the physical rather than *of* the physical. There was a shift of emphasis from the subject matter to the individual and his needs.

Play and recreation thus became an important educational activity because they could be used effectively to improve both the power of the mind and strength of the body. Personal health was also emphasized because of the influence of developmentalism and its concentration on child study. Athletic sports became more popular and began to be considered a part of the physical education program. This total program contributed to the social education movement through providing opportunities for the development of such social and personal qualities as ethical character, cooperation, honesty, friendliness, sportsmanship and fair play. These ideas and attitudes concerning health, physical education, recreation and athletics were much different from those which were prevalent during the old formal gymnastic regime. These new concepts were indicative of the "New Physical Education" formulated by Thomas Wood, Rosalind Cassidy and Clark Hetherington in 1922. (6:424)

As in education, so it is in physical education according to pragmatic belief. Learning is accomplished in a pragmatic way through doing and experiencing those things which are purposeful, creative and beneficial, those which spring from the interests and needs of the individual and are selected by him from his own level of experience. Meaning of a learning situation is conveyed to the student through practical and satisfying consequences. Social education which is considered an important phase of this philosophy comes through cooperative participation in life situations in a democratic society.

Physical education, seen through the eyes of pragmatism, might be interpreted as follows:

Aim

The aim of education is to interpret the Universe in terms of ever-changing, ever-developing human experience for more efficient societal living. The aim of physical education, as interpreted by pragmatism, is to develop the whole individual mentally, morally, socially, and physically in terms of human experience *through* the physical and not *of* the physical. Physical education considered in this concept is a phase of education.

Objectives

Some of the objectives of pragmatism are: (1) to approach education through experience; (2) to approach education through the study of the child and not through subject matter; (3) to develop social efficiency; (4) to develop the whole individual mind, body, and soul — total fitness; (5) to make learning more purposeful and creative; (6) to develop individual initiative, and individual and group thinking;

(7) to encourage thinking, acting, and doing; (8) to emphasize the importance of scientific procedure; and to develop social consciousness, democracy, and cooperation in societal living.

Program

The program of the pragmatist teacher is based upon the needs, interests, and desires of students. The teacher is likely to encourage students to choose activities in which they are interested and which they feel are most useful to them. There is, as a result, a noticeable shift from inclusion of activities in the program which emphasize effort per se to those which emphasize interest; from those that are formal to those that are informal, and to the ones that are socializing, challenging, creative, and problem solving. To accomplish these things necessitates a large program and a wide variety of activities; such activities as individual and team sports, aquatics, dance, recreational, and social activities would be included.

Method

The pragmatist teacher uses the experimental and constructive project method because they help attain the objectives of a pragmatic program. These methods, it is assumed, help make learning more purposeful and creative; develop individual initiative and individual and group thinking; teach students to recognize problems and to try to find solutions for them; encourage thinking and doing; stimulate the construction of better programs through student-teacher cooperation; bring about more satisfactory evaluation through student self-evaluation; and develop social consciousness and democratic living.

Discipline

A school situation in which the students are encouraged to participate in making the school program and to evaluate their work and to be creative shapes and fashions naturally an atmosphere in which students are largely responsible for their actions and behavior. If the meaning of a problem situation is in the practical consequences of experience, then unsatisfactory and annoying experiences as well as satisfactory and enjoyable experiences are some of the controlling factors which influence students to shape and restrain their behavior. Student behavior may also be directed through the use of guidance, counseling, and motivation. The pragmatist teacher does not use an autocratic approach to discipline.

The Teacher

The pragmatist teacher possesses certain qualities and characteristics that enable him to be a counselor, an advisor, and a leader. He does not have a dictatorial attitude when he teaches and works with students. He is understanding, helpful, and friendly. He tries to guide students through the use of motivating and stimulating techniques and cooperative effort.

The Administrator

The pragmatist administrator is a person who provides the kind of atmosphere and environment that is conducive to the attainment of pragmatic aims and objectives. He will encourage the successful employment of the project and experimental method. He is likely to favor the functional type of administrative procedure.

Evaluation

In a school situation where pragmatic philosophy is dominant learning and academic status of students is determined more by evaluation than by a limited measuring process. The teacher is not as much concerned about scores and records of performances as in the occurrence of behavior changes; in improvements in the ability to adjust to changing situations; and in an increase in ability to solve problems. Subject to and commensurate with age and maturity, students are encouraged to make their own evaluations and subsequent adjustments.

SUMMARY

In this chapter discussion has centered around the development of pragmatism by many philosophers over the centuries and the meaning of this philosophy for education and physical education. The root ideas contributed by ancient and modern philosophers of Europe to this new point of view were seen to be the concept of continuous change or movement; the skepticism of knowledge; the importance of the study of particulars and the pursuit of science by society for the common good; the principle of practical reason; and the theory of positivism. It was in the United States where these ideas found favorable environment in which to materialize and philosophers eager and capable to develop them into a full-fledged philosophy. It was learned that some of the favorable situations were the spirit of inquiry, the spirit of democratic living, and the three movements of scientific knowledge, educational developmentalism and social education. Important among the many philosophers in the United States who were associated with pragmatism were Peirce, James, and Dewey. Peirce was the originator of the idea from which this modern philosophy developed and he coined the name "pragmatism." In Peirce's philosophy, the meaning of an idea was found in its logical analysis or consequences. James changed the meaning of pragmatism when he advocated his theory of free will. It was through his efforts that pragmatism rose quickly and spread rapidly. Dewey deviated farther from Peirce's original idea and proposed theories of instrumentalism, experimentalism and social education. He was the person responsible for the great growth and development of pragmatism. Pragmatism, as interpreted by education and physical education, is concerned mainly with the experiences of people. Experience is the proving ground of all things. It is basic to all learning. In reality experience is always changing, influencing and enriching other experiences and reconstructing new experiences. Education is not concerned with facts alone. It emphasizes the process of acting more than the process of knowing. It is interested, however, more in the theory of knowledge than in the theory of reality.

QUESTIONS FOR REVIEW AND DISCUSSION

1, Discuss the meaning of pragmatism.
2. What is the connecting link between the theories of some of the early Greek philosophers and modern pragmatism? Name some of these philosophers. What were their beliefs?
3. Name at least two Sophists whose tendency toward skepticism of knowledge was similar to that of modern pragmatism. Discuss other characteristics of the Sophists which affected education.
4. What were the two ideas of Francis Bacon which influenced modern pragmatism? Explain them.
5. Some of Kant's ideas supported several philosophies: idealism, realism, and pragmatism. How could one man provide so many different theories? Can this be justified? What was his contribution to pragmatism?
6. Discuss Comte's theory of positivism. What phase of this theory contributed some meaning to pragmatism?
7. Who originated the term pragmatism? What was his theory?
8. What is William James' theory of radical empiricism, doctrine of of the will to believe and doctrine of meliorism?
9. What American philosopher was largely responsible for the growth and development of pragmatism? What is his theory of instrumentalism?

10. Discuss the meaning of pragmatism in relation to education and physical education.
11. Trace the origin and development of pragmatism in the United States. Show how various movements prepared the way for pragmatism to flourish.
12. Discuss the shift of emphasis from the formal type exercises of various gymnastic systems to the informal activities of the New Physical Education.
13. Discuss the pragmatist approach to physical education in relation to: aim, objectives, program, method, discipline, the teacher, the administrator, and evaluation.

Bibliography

1. BUTLER, J. DONALD. *Four Philosophies and Their Practice in Education.* New York: McGraw-Hill Book Company, Inc., 1950.
2. FROST, JR., S. E. *Basic Teachings of Great Philosophers.* New York: Barnes and Noble, Inc., 1957.
3. JONES, J. MORRIS. *The World Book Encyclopedia.* Chicago: The Quarrie Corporation, 1947.
4. RUNES, DAGOBERT D. *Dictionary of Philosophy.* Paterson, New Jersey: Littlefield, Adams and Company, 1962.
5. TITUS, HAROLD H. *Living Issues in Philosophy.* New York: American Book Company, 1946.
6. VAN DALEN, DEOBALD, ELMER D. MITCHELL, AND BRUCE L. BENNETT. *A World History of Physical Education.* New York: Prentice-Hall, Inc., 1953.

Philosophic History of Physical Education

6

The discussion to this point, has centered around the origin and growth of basic philosophy and the historical development of several philosophies in education: naturalism, idealism, realism, and pragmatism. In this chapter, additional data are presented which, it is hoped, will help the reader to understand more clearly the antecedents of a philosophy of physical education, will help him appreciate the heritage of physical education, and will prove useful to him in building his own professional philosophy. This chapter concerns the philosophic history of physical education; that is, an interpretation of the purposes of physical education throughout history.

Peoples of every culture through the ages have had certain feelings toward or views concerning the political events, social, economic, and religious forces of their time. Physical exercise is one of these forces. Physical exercise is the oldest of all forms of education of the human race. It has been used by different peoples for different purposes: for the development of physical fitness and for educational, religious, aesthetic, artistic, political, recreational, and/or military reasons. It has been an integral and important aspect of some societies and has been eliminated, restrained, or subjected to certain forces in others. Through a study of the mores, habits, customs, movements, forces, and personalities of peoples of all countries throughout history one can come to understand the various feelings about the value of physical exercise and can determine the purposes for which physical activity has been used. Using these sources of data, one can analyze and interpret the influence which different cultures have had upon physical education and upon the subsequent development of philosophies of physical education. Let us begin this analysis by studying, first, the status of physical education in primitive society.

PHYSICAL EDUCATION IN PRIMITIVE SOCIETY

The basic needs of man have been the same from primitive times to the present. The only way these needs differ is one of degree, or the manner or method in which they are obtained. Physical and biological needs are concerned mainly with the securement of food, clothing, and shelter. Mental and social needs are concerned chiefly with being accepted by one's society, having a chance to succeed, maintaining a degree of security, being given an opportunity to belong, securing a certain amount of happiness and well-being, and having an opportunity to think and to believe as an individual.

Taking care of biological needs in primitive society was dependent more upon the physical strength, skill, and endurance of the individual than it is today. It was necessary for primitive man to struggle vigorously against the elements of nature and fight the savage beasts of the forest and sea in order to provide the bare necessities of life. Thus, physical exercise was the order of the day. It was the important phase of daily life and of education for survival. While their physical exercise could not be identified formally with our types of physical education today, it did provide for them, in a practical way, a method to meet the physical, mental, and social needs of their society. They, like all peoples, had need to relax from the daily chores of providing life essentials and it is assumed they did this through their favorite forms of fun and amusement. Their interests were their needs. Their aims and objectives, while not declared formally, were in practice: physical fitness, security, and conformity. Upon these they depended for their survival. The forces which motivated them to strive for their objectives were those of combat against unfriendly tribes, wild beasts, and the elements of nature. Thus, we may interpret their philosophy as a practical one of meeting the needs of daily life. While we cannot claim that this makes a formal contribution to our philosophy of physical education today, nevertheless it is a clue to the building and development of the practical and workable.

ANCIENT MIDDLE EASTERN AND ORIENTAL COUNTRIES

The early middle eastern and Oriental peoples were those of Egypt, Mesopotamia, China, India, and Persia. Each had a society of a higher order than those of primitive peoples. Each made certain specific contributions to civilization. Each had definite aims of education which directly influenced their practices of physical exercise or physical education, a term used later to describe a program of physical activity.

The societies of the Egyptians, the Mesopotamians, and others of the Near East were the first to have direct influence upon subsequent civilizations. (3:12) Civilization is generally considered to have had its origin in Egypt. The aims of the Egyptian education were to teach reading and writing and to preserve and to perpetuate learnings of the past. These aims were concerned more with the practical and vocational side of life than with the cultural. As far as we know there was very little consideration given to health practices and physical exercise. Among the Orientals, China was one of the first to create the early beginnings of a civilized state. She was interested in training her people for social stability and this was maintained by educating a scholarly caste to the ideals of the ancients. The aged scholar and the concepts, customs, and traditions of the past were held in high esteem. This resulted in a static and nonprogressive society. In a narrow environment of this nature, physical fitness, exercise, and health received little attention. What consideration physical exercise received was through regular occupational pursuits of their culture (as of the soldier, the farmer, and other laborers) or resulted from military demands.

Nor did the ancient peoples of India place much importance on physical education. The climate was oppressive, disease and poverty were prevalent, and the death rate was high. This kind of an environment is not associated with an emphasis on physical exercise. Relief from the burdens of life was sought through the spiritual realm and since this placed emphasis upon the future life, physical exercise was opposed. Some physical activity came about, however, in the performance of dances at religious ceremonies. They, like the Chinese, were also interested in maintaining social stability. This was accomplished by educating the Brahman priests who enforced the religious ideals and kept the caste system intact. (3:27)

Persia, another early Oriental country, was different in an unique way. This was the country in which the civilizations of the Orient and the Occident met. This country served as a bridge which touched the cultures of two different civilizations. The Persians were aggressive and warlike people. To make strong armies, strong men were necessary. To make strong bodies, vigorous exercise, as well as proper food, clothing, training, and rest were required. Persia consequently emphasized the physical more than any of the other Oriental countries. Physical fitness was the primary aim of education. There was little education for the cultural or the vocational pursuit of life and this was the big defect in Persia's educational system. As China maintained social stability by training the scholarly caste, and India by educating the Brahman priests, Persia maintained social stability by training the warring class. It was with the Persians that the first spark of freedom and respect for the individual appeared. This concept of the individual was developed later more completely by the Greeks, Hebrews, and others. This is part of the heritage that the present day democracies received from these ancient peoples and made an integral part of their philosophy: respect for the worth, rights, and freedom of the individual. Other contributions these early peoples made to our society were their native forms of dance, art, and recreational activities. They demonstrated that physical education could be obtained in a practical way through the training and pursuit of their vocational activities. While all of the Oriental countries did not accord physical education the same degree of importance, they, like the primitive peoples, gave it a position of permanence which they passed on to subsequent societies. Furthermore, the Persians were the first to create a new philosophy of education. This resulted in the instruction of boys beyond the age of seven in physical education and military training under the direction of government officials. This was the first known instance of state control of education for the pursuit of political aims and prestige. (3:31)

THE HEBREWS

Modern civilization is indebted to the Hebrews for many philosophical, religious, and educational ideas and these have had profound influence on both modern and present day civilizations. These early peoples departed from the beliefs of the Orientals which were based upon the authority of the caste, ancestors, or military class, and developed a higher form of authority and religion predicated upon the conception of a monotheistic, omnipotent, and righteous God. The emphasis of education was placed upon the fear of God and the development of righteous living. They conceived the philosophical ideas of brotherhood of man, social justice, and universal peace, which form a part of our modern philosophies. These certainly are worthy ideals that can be incorporated in a philosophy of education, of physical education or in one's personal philosophy. Furthermore, the Hebrews elevated health and physical education to a higher plane than it had enjoyed in any earlier civilization. They employed the dance to express their feelings and emotions in worshipping God. They held a high regard for personal and community cleanliness and encouraged moderate physical exercise for the physical development of the individual.

All of these activities, however, were conducted in agreement with and subjected to the authority of their religion, rather than for the accomplishment of specified objectives in health, and physical education. At least, this was a start toward the recognition of the importance of this area of activity in the general field of education and contributed to the heritage of our profession.

THE GREEKS

The Greeks had the honor of being the first peoples in Europe to develop an outstanding form of civilization; in fact, it can be stated that western civilization had its origin in Greece. It was from this country that a rich heritage in science, philosophy, art, sculpture, architecture, education, games, and athletic contests have come down to us. They produced a society that was much more progressive and vigorous than any had been before and, in many respects, since that time. They developed a form of education that emphasized individual excellence and the concept of progressive change and adjustment. They were the first people to give positive consideration to the problems of philosophy and education. (3:41) They gave great recognition to the importance of the development of an integrated individual, mentally and physically — a "sound mind in a sound body." A greater understanding of Greek philosophy, education, and culture can be obtained by a more detailed study of Greek history.

The Homeric People

The Homeric Age began about 1000 B.C. when the peoples of the North began to invade Greece and mingle with the natives of the Greek peninsula. This period continued until about 750 B.C. (2:13) These rustic and pastoral people formed a primitive society, but one from which later institutions of Greek civilization were to arise. Religion played an important part in their lives, but not so much from the viewpoint of morality as from a love of beauty in nature and in man. However, religion did foster and encourage the development of the arts — music, sculpture, poetry, and architecture — as well as education and gymnastics. The Homeric people had many personalized gods whom they worshipped for their superior strength, physical ability, and mental capacities, and tried to excel them. This motivation and desire to excel plus their inherent love of competition were powerful forces in creating the spirit of individual excellence in mind and muscle which they pursued as a goal. From a meager beginning the concept of the individual was more fully extended and developed later in the Athenian society. The general aim, however, was to develop a strong physical being – "a man of action." (3:43) It was from Homer's ballads, the *Iliad* and the *Odyssey*, that a supposedly accurate account of the life of this early Grecian period was obtained. From these sources we learn that athletic sports, games, and contests held a prominent place in the lives of these early people. Competition was also held in poetry, music, public speaking, sculpture, and other arts. Pursuit of wisdom therefore was encouraged because of their interest in the development of the most excellent and complete individual, encompassing both the knowledge of physical action and knowledge of the mind.

The Spartans

The Spartans were an aggressive and warlike people and began to make their influence felt upon their neighbors about the eighth century B.C. They were not interested, as the Homeric Greeks were, in developing the whole man. They were guided apparently solely by militaristic aims, and thus directed all their attention to the physical excellence of man. Because of the militaristic aim they were interested in making strong obedient people who were subservient to the state – strong and healthy men to make strong and courageous soldiers and strong and healthy women to rear robust children. They had little desire or time to devote to the development of science, philosophy, art, or literature. Even though they rose to great political supremacy, the major cause of their downfall was their lack of a complete and well-rounded education. Other contributing causes were their fear of change, disrespect for individual freedom, and their unwillingness to mingle and exchange ideas with other people.

In his program of physical activity, the Spartan youth was trained to withstand hardship. Since he was to become a soldier, his program consisted mainly of military training. Gymnastics and other forms of physical conditioning exercises were included, together with vigorous games and contests. It is of great interest to note that, even in this early period, the Spartans employed a commendable method in presenting their program of activities, the grading of gymnastics and other forms of physical exercises proceeding from the simple to the complex and the gradual increase of dosage in time and repetitions. This is a practice which is employed in good curriculum building and in effective presentation of materials in modern education and in physical education. This we inherited from the Spartans.

The Athenians

The Athenians arose from cultures similar to the Spartans, but gradually their ideas and attitudes of life changed and they slowly developed a different society, one that was more democratic, progressive, and intellectual in character. While they were not as warlike and aggressive as the Spartans, they gave a good account of themselves in battle when military emergencies arose. The entire Athenian history, including the early and later periods, extended over the years from approximately 776 to 338 B.C. (3:42) During this time there was a gradual rise to greatness; the pinnacle of achievement, the Golden Age; and the fall and decline of their society. History has recorded this pattern many times since the Greeks, that of repeating this same cycle and ending in dissolution because of human failure and weakness: morally, socially, and physically.

The early Athenians, like the Homeric Greeks, were interested in developing the whole man, mentally and physically. They sought beauty and harmony in their work. They considered skill, form and grace of performance in athletics more important than establishing records. Sportsmanship, fair play, courage, and self-discipline were emphasized. Emphasis was placed on individual performance. There were no team games. This was an age of individualism. While the Athenian society had the embryonic beginnings of democracy, however, only about twenty per cent of the people were free and qualified as citizens. The culture and environment necessary for the germination and development of the team games and team spirit of later democracies had not yet appeared.

Much more complete education was provided for the boy, beginning at the age of seven and extending through to adulthood, than for the girl. The boy's early physical education was received from a teacher at a private school, called the "Palaestra," and his early education in academic subjects (music, literature, and arithmetic) was obtained in the "Didascaleum." No formal education, either physical or mental, was provided for the girl. She was trained in the arts of housekeeping by her mother and led a life of semi-seclusion, similar to the girl in Oriental societies. (2:27)

A noteworthy method of teaching employed by the Athenians, and one which has received considerable attention in methodology today, was that of general ability grouping. This method was used in preference to a strict age classification. (3:66) Like the Persians, they also graded their exercises commensurate with the ability of the individual.

The society of the later Athenians embraced the Golden Age and the decline of Greek civilization. Many factors set the stage for the Golden Age: the defeat of Persia, the decreased power of the agricultural ruling class, the beginnings of commerce, higher standards of living, and increased power of the lower masses. This stimulating environment created political and social changes which encouraged people to develop their talents and abilities for their own self aggrandizement.

After the Persian Wars, the Athenians gradually lost much of their respect for the "man of action," and consequently their interest in physical fitness declined. Soon the emphasis was shifted almost entirely to the "man of wisdom," and great importance was placed upon intellectual education. Old beliefs, customs, and traditions were challenged, and new philosophies arose. Spearheading this new movement of liberal thought were the Sophists who were wandering teachers of that era. Aristophanes and Xenophon, then conservative philosophers, tried to warn the people against the pitfalls of this as a total philosophy and insisted that they return to the old theories and ways of living. Socrates, Plato, and Aristotle, and other philosophers thought that greater advancements could be made not by returning to the old order of things, but by discovering new knowledge and ideas and new ways through which the individual could adjust and make a contribution to society. The decline of the importance of physical fitness, the complete stress upon intellectual education, the luxurious and easy life gradually began to change habits of thinking and acting with regard to physical activity. No longer were these people interested in the vigorous pursuits of former times. They sought the lighter and more pleasurable type of activity or preferred lounging around in the gymnasia or at the pleasure resorts. Now the people were more inclined to watch someone else play than to participate themselves. This attitude encouraged the advent of professional athletes who were paid for playing and the professional coaches who were paid for their services. Gambling, dissipation, and corruption were freely indulged in. One important contribution that this last period of Athenian society made to physical education, however, was the innovation of the "coaching method" of teaching. This we inherited from the Greeks.

Thus we see that the Greeks as an entire group of people contributed many things to posterity: art, music, sculpture, literature, education, philosophy, and pedagogical methods, to name a few. They elevated physical education and athletic sports to a higher place in their society than has any other nation since their time. They called attention to succeeding generations of the importance of the all around development of body and mind, and the pursuit of excellence in both. They gave to the world a deep appreciation for form, beauty, and symmetry in man and in nature. They originated the Olympic games in 776 B.C. with the intention of fostering peace and friendship among the various groups of people of their known world. These games with the same original purpose, with interruptions, have continued throughout the ages sowing seeds of friendship among nations. They were abolished by Emperor Theodosius I of Rome in 394 A.D. and revived by Baron Pierre de Coubertin of France in 1896. They have been held every four years since that time with the exception of the years 1916, 1940, and 1944, when they were not held because of World War I and II. (1)

THE ROMANS

The Romans held a different philosophy of education and physical education than did the Greeks, but like the Greeks, their philosophy changed considerably from the early to the latter period of their history.

The Early Romans

In the early days of the Republic, the education of the Roman was concerned mainly with producing a citizen-soldier. A person was prepared for an occupation, trained to be diligent and industrious, taught to respect his parents and to worship his gods, as well as to serve the state efficiently. With these aims, it was natural for his education to be practical and serve specific goals. To do the things required of him, the individual had to be rugged physically, healthy, courageous, and a skillful warrior. This meant that the aim of physical education was to build a strong soldier skilled in the arts of war.

Absent in the Roman education and physical education were the aesthetic and cultural ideals of the Greeks. No interest was shown in the beauty of physical poise and form or grace of movement. More attention was given to moral, physical, and military training than to intellectual education; however, everyone did love to participate vigorously in games and physical exercises. These early Romans were real participants, not spectators. The home was the center of the early education for children, and this education was conducted mainly by the mother. Like the Spartan woman, but dissimilar to the Athenian woman, she enjoyed an honored position and was held with high esteem and respect. There were a few private but no public schools. No promotion, direction, or support, however, was given by the state to these educational institutions.

The Later Romans

The Romans were a conquering people. With each conquest they seized riches and slaves from the countries they overran. They learned about various cultures and brought back new ideas about government, education, commerce, and trade. The use of slaves created cheap labor, thus reducing the number of jobs of the free laborers and forcing many into idleness. In time, the professional soldier replaced the citizen-soldier. The Romans' contact with intelligent people made them realize the shortcomings of their own educational system, and pointed out to them the necessity of establishing schools of their own with which to produce orators, lawyers, educators, and politicians. Education, however, was limited mostly to the wealthy and to the ruling class. The common people received only a meager amount of job training. Education was sponsored, directed, and supported by the cities or provinces.

Wealth from trade and commerce, rich loot from conquered countries, and slave labor produced an easy life. Luxurious conditions and idleness led to licentious living, poor ethical standards, bribery, gambling, and corruption in government. Physical education changed from vigorous individual participation to that of watching, or, if engaged in, it was merely for amusement. Politicians employed professional athletes to put on exhibitions in large stadiums (colosseum) to influence people and curry favor for political and monetary advantages. They were not interested in the physical fitness aspect or the athletic ideal of physical education. Circuses, jousts, and tournaments were held in which brutality and bloodshed were encouraged and were commonplace. Since there was a professional army, the citizen no longer was required to train vigorously as he once was as a citizen-soldier. There was a disregard, even contempt, for exercises with the exception of mild exercise in connection with the use of luxurious baths (Caracalla).

Many thinkers today draw a parallel between our civilization and that of the rise and fall of the Romans. Since history indicates that no nation can survive long unless its citizens keep mentally alert, morally sound, and physically strong, it behooves us to heed this warning while there is yet time. While the later Romans did not value physical exercises very highly, they did make certain worthwhile contributions to society and to health and physical education generally. They provided clean water (via Roman aqueduct) for baths and drinking purposes; instituted street cleaning; formulated food regulations, and produced written manuscripts on scientific exercises. Galen, a Greek philosopher and student of medicine who lived in Rome, called attention to the importance and relationship of physical exercise, nutrition and health. (3:86) They made other outstanding contributions in government, law, and good roads (the Appian Way). It is impossible to chronicle in these short pages the extent of the Greek contribution to civilization.

THE MIDDLE AGES

The philosophy of physical education in the Middle Ages (approximately A.D. 500 to 1500) changed considerably from that of either the Greeks or the Romans. Conditions in the world had changed and, in turn, had affected the activities and thought of the people. The moral and civil decay of the Roman civilization and the invasion of the Teutonic barbarians from the North quickened the decline of the Roman Empire. This created chaos, confusion, and bewilderment. Civilization dropped to its lowest ebb and experienced its darkest hour. Some historians refer to this period as the Dark Ages. Some prefer to call it the Age of the Educational Plateau. Whatever the name, however, this was the period during which Western Civilization gradually was built from certain fragments of the Roman civilization and component parts of the barbarians' society molded together by the influence of Christianity. At first thought, it may appear that the barbarians did a disservice to mankind by practically destroying the implements of the only civilization at that time, but history has borne out the fact that they actually added life to a fast dying society by contributing their strong, vigorous bodies and the concept of a closely knit family life. These people were the ancestors of some of the greatest civilizations of today. (2:49)

During the Dark Ages, the only light of civilization left burning was found in the monasteries. Through the efforts of the monasteries and the church, the small flame of civilization was preserved and nurtured until it was gradually developed again by future generations. The attitude toward physical education was influenced by the early Christian belief. It was thought that individuals needed to be reborn spiritually, morally, and socially, and to live in fear of and by the will of God. They were also directed to have compassion and consideration for their fellowman. This latter thought was the continuation of the concept of brotherhood of man conceived by the Hebrews.

The Christians believed that the good things of life came by way of the spirit or the soul and that there was something evil in the character of the body. This idea of the body came as a natural reaction against the debased conditions of the luxurious baths and the corrupt nature of the Roman games. Life on earth was merely a preparation for the life to come. The best way to make this preparation was to subject the body to the soul, to deny oneself of all physical and worldly pleasures. This asceticism was the highest ideal of the Christians in this period. There was no place in this belief or education for the physical. The only physical exercise approved by them came through the program of work, which dignified labor. This was known as the Doctrine of

Labor, which helped to make strong bodies and indirectly achieved some of the objectives of physical education. Not only were games and recreational pastimes rejected but also cleanliness of the body. This was another way to subject the body and glorify the soul. All in all, it can be stated that there was no direct contribution made to physical education.

Philosophy is a changing thing. It changes with varying conditions of political, economic, social, and religious situations of life. The philosophy of physical education therefore was different in the feudal period from that of the early Christian era. When the Teutonic hordes overran Rome, they disrupted the weak Roman government. With no central government to control civil affairs, conditions became chaotic. There were banditry, uprisings, and lawlessness of all kinds. The weak sought the protection of the strong. Thus evolved a system of serfs, vassals, and lords known as feudalism. Feudalism embraced two areas of activity from which the sons of the noblemen might choose: the church and chivalry. The training for the church revolved around the study of religion and literature and took place in the monastery or cathedral schools. There was no training in physical education. The duties of the bishops were to pray, bless, and conduct religious services. The training for chivalry concerned the education of the page, squire, and knight, the goals of which were religion, gallantry, and war. The curriculum which included moral and social education was heavily weighted with military and physical training and was conducted in the palace or castle school. The heart of the active curriculum centered around vigorous forms of physical activity, games, and contests which prepared them directly for battle, conquests, and challenges. The aims were largely military and for the preservation of the individual. Little or no attention was given to intellectual education or to personal hygiene and public sanitation. This philosophy was very different from the artistic and aesthetic idea of the Greeks and the patriotic concept of the Romans. In one respect, however, they were similar: each included some form of physical training in its military preparations for war.

During the latter part of the Middle Ages, definite scientific, political, and social changes occurred with accompanying changes in philosophical attitude toward elements of life including that of physical education. Many factors brought about the decline of feudalism and ushered in a new society built on the cornerstones of vocation and education. Some of these influencing factors were the invention of gunpowder which made the serf equal in combat with the knight; the Crusades which created a desire for trade, commerce, goods, and knowledge of foreign countries; the subsequent realization of the need for education; the invention of the printing press, which made easier the dissemination of information and knowledge for study and discussion; the growth of towns with guilds and schools; and the development of royal law as a substitute for feudal law. In all this activity, people seemed to be too busy for, or not interested in, physical education. The sports and games they did participate in were informal and for merriment and gaiety in connection with some celebration or community function. These sometimes became riotous and ended in brawls. There was no formal physical education in the schools. Physical education was not important in the lives of the common people as it was in the knights' lives.

Progress seems to be dependent upon continuous change. Other developments were occurring. As the cities continued to grow, there was more and more need for educated men to fill the positions of the clergy, government officials, lawyers, and physicians. Thus, there was a demand for schools and universities of theology, law, and medicine. At first, there was total acceptance of the church doctrine, but with the return of the Crusaders from Spain, the Holy Land and other foreign countries with new ideas and information on education and religion, the beliefs of the church were challenged. The theologians tried to show by logic and reasoning that these doctrines were defensible and justifiable. This philosophical attempt to reconcile the dogma of the church with the ideas of Aristotle, Plato, and other Greek philosophers was called scholasticism. With great emphasis placed upon the intellectual pursuit of theological scholasticism, there was little concern for physical education or hygienic care of the body. The views of asceticism toward the body still continued. Only a few schoolmen, such as Peter Abelard and Saint Thomas Aquinas, regarded physical education as having any value and then only as it contributed to religious education.

THE RENAISSANCE AND THE REFORMATION

Some of the social, political, cultural, and economic conditions which hastened the end of the Middle Ages served to usher in the period of the Renaissance. The Renaissance was the age of the intellectual awakening and the restoration of the ancient cultures of the Greeks and Romans. Humanism, a movement which shifted the emphasis from things divine to things human, was a part of the general renaissance. It centered attention on the value of present day life, encouraged individual development and recognized the need for preparation for life now, not just preparation for life hereafter. It opposed the limited and narrow fields of knowledge of theology, logic, and doctrines of scholasticism and proposed that the classical literature, philosophy and art of the Greeks be studied. This new outlook on life encouraged study and activity in many fields of endeavor: literature, painting, sculpture, writing, anatomy, physiology, and other fine arts and sciences. This created an environment which was stimulating to education. Schools, where many of the subjects in arts and sciences were taught, were opened for the sons of the aristocrats and others, but not to the masses. Since humanism recognized the importance of the individual and things human, it was natural that some thought be given to the care and development of the body. Attention was called by many men to the value of games and exercises. da Feltre, at his school at Mantua, Italy, devised exercises and games for children. Mercurialis, da Vinci, and others believed that physical exercises were valuable for maintaining health. Practically all humanists favored physical education and by their writings or teachings helped to restore it to a respected position in education.

The height of esteem in which physical education is held always seems to be related to the changing beliefs and philosophies of other fields of knowledge and environmental conditions. During the early Christian period, because of the religious belief that the body should be subjected to the soul, physical education received no attention except through the physical exercise involved in the work program of the Doctrine of Labor. The main philosophy during this era would be identified as idealistic and the attitude held toward physical education would be characterized as religious. During the feudal period, physical education was emphasized for the first time during the Middle Ages and began to swing back into prominence. It did not have, however, the full concept of the harmonious development of mind and body of the Greeks, but a narrow one, that of specific training for knighthood. The philosophy in this era would be classified fairly well as humanistic realism and the attitude held toward physical education would be military and social. Again, during the Renaissance, because of the revival of Greek culture, physical education was restored once more to a respected position in society and in pedagogy, particularly in the early days of humanism, but as the period of Reformation dawned, it was relegated again to a lower status. Elements of several philosophies of idealism, naturalism, and realism existed during the Renaissance and the attitude toward physical education was intellectual, physical, and scientific.

Humanism, which was responsible for creating a higher respect for physical education, was also indirectly responsible for the beginning of the Protestant Reformation and consequently a lower respect for physical education. During the period of Humanism as thinking proceeded more along secular lines and more knowledge and information were available, people began to challenge the ecclesiastical activities of the church on religious and moral issues as well as on political and economic questions. This conflict to break the civil power of the church and to obtain the right of the individual to discover for himself the meaning of the Bible culminated in the Reformation.

During the period of the Reformation motives and attitudes which had been prevalent as a result of humanistic ideals changed considerably. No longer were the classics read for their style, form, and pleasure, but for the meaning they might give in understanding the Bible. Attention was again concentrated upon saving the soul rather than upon the pleasures of life. The Bible was the source of all religious knowledge. Schools were established to teach reading, writing, and religion in order to assure a complete understanding of the Bible. While Luther, Melanchthon, and a few other leaders of the Reformation believed in the value of games and physical exercises during the free hours after school, they reserved no place in the regular school curriculum for them. Physical education was kept in the background and placed in a position inferior to other subjects. The emphasis was still upon the soul, not upon the body. The philosophy subscribed to was idealism and the attitude toward physical education was religious.

Physical education received a little more consideration during the period of the Counter Reformation, particularly by Loyola, the leader of the Jesuits. He encouraged games and physical activities for physical fitness and recreational purposes as part of the instructional training for the Order, but they were not participated in for the enjoyment and fun they provided. They were used to build strong and healthy bodies to glorify God and to obtain greater spiritual and moral goals. Physical education still had a limited and narrow meaning.

EARLY MODERN AND MODERN TIMES

The period of the Renaissance and the Reformation was the transitional period between the Middle Ages and the early modern times. The social, political, economic, and religious developments which began during the Renaissance and continued through the Reformation and the early modern times prepared the way for the modern period. Humanism began in Italy because it was the only place where the culture of the Greeks and Romans had not been snuffed out entirely during the Middle Ages. When humanism crossed the Alps, it found some favorable places to grow and influenced the thinking of some men toward human, individual, and secular things. Thinking in this vein helped to lay the groundwork for the early modern and modern times and influenced both education and physical education. This affected the ideas of such men as Milton, Locke, Rousseau, and Basedow who helped to gain recognition for physical education and made it possible to build a good program. Progress toward building a good program of physical education was slowed down considerably during the Reformation because emphasis again was placed upon the soul and the individual's salvation and less attention was given to the care and development of the body. Freedom of the individual to interpret the meaning of the scriptures, according to his own dictates, was at issue.

Paradoxically, the religious revolt against the Catholic church to gain religious tolerance served only to initiate strict intolerances within the new Protestant faiths. Nowhere within the political government of states or religious faiths was there much consideration for individual freedom of thought. The Protestants were just as adamant and autocratic, if not more so, than the Catholics, in demanding strict observance to their creed. Physical education and amusements were not generally favored during the Reformation and Counter Reformation. Puritanical concepts were prevalent: physical exercise, unless connected with work, was not only a waste of time, but sinful.

The normal physical, mental, and social needs and desires of people persisted, however, as they always will, and demanded an outlet through some kind of expression. Whether or not natural impulses are expressed in a wholesome or detrimental way depends largely upon intelligent leadership and an environment of freedom commensurate with the maturity of the individual. The Reformation and its religious views did not restrain the people from their natural urges for long. These urges for individual freedom of religion carried over in the social and political life of the people. They wanted more privileges and more individual rights. Rousseau, in his writings, called attention to these inequities. His ideas of freedom and democracy helped to foment the French Revolution and the eventual rise of nationalism. The struggle of the masses against their rulers for more liberty and equality and the insistence of the people for religious tolerance were some of the important factors which laid the approaches to the modern era and subsequently affected the philosophy of physical education in the modern era.

Many factors contributed to the rise of nationalism. A few important ones, enough to show the resultant effect upon the attitude toward physical education were: the development of stronger government by the ruling monarchs, the Commercial Revolution, the French Revolution, and the Industrial Revolution. Nationalism needed certain common ingredients in order to exist and thrive. Loyalty and patriotism were essential qualities the citizen must have for his state. He must have pride in it and want to serve it to the best of his ability. There must be high commonality of purpose, language, race, culture, religion, and universal education. While all of these characteristics may not be present in all nationalistic nations, there must be enough of them to bring about a high degree of group pride and group feeling. Universal education is extremely important to a strong sense of nationalism. It is usually state supported and state controlled in order to produce citizens who are loyal and willing workers for the state.

In the early European countries success of a nation in commerce and trade, stronger governments, larger armies, accumulation of colonies and other national accomplishments increased the interest and pride of citizens in their states and this, in turn, developed a greater feeling of nationalism. It was natural that greater attention was directed toward a stronger military force for either defense or aggression. This meant that physical conditioning of the soldiers was necessary. Consequently, systems of physical exercises were devised for military purposes. Some of these were the outstanding gymnastic systems of Europe, which were organized in Germany and Sweden. Other notable ones, but less popular, were those of Denmark and Switzerland. The exercises of these gymnastic systems were formal, precise, vigorous, and conducted with autocratic authority. There was no consideration given in these programs for freedom of thought, self-expression, choice of activity or interest. Special attention, however, was given to effort, discipline, obedience, and loyalty. The motive was not only to strengthen the body but to develop patriotism, loyalty, and group feeling for one's country. These were the things that made for unity under nationalism.

These gymnastic systems met most of the needs of that time and of the nations for which they were built, but they would fall far short if applied to today's standards for physical education programs. They did, however, make beneficial contributions to our present day programs. Many new and useful techniques of teaching and methods of organizing materials were employed such as grading exercises according to degree of difficulty, adapting them according to age, sex, and individual needs, as well as arranging them for mass performances and demonstrations. These programs were built scientifically from a study of anatomy, biology, and physiology, and included corrective and medical exercises in addition to the regular physical conditioning ones.

Nationalism spread to European countries other than those just mentioned and to many other nations throughout the world. In each of these countries, some system of gymnastic or physical education exercises was formulated as an adjunct to nationalism. None of these nations, however, originated its own system, but borrowed certain aspects from the major programs of Europe, making an eclectic order of exercises adapted to its own particular needs. During the period of nationalism, much attention was given to the military attitude of physical education and to civic aims rather than to the aesthetic, religious, social, and humanistic ones of earlier periods. While the European brand of educational nationalism was developing and expanding in Europe, another form was unfolding in England.

All nations must have some common bonds which make for unity if they are to develop and grow strong. The European countries achieved this unity, for the most part, through state supported and controlled schools, through formal and strict systems of gymnastic exercises and through militarism. Because of certain geographical, climatic, governmental, and philosophical factors, England was able to achieve group feeling and loyalty to the state in a less formal and more democratic manner. Located on land surrounded by water and protected by a powerful navy this country was more secure and less likely to be attacked by aggressor nations. This was in contrast to the continental nations which had more reason to fear invasion by other countries. In England, it therefore was not necessary to have state controlled schools and to devise a gymnastic system of exercise to gain unity of feeling and action. The type of government was representative and democratic in its aspects rather than autocratic as in Europe. This encouraged individual initiative and fostered freedom of thought and action. Schools were decentralized and conducted largely by the authority and efforts of the local community. This type of environment, together with the mild weather, was conducive to the growth and development of games and sports instead of a nationalistic gymnastic system.

While the English people enjoyed their recreational pastimes, sports, and games, they did not always remain free from the influence of Europropean nationalism. After the Napoleonic period, around the early 1820's, Phokion Clias and later Archibald Maclaren were invited to England by the British military authorities to devise a system of gymnastics for the armed forces. (3:290) The over-all emphasis, however, throughout English history has been upon recreational sports and games dedicated to liberty loving, free thinking people, with accent on joy of participation and not so much on winning; on moral and social qualities; on all around physical well-being and on democratic principles. Sports and games have been associated historically with democratic forms of government. Both have similar characteristics. They encourage, give opportunity and promote co-operation, competition, leadership, sportsmanship, loyalty, individual initiative, and other characteristics necessary to successful performance. It is to the British that the United States must give credit for her heritage in sports and games.

THE UNITED STATES

The Colonial Period

Many European immigrants came to the United States after the Reformation because of religious and political intolerances. They sought freedom of worship according to their own beliefs, freedom from the tyrannical government of the monarchs, and a chance to start life anew in a new country. Not all people came for these reasons. Some came for adventure and fortune, and some came for the expressed purpose of establishing a new type of government and a wholesome society suited to the needs and desires of the people of a new land. The people who came here by choice were much more than refugees. They came seeking independence in all affairs of life and an opportunity to follow the principle of voluntary action. It was this kind of thinking people who were to assist in setting up a democratic form of government and make America great. They came with all the beliefs and customs of their former country. They came as Puritans, Quakers, Catholics, and members of other denominations. They established institutions similar to those of their homeland, but later gradually adjusted them to the different conditions of a new country. These early pioneers were occupied with the labor, toil, and privation of frontier existence: the need for food, clothing, and shelter, the urgency of protection against wild animals, unfriendly Indians, and the elements of nature.

Pioneers in America had little time or energy for play and recreation. If there had been time for self-expression in recreational activities, some would not have engaged in it because of religious objection. The Puritans thought play was not only a waste of time but sinful. The concept of frugality of time, energy, productivity and dignity of labor was one of the early roots of capitalism, which was later to help direct the physical education system of the United States toward a sports and games program. It is true, however, that the pioneers did receive some relaxation in forms of activity simulating their daily work, such as in corn husking bees, plowing contests, log rolling, rail splitting, and similar activities. This was not recreation, however, in the present sense of the word, but these daily duties of every day life were vigorous physically and served to keep the body strong. Occasionally there was informal participation in some of the sports and dances of their mother country. There was no provision for physical education, however, in the curriculum of the early schools. Generally speaking, therefore, the attitude toward physical education in the Colonial period, with the exception of that dictated by religious views, was not definitely formed.

The Early Modern Period

The Revolutionary War united the colonies with just enough nationalistic spirit to win the conflict. Greater unity was needed before a strong full-fledged nation could be molded out of separate states. This would depend to a great extent upon the effectiveness of the melting pot process of the English language, schools, churches, politics, trade, and commerce in blending a strong nationalistic spirit out of the varied interests, philosophies and education of so many different people. Many social, political, and economic forces tended, however, to interfere with the growth of national unity: the unwillingness of the states to surrender any jurisdiction to the central government, the problem of slavery, the economic struggle in industry and agriculture, the question of more democratic rights, and the extension of these rights to more people and many other similar forces. Many factors operated, nevertheless, to inject more energy into the weak spirit of nationalism and helped to develop it into a strong movement. These included the organization of a national army and navy after the War of 1812, the issuance of a national currency, the passing of tariff laws to protect American commerce, and the beginning of a national literature. (3:362) Since the federal government was not very strong, most educational supervision and administration was performed by the local boards. Because of little or no governmental direction of education, physical education was not influenced by governmental authority except in time of war, and then only the military aspect was emphasized.

While there was no great interest in physical education in this period, there were a few encouraging developments which indicated a growing importance for the future and the embryonic beginnings of a profession. The favorable stand taken in speech and in writing by a a few outstanding citizens provides examples. Benjamin Franklin, Noah Webster, Thomas Jefferson, and others expressed their views on the value of exercise to the mind and to the body. These views had considerable influence on the thinking of the public.

Other events were occurring. Several attempts were made to establish physical education systems in some public, but mostly in private, schools and in some colleges. Charles Follen, Charles Beck, and Francis Lieber, all German immigrants, introduced the German Gymnastic System to the United States around 1825-1830 with meager success at first. Greater gains were made in the 1880's. The time following the 1825-1830 period did not seem conducive to the growth of the German system either because the interest was beginning to be focused on hygiene and physiology and/or it did not meet the needs of the people. Around the 1850's the earlier interest in sports, particularly football and baseball, began to increase, but there was no great respect or consideration given to recreation. Catherine Beecher and Dio Lewis made further attempts to popularize physical education around the 1850's and 1860's, and Edward Hitchcock, at Amherst, developed the first outstanding college physical education program in 1861. (3:368) The interest which was generated for physical education and sports in this period was abruptly terminated by the outbreak of the Civil War and was not revived until after the war was over.

The Modern Period

The status of physical education in the schools during the Civil War dropped to a low level. In many schools, physical education was replaced completely by military training. Even after the war, military training remained in some schools, but this requirement gradually diminished under pressure from the students. The period after the Civil War was one of great adjustment and change. As the shock of war gradually subsided and the people of the North and South began to live more peacefully together, great changes began to occur in agriculture and industry. With this growth and development, the people became more nationalistic in feeling. The federal government, to meet the demands and solve the problems arising from the great expansion of business, assumed more authority. All these changes indicated that nationalism was growing strong.

Around the 1880's, there was a new surge for recognition of the European gymnastic systems, particularly the German and the Swedish. There were American programs also in existence, thus adding to the conflict of competing systems: those of Catherine Beecher, Dio Lewis, Edward Hitchcock, Dudley Sargent, Luther H. Gulick, and others. In all this confusion, authorities in physical education began to realize that the intelligent way out of this dilemma was to study all programs to determine their strengths and weaknesses. Some suggested that the good characteristics from each, those applicable to life in the United States, be selected to make one best system. This controversy did not end here, but was to continue for years to come.

There were many encouraging signs, however, that physical education was growing in stature and popularity and was becoming more respected. It was during this period that the unification of separate movements of school hygiene, health instruction and health service took place. Other related movements grew independently, but their differences were never resolved. The gymnastic movement which was instrumental in placing gymnastics in the curriculum of some of the schools was administered by the schools. The athletic sports program enjoyed a phenomenal growth. It originally started with the students as a pastime activity; it went through the informal stage as a club, and finally entered the formal stage of sponsorship by the college faculty. These were the preparatory stages of our athletic sports program today. The recreation movement was even less energetic and made only a weak start. It was not connected in any way with the schools or colleges, but was sponsored by interested citizens and philanthropic organizations. There was no great acceptance of any of these movements by the educators or the general public. A good foundation was laid, however, upon which the structure of the physical education profession could be built in the succeeding period.

Other forces were at work which influenced the direction and nature of physical education. The scientific movement stimulated by Charles Darwin and Herbert Spencer caused more emphasis to be placed on the natural sciences and less upon classical subjects. The natural sciences led to greater interest in physiology and related physical activities of strength testing, body measurement and athletic achievement testing. This was a strong movement and encouraged many of the leaders in physical education to seek medical degrees. The developmental movement spurred on by the efforts of Johann Herbart, G. Stanley Hall, and others stimulated better teaching methods and held that physical education was essential to the normal growth and development of the individual. Education, with emphasis upon respect and worth of the individual, was deemed necessary in order to prepare a person for membership in the society of the new American brand of nationalism. The social education movement showed evidence of growing significance in the rise of interest and participation in athletic sports. Influenced by these movements and other changes in society, physical education, as a profession, grew in strength and character.

The Late Modern Period

This period was one in which there was not only the extension of many of the social, political, and educational forces of the past period which made for strong nationalism but strides in new fields of endeavor. Business in the home markets had been good. Demands for most domestic commodities had been satisfied. New foreign markets consequently were sought and export trade and commerce expanded to meet these needs. The United States participated in many international activities: the signing of treaties, the acquisition of colonies after the Spanish-American War, overtures of international peace at the Hague Conferences of 1889 and 1907, the involvement in World War I, and other events. (3:421) Citizens contributed to the movement abroad through the missionary work of churches and the activities of philanthropic groups. All of these movements heralded the coming of the period of internationalism. After the war was over, new growth in economic conditions occurred and with these came a higher standard of living.

Education experienced new expansion and developments: the consolidation of schools, the construction of more buildings, increased attendance, and a change in philosophy and curriculum. The change in philosophy and curriculum was influenced mainly by the continued development of the three movements: scientific, education developmentalism and social education. These changes were evident in the shift of emphasis in the method of study from the concentration on "effort" to the "interest" of the student, the realization that individuals are different in their mental and physical abilities, the recognition of the importance of understanding the nature of children, the tendency toward a child-centered curriculum rather than subject centered classes, the addition of "interest" subjects to the curriculum and the fostering of activities outside of the regular school curriculum. (3:422) These forces made deep impressions upon physical education. Methods of study, techniques of teaching, and the solution of research problems were approached more scientifically. Educational developmentalism and social education with emphasis on the nature, needs, interests, and differences of the individual served as the cornerstones of the New Physical Education formulated by Thomas Wood and Clark Hetherington in 1910, and later advocated and elaborated upon by Rosalind Cassidy, Jesse F. Williams and Jay B. Nash. (3:424)

The interest generated in physical education and athletics during the last period was stimulated by several events to reach a new high in this era. Examination of draftees of World War I revealed many physical defects and mental illnesses. This naturally created a greater concern for a better program in physical education, in health education, and in sports in order to correct these deficiencies and to prevent a repetition from occurring in the next generations. The social education movement with its emphasis upon society as well as upon the individual and the improvement of the moral and social values of life within the community were other influences contributing to the growth and popularity of the total physical education, sports, and recreation program. In addition, because of the new philosophy of education in combination with developmentalism and social education, leaders in physical education became critical of the formal and autocratic gymnastic programs based upon effort. There was a definite swing away from this system to a program built on interest, self-expression, self-selected activities, and cooperation, as well as upon the needs of the individual. This further emphasized the physical education, sports, and recreation movement.

The profession of physical education was maturing, growing in stature, and gaining greater respect in education and with the general public. Athletic sports became a phase of the general physical education program; recreation, playground and camping activities became more popular; health education and personal hygiene received more attention and intramural athletics were initiated. There were indications of a closer relationship among physical education, health education, athletics, and recreation, but conditions were not yet ready for full integration. There was little emphasis on the military aspect of physical education except during the period of World War I.

The Ultra Modern Period

The previous period brought forth many changes in social, political, and educational situations. There was a swing away from strong nationalism to the beginnings of internationalism. These beginnings were indicated by governmental and civilian activities through international trade, treaties, conferences, and missionary work. Unlike the political, industrial, and economic advances made in internationalism, the forces of education were slow in making progress in this era. There was some marshalling of forces, however, for entry into this realm, the results of which appeared later in the ultra modern period of internationalism. In the early part of ultra modern period, the United States was faced with many difficulties: the depression of the early 1930's, World War II (1941-1945), and the start of the Cold War with Russia. After much controversy, hesitancy, and vacillation in national policy regarding the alternatives of complete isolationism, internationalism, or some relative position between these two, an international policy was finally initiated under the leadership of the late President Franklin D. Roosevelt through the "Good Neighbor" policy "based on equality and mutual understanding between all the nations of the New World." (3:469)

In all these emergencies and periods of stress, social, political, economic, and educational forces and agencies were disturbed. Physical education experienced difficulties, too. During the depression, because physical education was considered a "frill" subject and not essential to education, it was reduced or eliminated entirely from the school curriculums. It was retained in some schools and later restored to others by the support of several organizations, among them the American Legion, some labor unions, Turners, and others. The urgencies of World War II, however, created a different attitude toward physical education. While the main emphasis was on the military aspect of physical education, military leaders encouraged the schools and colleges to enlarge their physical education and sport programs and build them around the theme of physical fitness rather than military training; in fact, the armed forces included athletic sports and some recreational activities in their regular training programs. Because of the war, more attention was paid to many aspects of health, nutrition, immunization, prevention of disease, and medical examinations, to mention a few.

Attitudes toward science, psychology, and sociology became more firmly imbedded in the educational philosophy of this period. More research was conducted in physical education than ever before during and after the war. A program of physical activities and sports, participated in regularly, was considered necessary for an abundant and happy life. Attention was given to life "at present" and adjustment to society as well as preparation for future life. More educational value was seen in recreation because of the presence of increased leisure time and the beneficial influence pastimes have upon mental hygiene. In this period, physical education was becoming more informal and democratic. This was indicated by the inclusion in the programs of athletics, games, recreational activities, intramural sports, dance, camping, outdoor education, physical education for exceptional children, and others. The emphasis was more on social, moral, and healthful outcomes and less upon the perfection of skill. Earlier, as a part of the new philosophy, there was a shift of attention from "effort" to "interest" so now there was a movement toward more emphasis on the educational part of physical education, and less upon the physical. It was education *through* the physical rather than *of* the physical. Physical education was now being considered a phase of general education.

Physical education has contributed and is still contributing generously toward the "Good Neighbor" policy and toward international peace and mutual understanding among nations of the world. This has been and is being accomplished through international games such as the Olympics, Pan American games, and others and through various organizations and institutes such as the International Council on Health, Physical Education and Recreation, the International Congress for Physical Education for Girls and Women, the Pan American Institute of Physical Education, and many others. This is the great period of internationalism.

Today, while sports, physical education, and recreational type programs are still very popular, great emphasis is being placed upon physical fitness. This has resulted from demands and emergencies of the cold war, and a revelation through tests, Kraus-Weber and others, that young people in the United States are "soft" and "flabby" and do not compare favorably in strength and agility with young people of European countries. Many conferences were called by former Presidents Dwight D. Eisenhower and John F. Kennedy on physical fitness. Many organizations have held conferences on this subject, among them the American Association for Health, Physical Education, and Recreation and the National Collegiate Athletic Association. All in all, physical education has given a good account of itself in this present period. Closer integration needs to be made, however, with the allied departments of physical education – health education, athletics, recreation, school camping, outdoor education, and safety education. Greater cooperation also needs to be effected with education and other subject matter areas; with school, public and community organizations and agencies.

SUMMARY

In this chapter, a study of physical education has been made to determine what effect various forces, such as the social, economic, religious, and political, have had upon its history and its philosophy throughout the centuries. We have seen that these forces have operated in each period of time to bring different meaning to physical education. Physical education, in turn, has contributed value and meaning to these forces and has left its own impressions upon society. To summarize briefly, here are interpretations of physical education in various periods of history.

In primitive society, people derived physical exercise from their daily chores and it was an important part of education for survival. Philosophy was a practical one — that of meeting the needs of daily life in order to survive. The educational philosophies of the middle eastern countries of Egypt and Mesopotamia also were practical and vocational, with the aim of preserving and perpetuating the learnings of the past. Little formal consideration was given to health practices and physical exercise. The main aim of education of the Oriental countries of China, India, and Persia was to maintain permanence or social stability in their respective societies. This each country did in its own way. None gave much attention to physical education except the Persians, who emphasized the military aspect. The Hebrews elevated health and physical education to a higher plane than ever before through the employment of the dance and the observance of personal and community cleanliness in connection with the performance of religious beliefs.

The Greeks contributed many things to future civilizations: art, music, sculpture, literature, education, philosophy, and teaching and coaching methods. They elevated physical education and athletic sports to a higher place than has any other nation since their time. They called attention of succeeding generations to the importance of the all around development of body and mind and the pursuit of excellence in both. They gave to the world a deep appreciation for form, beauty, and symmetry in man and in nature.

The Romans as a whole were energetic and practical people. They were not philosophers. They were organizers and collectors of culture and knowledge and the transmitters of this information to other peoples of the world. In health and physical education, they emphasized the hygienic value of the bath, provided clean water for bathing and drinking purposes, and called attention to the importance of physical exercise and nutrition to health.

Many different religious, political, and educational philosophies appeared during the middle ages: Christianity, asceticism, feudalism, and scholasticism. None of these beliefs made any direct or formal contributions to health and physical education. In feudalism, the educational program for the page, squire, and knight did include vigorous forms of physical activities, games, and contests, which prepared them for battle, conquests, and challenges. The aims were largely military and the preservation of the individual. Little or no attention was given to intellectual education or to personal hygiene and public sanitation. During the period of the Renaissance and its emphasis upon humanism, the importance of the individual and things human were emphasized, and there was some thought given to the care and development of the body. Practically all the humanists favored physical education and by their writings and teachings helped restore it to a respected position in education and in society. In the period of the Reformation and Counter-Reformation, physical education had a limited and narrow meaning. Physical education was kept in the background and placed in a position inferior to other subjects. The emphasis was still upon the soul not upon the body.

In the early modern times in Europe, nationalism arose with its characteristic concepts of loyalty, patriotism, and pride for the state. Formal, precise, vigorous gymnastic systems were organized as an adjunct to nationalism. The aims of these systems were to strengthen the body and to develop patriotism, loyalty, and group feelings for one's country. The stress was upon the military aspects of physical education and upon civic objectives. In England, however, nationalism was accomplished in a less formal and more democratic manner. Protected by a natural water barrier and a strong navy, she was fairly safe from attack by other nations. It was not necessary for her to have state controlled schools and to devise a gymnastic system of exercise to gain unity of feeling and action. Her government was democratic in nature, her schools largely decentralized, and her weather mild. She had a tradition in sports and games. All of these factors were conducive to the development of a sports and games program rather than a gymnastic system. It was from England that the United States inherited the sports and games that form a large part of the physical education program today.

Physical education in the United States has had many meanings throughout history. In the Colonial period, the attitude toward physical education, with the exception of the religious views, was not definitely formed. During the early modern period, nationalism was not very strong. Because there was little governmental direction of education, physical education was not influenced by federal authority except in time of war. Otherwise, there was little interest in physical education except that shown by a few renowned citizens in speech and writings. It was during this period that the German gymnastic system was first introduced to the United States. Sports, particularly football and baseball, began to attract more attention. However, the growth that had taken place was interrupted by the Civil War. In the modern era, after the adjustment period of the Civil War and the revival of industry and commerce, nationalism grew stronger. The federal government asserted more authority to meet the demands of a growing economy. Physical education increased in importance and popularity. Many systems of physical education competed for recognition. It was a period of unification of separate health organizations, but not for the related areas of health, physical education, athletics, and recreation. Regardless of the problems of a growing organization, physical education was in a period of great professsional growth.

In the late modern era, there was a movement toward internationalism. After the close of World War I, new growth occurred in economic conditions, and with it came a higher standard of living. New expansion and developments in education took place. Physical education followed the lead of general education and shifted the emphasis from "effort" to "interest" and the subject-centered to the child-centered curriculum. This was the period of the formulation of the "New Physical Education" by Wood, Cassidy and Hetherington, not only as a protest against the formal gymnastic program but as a conscientious effort to build an integrated program based upon the current needs, interest, and desires of children. This was a period of still greater maturity and advancements toward an established profession in physical education.

The ultra modern era is the period of strong internationalism and the pursuit of the "Good Neighbor" policy. More attention is being paid to many aspects of health at home and abroad. Advancements in knowledge gained through science, psychology and sociology are being more firmly imbedded in the educational philosophy. Physical education is now considered a phase of general education. While the sports, games and recreational type programs are still popular, great stress is being placed upon physical fitness.

In retrospect, therefore, we have seen that throughout the ages physical education has been influenced by the social, political, religious, educational, and economic forces which operated in each particular period and, in turn, has left its own impressions upon society.

QUESTIONS FOR REVIEW AND DISCUSSION

1. Discuss the main aims of physical education in the primitive society.
2. Discuss the importance accorded physical exercise activities by the societies of the ancient, middle eastern and oriental countries.
3. What contribution did the Hebrew society make to philosophy and to physical education?
4. Discuss the physical education heritage that came to us from the Greeks: Homeric, Spartan and Athenian.

5. Compare the early and later period of Rome with regard to education, physical education and philosophy of life.
6. Discuss the changing status of physical education during the Middle Ages. What were some of the factors which influenced the change?
7. Describe the position physical education held during the Renaissance and Reformation. Compare physical education in the two periods. Describe the social, political, cultural, and economic conditions during these periods.
8. Name and discuss several factors which contributed to nationalism. What place of importance was accorded physical education in Europe during the early modern ages?
9. Compare nationalism in Europe with that in Great Britain during the early modern period.
10. Discuss the effects of the various European gymnastic systems upon physical education in the United States.
11. What effect did the culture and the sports and games of Great Britain have upon physical education in the United States? How did these affect the philosophy of physical education in the States?
12. Describe the attitude held toward physical education in the Colonial period.
13. What factors operated to blend a strong nationalistic spirit in the United States during the early modern period? What forces interfered with this growth? What influence did this have upon physical education?
14. Discuss the attempts that were made to establish European gymnastic systems in the public schools of the United States during the early modern and modern periods. What other physical education systems were presented during these periods? What effect did any of these systems have upon the philosophy of physical education?
15. Name and discuss some movements during the modern era that influenced the direction and nature of physical education. How did they influence this change in philosophy and curriculum of education and physical education?
16. What is the philosophy of the "New Physical Education"? Compare it with that of the formalism of the old gymnastic systems.
17. Describe the contribution made by physical education and sports to national and world affairs during the period of internationalism; during the depression of the 1930's.

18. What phase of the physical education program in the ultra modern period today receives the greatest amount of emphasis? Why?

Bibliography

1. *Games of the XVII Olympiad.* Rome: Olympia Edizioni Sportive, 1960.
2. Rice, Emmett A., John L. Hutchinson, and Mabel Lee. *A Brief History of Physical Education.* New York: The Ronald Press Co., 1958.
3. Van Dalen, Deobold B., Elmer D. Mitchell, and Bruce Bennett. *A World History of Physical Education.* New York: Prentice-Hall, Inc., 1953.

Part II

Building a Personal Philosophy of Physical Education

Origin and Meaning of Physical Education and Related Phases of the Profession

7

ORIGIN AND MEANING OF PHYSICAL EDUCATION

Physical education in some form or another is as old as the human race. Primitive societies employed it mainly for survival and group unity, but also participated in the physical for recreational purposes. Subsequent societies added other reasons such as military, art, religious, scientific and social. The study of history indicates that physical activity in all societies or lack of it has been purposeful. Sometimes it was conducted informally, sometimes formally, and sometimes it was incidental only, but it was not until modern times with its educational aim that it has advanced to academic status and has been included in a curriculum of study.

There has been much controversy over what to call this part of education and of what it should be composed. In the ancient period the Greeks called it "gymnastics" (from the Greek "gymnastikos" and the Latin "gymnasticus") as did the Germans and other Europeans later in the nineteenth century. Indeed the word in Germany and in some other European schools was synonymous with the total concept of "school." Throughout the ages the military has called it "physical training," as have some schools in the United States, perhaps a proper term for that which was done in many cases. The term has been, however, used little in recent years.

"Physical culture" is a term which was used in the latter part of the nineteenth century by some organizations and faddists and its use continued for some time, but the term is sparingly employed now and carries with it a noneducational connotation. (7:398)

The development of the scientific movement with its interests in anatomy, physiology, and biology; the social education movement with its interests in sociology; and the educational developmentalism movement with its interests in psychology influenced the change of the name to "hygiene" for some people, to "health education" for others, and finally to "physical education." These names still are used in many communities today, but the most prevalent is physical education. With continued developments and expansion in the profession "health" was added and then "recreation" until now the complete term of the professional organization in this country is "health, physical education, and recreation," a designation encompassing the broad aspects of this field. It is recognized that health and recreation are in no sense completely synonymous with physical education but are unique fields by themselves; however, physical education does contribute strongly to each and there are many intimate relationships among the three.

Changes in the name have been accompanied by changes in meaning, and sometimes the same term meant different things to different people. Gymnastics to the Greeks meant such activities as running, jumping, wrestling, boxing, discus and javelin throwing. Gymnastics to the Germans and Danes meant similar activities but, in addition, a great variety of stunts and games and formal exercises with and without equipment and apparatus. (4:88-89; 115) Gymnastics to the Swedes meant formal exercises supplemented by games with special emphasis on medical uses of movement. (4:121) Throughout all periods of history gymnastics has been employed in preparing for war by the military when emergencies have arisen. This has been true in all societies throughout the ages, regardless of the system of physical education. At these times the military simply adapted the system to its particular needs and called it physical training. Hence, physical training has the connotation of authority, formality, and obedience with emphasis on training for skill, for physical fitness, and conditioning of the body for the development of strength and endurance. In such training there is little opportunity for the development of self-initiative, self-expression, or enjoyment by the individual. It serves only one definite purpose — preparation for military duty.

Physical culture was and is a term used mainly by faddists to popularize strength-building exercises with weights and to glorify the body through muscular development. It does not embody in its concept the variety of activities of other systems and was a term used little by the schools in early American history with the exception of the Delsartian School. The term physical education developed as a protest against the formal activities of gymnastics with its accompanying formal method of teaching and is a more descriptive term mirroring its current objectives. This term encompasses the objectives of expression of the individual through creative forms of activity by participation through joy, through reflective thinking and self-discipline. It also includes vigorous activities, sports and games for the development of strength, skill and endurance; rhythmical activities and dance for the development of poise, skillful movement, social graces and artistic expression. Physical education identifies itself with general education and, as such, its objective is to develop students as integrated individuals through the physical to "live most and serve best."

Physical education, then, is a phase of general education which employs motor activities and related experiences in developing an integrated individual, mentally, physically, morally, spiritually, and socially to be a useful citizen of his country and of the world. It should provide joy, help and assistance to all people of all ages, the strong, the weak, the ill, and the handicapped according to their needs and interests. The purpose of physical education is to give instruction and practice in the basic skills and knowledges, to develop social, ethical, and educational values through the various games and physical activities, and to develop that degree of health, physical fitness, and safety necessary for daily requirements and immediate emergencies. Physical education was officially recognized in the United States when the first significant program was initiated at Amherst in 1861 by Dr. Edward Hitchcock. It was, however, organized in the private schools as early as 1825 under the name of gymnastics. In that year, German Gymnastics were taught at the Round Hill School at Northhampton, Massachusetts, by Dr. Charles Beck. (7:369)

Perhaps because the term for physical activity has changed in name as well as in content and meaning over the centuries, the new term "physical education" has different meanings for different people. To some it means varsity athletics, or intramural sports, to others health education, and to still others recreation. Other related fields, school camping, outdoor education and safety education, have been incorporated. What are all these activities and how are they associated with physical education? Most of these, while related, developed independently in an informal way between 1825-1885. This is particularly true of physical education, health, recreation, and athletics. During the latter part of the nineteenth century, all these phases of the program were conducted in many colleges under one director who was usually a physician and the combination was considered a total physical education program. Later when physical examinations and medical services were moved out of the department and formed into the health services program of the school, the director of health, physical education and recreation became more of an educational administrator than a physician. This practice has continued until recent times. Health education and recreation too are now recognized as special fields with established specific and unique objectives.

ORIGIN AND MEANING OF ATHLETICS

From the standpoint of formal recognition athletics was the first of these groups to be conducted on an organized basis. The crew of Harvard University rowed against the crew of Yale University in the year 1852. (2:29) Williams defeated Amherst College in the first intercollegiate baseball game in 1859 (7:379), and the first intercollegiate football game was played between Princeton and Rutgers at New Brunswick, New Jersey, November 9, 1869. (7:409) Athletics organized under regulations similar to those of today, however, did not occur until 1870 when the Rowing Association of American Colleges was formed. (7:400)

Athletics did not have a very promising beginning. They began informally when the energetic and lively students of the early universities sought relaxation from their studies and release from their tensions and emotions by forming teams for competition within the school, and occasionally with other universities. These affairs many times ended in fights and boisterous activities which resulted in injuries, damaged property, and unethical practices. Athletic activities were organized and conducted by the students without sanction or approval by the faculty; in fact, many times they were carried on against the wishes of the faculty. It is understandable, due to the Puritanic belief in that period which considered play purposeless and sinful, that the faculty would oppose athletic games. Faculty failed at first to realize that students needed some kind of physical activity and that the best way to solve this problem was to make provision for wholesome and vigorous sports and refreshing physical activities. Eventually faculty guidance, supervision and support came about.

Unfortunately, faculty control did not eliminate all the problems connected with athletics. Throughout history, problems of subsidization, proselyting, gambling, commercialism and unethical practices have appeared and reappeared; in fact, they are unfortunately still present today in one form or another. How is it possible to eliminate these difficulties or at least to decrease their effectiveness? In the first place, athletics must be an integral part of the general educational experience, not just in name only. If athletic activities cannot contribute educational values, they have no legitimate place in the institution. Winning at the expense of health, life, and character, and equivocating of moral and spiritual values cannot be accepted. In addition their main purpose should not be for publicity or entertainment. Too many colleges and universities today depend upon their athletic prowess to advertise their schools, to make money, and to attract prospective students. Athletics in many institutions are big business, almost as commercial and competitive as general public enterprises. This is not education and should not be the main purpose of athletics. The coach who has to win to hold his job and must fill the stadium with paying spectators every Saturday cannot be expected always to use accepted teaching methods. Methods which are dictated mainly by motivation from the outside are properly open to question. When the coach uses all formal training methods and calls all of the plays in the game from the sideline, then the player becomes a robot, not an individual learner. Why not give athletics back to the athletes so that they can be a real source of enjoyment and an educational experience?

One way to lessen the big business aspect would be to funnel all the money raised from gate receipts to the general school fund and appropriate money from this fund to conduct all athletic sports, not just the so-called major sports. The coach should be a regular and respected member of the faculty and paid a salary commensurate with other members of the faculty of his rank. To attain his rank, he should be required to meet not only the qualification of skill in coaching his sport but also educational qualifications equivalent to other faculty members of his academic rank. Too often, the coach is selected on the basis of his skill as a varsity player and not upon his educational qualifications. Many coaches have no degree or only teaching minors in physical education. Think, then, of the havoc this individual can do to the physical education program if, after he has been a successful coach, he then becomes director of athletics and physical education, or, if he has been an unsuccessful coach, he is assigned as a faculty member in the physical education department. Is it any wonder that many programs today are questionable and below par? While good leadership will not solve all the problems which exist in athletics and physical education, it certainly would eliminate the major share of them.

There are other ways to eradicate some of the overemphasis on athletics and make them more educational. One is to make them available to as many participants as possible. This does not mean cutting the varsity squad. If athletics are good for a few, they are equally good for as many others who wish to participate. The coaches and school officials may say, and often do, that we do not have sufficient time, space, or the money to support a program like this. Two ideas which might help to solve the problem of obtaining varsity material without the high cost in time and money now involved in the solicitation and subsidization system employed in the colleges and universities today are: (1) to appeal directly and earnestly to the student body of the institution for players from its own ranks and (2) to select varsity players from the corresponding sports in the intramural program. The intramural program, however, must never be used or even considered as a "farm system" to the varsity program. If this were a universally accepted plan, the colleges would drop the idea of soliciting athletes from other communities, states, or countries. If conscientiously practiced, this plan would do away with proselyting, subsidizations, and tenders. Scholarships for athletes would be on the same basis as those for other students in the school. A most desirable situation of "athletics for all" would then be approached. One could venture to go one step further and say that in time, as the university alone became financially responsible for athletics from its general fund, gate receipts could practically be eliminated altogether. Support for this program could come from student athletic and physical education fees which would be paid by the student as part of his tuition. The public could be invited to make donations or at least be charged only a nominal fee for admission to athletic events.

Varsity athletics are various sports conducted on a high competitive level between teams of different schools. They are for students who have high ability and the desire to excel. Naturally, not every student can be on a varsity team; however, varsity athletics are very important and are an extremely useful part of the total physical education and education program *if conducted properly and kept within limits commensurate with the value they contribute.* They are the cap sheaf of a comprehensive physical education program but not the whole of a good program.

ORIGIN AND MEANING OF HEALTH EDUCATION

It is difficult to determine the exact beginning of the teaching of health within either the public schools or institutions of higher learning. It is possible, however, to cite some early scattered activities which indicate the approximate origin. In the early part of the nineteenth century interest began to shift from gymnastics to physiology, anatomy, and hygiene. Some universities began to offer courses in these subjects. In 1818 Harvard offered a course in hygiene and later a course in human anatomy. Hygiene was emphasized in the training of prospective teachers at the first state normal school, Lexington, Massachusetts, 1839. (5:27) Subsequent motivation was given to this area of teaching by the Women's Christian Temperance Union around 1890 as a result of their campaign against alcohol and narcotics and the harmful effects of these drugs on the human body. (7:398) The efforts of this group were powerful enough to influence state legislation, as evidenced by Ohio in 1892 which designated that its state program in physical education include these subjects. This action naturally emphasized the teaching of hygiene, physiology and anatomy, subjects associated and related to health education. Subsequent legislation was passed by other states, North Dakota in 1899, Idaho in 1913, and in quick succession by many states after 1916. (5:29)

Different aspects were emphasized as the health movement developed: knowledge of structure, function and mechanical movement of the body; sanitary conditions and prevention of disease; and later around the beginning of the twentieth century methods for better personal and community living in order to acquire proper attitudes and form healthful habits. Today the concern is centered around total fitness of the individual and positive mental hygiene. The total health education program as it exists today in the schools consists of health instruction, the provision of healthful environment and healthful school living, and health services. Health instruction provides knowledge related to personal health, the function, care and maintenance of the body and mind. Healthful school living consists of factors in the environment which influence the health of students, such as the physical condition of the school buildings and school grounds, the school personnel, methods of teaching, types and kinds of academic curriculums including physical education, health, and recreation. Health services are concerned with the preservation and maintenance of the health of students through examination, prevention and control of communicable diseases and injuries, and care of the ill, injured and handicapped.

Several purposes of health education form the basis for a suggested definition. None of these is complete, but together give a fuller meaning:

1. The concept of freedom from disease and defects.
2. Sanitation and favorable environment.
3. Acquiring knowledge and attitudes and forming habits.
4. Good mental health; a positive attitude of mind.
5. Physical fitness.
6. Happiness and success.

With these purposes in mind, health education can be defined as a phase of education which is concerned with developing in individuals the positive concepts, attitudes and habits which will produce a level of total fitness sufficient to insure efficient performance of one's daily duties and leisure activities without danger to one's own well-being or that of others.

ORIGIN AND MEANING OF RECREATION

Recreation is not new; historically it has been a part of the mores and folkways of all races in some form or another. All peoples of all time have engaged in various forms of organized and unorganized recreational activities. Whether civilized or not, youngsters everywhere imitate in play the daily work and activities of their elders.

Organized recreation in the United States originated around the latter part of the nineteenth century with the beginning of playgrounds. In 1885 the Massachusetts Emergency and Hygiene Association of Boston opened a sand garden for children. Playgrounds were opened by New York in 1889 and by Chicago at Hull House in 1892. (2:95) Because of the interest generated in these cities, the movement spread quickly to other cities in the Midwest and the Pacific Coast and influenced the founding of the Playground Association of America in 1906. Dr. Luther H. Gulick was the first president of this association. Through various stages of development and some changes of name this organization became the present National Recreation Association. The recreation programs conducted during the years of World Wars I and II and the depression of the early 1930's gave impetus to the growth of recreation as an organized movement. The word "recreation" was added to the name of the national organization of Health and Physical Education in 1938. It thus became the American Association for Health, Physical Education and Recreation.

Recreation has many facets and the word connotes different meanings to different individuals. An activity that is fun and enjoyable to one person may not be to another. A vigorous game of football may be recreation for one individual and the quiet activity of reading or listening to music for another. Even work may be recreation for some. It can be seen that one's attitude affects whether or not a thing is recreation. Recreation must be pleasurable and relaxing to the individual and participated in when he wishes. Recreation should be wholesome, healthful, and stimulating to the individual. Recreation therefore can be defined as a phase of education dealing with any wholesome, healthful, worthwhile and enjoyable activity which an individual chooses to engage in during his leisure time.

Recreation is anything chosen by individuals: astronomy, gardening, photography, and so on. Recreation also has, however, certain definite relationships with education and physical education, health, athletics, physical fitness, and total fitness. It is related to education and to physical education by serving as a laboratory for the application of principles, facts, rules, and skills learned in physical education. Whether activities learned there "carry over" depends to a large extent upon the personality and methods of the teacher or leader and the level of skill attained by the learner. Recreation is related to health. One should play golf, for example, to enjoy it and not strictly for health's sake. Indirectly, one gains healthful benefits – physical and mental – from the fresh air, sunshine, exercise, and agreeable companionship. Recreation is related to athletics. Young people like to participate in competitive sports. This is a challenge to their mental and physical abilities when conducted on a level which is invigorating and pleasurable. Important consideration must be given, however, to assure that emphasis on winning the game at any cost does not substitute drudgery for enjoyment. Recreation is related to physical fitness. Physical fitness is a phase of total fitness and means attainment by the individual of strength, skill, endurance, agility, coordination, proper nutrition, rest, exercise, and relaxation. Other phases of total fitness include the social, mental, and emotional. Total fitness means sufficient ability in all of these phases to accomplish the maximum daily tasks with the greatest amount of efficiency and success. All phases of total fitness are necessary for a full and abundant life. Recreation plays an important role in bringing about these various phases of total fitness.

ORIGIN AND MEANING OF INTRAMURAL SPORTS

Intramural sports were participated in informally in the early part of the nineteenth century before varsity athletics were officially recognized, but were not formally organized until the early part of the twentieth century. The colleges were the first to develop a program; in 1913 the University of Michigan and Ohio State University each appointed an intramural director. High schools did not initiate intramural sports programs until around 1925. (8:14)

The term intramural is derived from two Latin words, "intra" meaning within, and "muralis" meaning wall. Therefore, when used in conjunction with sports, athletics or recreational activities, it refers to competition between members of one school or free play within the school walls or boundaries. The term "intramural athletics" was used at first because of its close affiliation with varsity athletics. A few schools still prefer to use this designation. As time went on, however, so many games and recreational activities other than varsity athletics were added to the programs that it seemed more appropriate to call it "intramural sports." This latter term is more popular today except in some high schools where the program is still closely associated only with varsity athletics and is, therefore, called intramural athletics. In some places today people use the single term "intramurals."

The main purpose or objective of intramural sports is to provide an opportunity for all students within the school to participate voluntarily in some sport or physical activity for fun and enjoyment. Many concomitant benefits and values may develop indirectly in the individual participant; these may include a higher level of health, improved mental and social attitude, greater physical fitness, higher level of cooperation, honesty and fair play and a desire to "carry over" some of these sports or activities into later life.

Individuals have different interests and needs. While some wish to compete on teams, others wish to participate as individuals; some desire organized tournament play, others prefer informal competition or just individual "workouts" or free activities. Still others may wish to spend their time and energy with organized clubs such as badminton, squash, weight lifting, archery, judo, scuba, and sailing. Some may use intramurals as an opportunity to improve their skill in order to "try out" for a varsity team in some sport. This, however, should not become the main objective of the intramural sport programs.

In summary, intramural sports are athletic games and physical activities which are either competitive or noncompetitive, informally or formally organized, between individuals, groups of individuals, or teams within the walls or confines of one school. This is just the opposite of interscholastic or intercollegiate athletic competition, in which competitors represent different schools. The situation in intramurals is similar to recreation in that activities are engaged in during free time for fun, are not required, and serve as a laboratory for the required physical education program, which should be largely instructional. (8:15)

ORIGIN AND MEANING OF SAFETY EDUCATION

Safety education is another subject related to the general area of education and is an important phase of a comprehensive program in physical education. In many places it is included in the subject matter of health education and taught in that area sometimes as a special course or sometimes is integrated or correlated with other courses in health and physical education. In any case, however, safety education is an important phase of *all* education, cutting across the boundaries of all education. It is not synonymous with nor limited to formal course work in physical or health education. The idea of safety and interest in it has been in the minds of men through the centuries, but it has been in only comparatively recent years that the organized movement was initiated, and still more recently that safety education has become a part of the school curriculum.

Progress was slow in the early stages because of greed and selfishness and because of the fatalistic belief that accidents were predetermined and unavoidable. Because of much suffering and loss of life during the Industrial Revolution there began to develop an awakening that something must be done to alleviate this situation. Early codes and workmen's compensation laws, first in Germany in 1884, then Great Britain in 1897, France and Italy in 1898, Maryland in the United States in 1902 and Russia in 1903, were among the first official measures taken to correct this condition. (6:4) Other factors contributing to the advancement of the safety movement were the inspection and advice given by insurance companies which were protecting their interests with industrial organizations insured by them, and mechanical safeguards which were installed in industrial plants. In 1912 action initiated by Lew R. Palmer and his committee of the Association of Iron and Steel Engineers led to the organization of the National Council for Industrial Safety. In 1915 activities were extended to include public safety and the name was changed to what it is today, the National Safety Council. It was soon found that something was needed in addition to laws, insurance, safety devices and mechanical safeguards: education. The employee needed to be informed, he needed to be taught how to acquire the proper attitudes and form correct safety habits. This thought prevailed in the discussions of the Council's meetings for a number of years and finally in 1919, through the efforts of Albert W. Whitney and E. George Payne, programs of instructions were worked out. Among the first programs which were organized in the public schools were those of Detroit in 1919 and Kansas City in the early twenties. (6:5, 7, 8)

Safety is a phase of life which is involved in all activities of the human race whether indoors or outdoors, in work, play or leisure time activities. It is a positive way of living in a safe and sane manner but without eliminating all of the adventure of life.

Safety education as a general term is a phase of general education which is concerned with developing the knowledge, attitudes and habits of safe behavior of the individual wherever he is and whatever he is doing. General safety education includes public safety education and school safety education. Public safety education is a phase of general safety education which is concerned with safe behavior in the home and community. It involves adults as well as children through various public, semipublic and private agencies. School safety education is a phase of general safety education which is concerned with the safe behavior of pupils going to and from school and in all school activities. Since it operates closely with the home and community it is related to public safety education.

School safety education includes safety instruction, safety service and safe school living. Safety instruction is organized teaching and educational experiences in the school designed to disseminate essential information, develop adequate knowledge, acquire favorable attitudes and form desirable habits about safe behavior and safe living. Safety service is concerned with the appraisal of the pupil's safety status, his proneness to accidents, his ability to cooperate with safety measures and the correction of improper attitudes and habits. It also involves inspection, accident prevention, and informing parents of the safety status of their children. Safe school living means organizing the school environment so that hazards and resulting accidents are reduced. This includes selection of desirable sites for buildings and grounds, proper construction and maintenance of buildings, favorable school schedules and friendly pupil teacher relationships.

ORIGIN AND MEANING OF SCHOOL CAMPING AND OUTDOOR EDUCATION

Man's first existence was in the out-of-doors hunting for food, finding shelter, fighting wild animals and coping with the elements. Camping in the out-of-doors whether in a cave or in native shelter was a necessity. As civilization progressed, activities which once were a serious part of life were used by subsequent peoples as forms of recreation. Camping as an informal recreational activity therefore has been in use by all races for a long time. In the United States, camping was probably first organized in 1861 as part of the school program by Frederich William Gunn, founder and headmaster of the Gunnery School for Boys at Washington, Connecticut. (7:407)

Philanthropic societies in New York City in 1872 continued to keep the camping idea alive by promoting "fresh air" vacations in the country for underprivileged children. (7:408) Playgrounds at the turn of the twentieth century promoted camping activities as well as sports. More summer camps were organized and conducted between 1900 and 1910 by schools, churches, Y.M.C.A.'s, Y.W.C.A.'s, Boy Scouts, Girl Scouts, industries and others. This was the beginning of the real development of the camping movement. Other occurrences, also, added to the movement. The first public school camp was conducted by Chicago in 1919. The Girl Scouts started day camps in 1921. Columbia and Boston Universities offered special courses in camping that same year. Lloyd Sharp between 1925 and 1928 conducted a scientific research project in camping and concluded that the camping program was based on sound educational principles. (7:451)

Between 1930 and 1950 camping was integrated more closely with education. Day camps and public school camps became more common. The CCC camps were formed and in 1934 the Youth Hostel movement was brought to this country from Europe. Writers called attention to this movement: Dimock and Henry in their book on *Camping and Character* and Mason in his book on *Camping and Education*, for example. All along, since the beginning of the organized movement in camping, there was an increasing relationship with education. School officials began to realize the educational value of experiences in the out-of-doors and started to refer to it as "outdoor education." The term was officially used in 1947 when a monograph on *Camping and Outdoor Education* was published by the National Association of Secondary School Principals. The states of California, New York, and Michigan were early leaders in school camping. The city and county of San Diego, California, established an outstanding program in outdoor education in 1946. Michigan, through the combined efforts of the Kellogg Foundation and the State Department of Public Instruction, has pioneered in school camping. (7:499)

The term outdoor education has general acceptance among educators today. In 1955 the American Association for Health, Physical Education and Recreation initiated the Outdoor Education Project with Julian W. Smith as its director. (1:127) More books were written: *Outdoor Education for American Youth* in 1957 by Julian W. Smith and *Leisure and the Schools* which was published by AAHPER in 1961. More schools and organizations have year-round educational activities in the out-of-doors. This does not mean, however, that outdoor education is replacing general camping or school camping, but it does mean that there is growing emphasis today upon the use of the out-of-doors as an educational laboratory. There also is considerable relationship among the various activities and experiences of school camping, recreation and physical education. None of these can be substituted for the other, but they do complement each other. Perhaps it would be useful to identify meanings for purposes of discussion.

The general term camping means learning to live or living in the out-of-doors either through necessity or for pleasure. School camping is an experimental part of the total school curriculum which is planned cooperatively by the teachers, students and parents and takes place in an organized and supervised camp. Outdoor education is a more general term than school camping and encompass all learning about natural resources and living situations which takes place in the out-of-doors. This may be in school camps, in parks or the countryside near the school; it may occur at all times of the year, it may be a part of the school curriculum or the program of some organization; it may be participated in individually or with groups. Outdoor education is definitely planned and is conducted for enjoyment, usefulness and education.

SUMMARY

All of the phases discussed are important parts of an educational program and specifically of a comprehensive physical educational curriculum. No one is more important than another. They are closely related yet have their own special objectives, but all are directed toward the general aim of educating the individual *as an individual* and developing the most useful and worthwhile citizen.

Today this means a citizen not only of the state and nation but of the world. Physical education assists in helping this citizen to obtain total fitness, which includes social, emotional, mental, spiritual, moral and physical fitness. All of these are important and contribute in making a well-adjusted and well-integrated individual. It must be remembered, however, that the important thing in physical education is not the exercise per se but the improvement of the total body-mind relationship. The strength of our country depends upon strong, courageous, industrious and intelligent citizens. To have weak, soft and lazy citizens would weaken the framework of our society and hasten the downfall of our republic.

We must not make the same mistakes the Greeks did. They created the greatest civilization which ever existed and maintained it for a long time. When, however, they let slackness, softness of life and luxurious living creep into their society, when they wanted security and comfort more than they wanted freedom, they lost all: security, comfort, and freedom. (3:24) Let us not let that happen in this country! All forms of good, wholesome and worthwhile physical activities, a complete and well-rounded physical education program including varsity athletics, health, education, recreation, intramural sports, safety education, school camping and outdoor education will assist our young people in obtaining total fitness for useful citizenship and more enjoyable individual lives.

QUESTIONS FOR REVIEW AND DISCUSSION

1. Discuss the origin and meaning of the term "physical education."
2. Define "physical education" as stated by a few different authorities, then define it in your own words.
3. How, when, and where did varsity athletics originate? Discuss the meaning of athletics.
4. Name and discuss some of the perennial problems which have plagued athletics from almost the time of origin to the present day? How would you combat some of these problems?
5. Do you thing varsity athletics are overemphasized today? If you do how would you de-emphasize them and make them educationally sound? If you do not think they are overemphasized explain how they contribute to the complete educational picture.
6. Define in your own words the meaning of the term varsity athletics.
7. Discuss the origin and development of health education. Explain how it is related to physical education. Define health education.
8. Describe the origin and development of recreation. Discuss its characteristics and purposes. How is it related to physical education?
9. What is the meaning of intramural sports? When and where were they first organized? Are they different from or a part of physical education?
10. What is safety education? How is it related to education and physical education? How does this area of education affect one's philosophy of physical education?
11. What is the meaning of school camping and outdoor education. How are they related to physical education?

Bibliography

1. ——— *Leisure and the School.* Washington, D. C.: American Association for Health, Physical Education and Recreation, 1961.
2. BUCHER, CHARLES A., *Foundations of Physical Education,* St. Louis: The C. V. Mosby Co., 1952.
3. HAMILTON, EDITH, "History's Great Challenge to Our Civilization," *Reader's Digest,* 74:160. March, 1959.
4. RICE, EMMETT A., *A Brief History of Physical Education.* New York: A. S. Barnes and Co., 1926.

5. SNYDER, RAYMOND A., AND HARRY A. SCOTT, *Professional Preparation in Health, Physical Education and Recreation*. New York: McGraw-Hill Book Co., 1954.
6. STACK, HERBERT J., ELMER B. SIEBRECHT, AND DUKE J. ELKOW, *Education for Safe Living*. New York: Prentice-Hall, Inc., 1949.
7. VAN DALEN, A. B., ELMER D. MITCHELL, AND B. L. BENNETT, *A World History of Physical Education*. New York: Prentice-Hall, Inc., 1953.

Some Factors Influencing One's Philosophy of Physical Education

8

In building a personal philosophy of physical education consideration must be given to certain factors and forces which may influence or shape one's ideas and ways of doing things. These may not all operate at the same time or be of the same importance. Also, they may be more influential at one time than at another. There are many forces impinging upon man which tend to change or modify his outlook upon life. To discuss all of these would not only be an impossible task but would lead to much repetition, overlapping and confusion. Only certain major relationships, therefore, have been selected for study. These include, as samples, brief examples drawn from anatomy and biology, sociology, politics and economics.

ANATOMICAL AND BIOLOGICAL FACTORS

There are certain basic facts man must know about himself before he can understand not only how he thinks, acts, and lives, but why he holds certain beliefs and why he acts in certain ways. An appropriate place for the physical educator to begin is with a study of the structure and function of the human body. Anatomy and biology reveal basic principles which become important parts of a philosophy of physical education. These principles aid the physical educator in choosing activities which seem appropriate for people of various ages, in selecting methods for presentation of material and in organizing the program.

Anatomical Characteristics

Human anatomy is concerned with the structure of the body and the relationship of its various parts. From the study of this subject various purposes and principles are disclosed. For instance, the skeleton serves as a framework to house and to protect the vital organs and the many systems of the body. The size, shape, and conditions of this framework together with the tissues of the body help determine the body type of the individual man and woman. Body build is influenced by both hereditary and environmental factors. Heredity contributes familiar characteristics and environment provides food, rest and development activities, which help in building physique and aid in forming body contour. Many attempts have been made to classify body build into various types; popular classifications include those by Kretschmer (asthenic, pyknic, and athletic) and by Sheldon (ectomorph, endomorph, mesomorph). The asthenic and ectomorph refer to individuals who are tall and thin and have short trunks. The pyknic and endomorph describe, in general terms, individuals who are short and fat. The athletic and the mesomorphic classification indicate persons who are strong, solid, and muscular. Obviously, there are also intermediate types between each of these classifications. The physical educator should know about body types for individual needs and probable physical abilities and interests are often closely related to physical structure. This kind of knowledge gives purpose and "reason why" to the physical educator. It encourages a way-of-thinking about facts. The way-of-thinking about things is an integral part of one's philosophy. The process of philosophizing demands analysis, synthesis, and judgment.

While both men and women can be classified into the general types described, there are skeletal differences between men and women which shape our thinking about physical education and assist in formulating our theory about this discipline. Here are a few examples of anatomical generalities. The shoulder girdle of the man is broader and stronger than that of the woman. The pelvic girdle of the woman is broader and the femur more obliquely arranged than in the man. The center of gravity is higher in the man and lower in the woman. The muscles of the arm and shoulder of the man, as related to age, size and weight, are larger and stronger than in the woman. These facts help determine the type of physical education program which is appropriate for men and for women and aid us in answering professional questions. The following question serves as an example: Should provision be made in the program for co-physical education, or co-recreation activities? In what activities and at what age level does this kind of teaching appropriately begin? What are the advantages and disadvantages of this type of instruction? The physical educator should, of course, adjust the program according to differences in sex and growth patterns of individuals.

Other facts form the basis of general principles which operate with reference to posture, health and safety. The bones of young people are composed of more organic matter and cartilage, and therefore are more flexible and are not so easily broken as those of adults. While this quality of children's bones helps to prevent breakage, it may contribute to problems of body mechanics. If a child in his work, play, and rest periods does not walk, run, sit and lie correctly the power of the muscles pull the flexible bones in the wrong direction, causing poor posture and faulty body mechanics. This causes, at first, a functional deviation that could have been prevented by proper habits. If this functional deviation is allowed to continue, however, structural defect may occur making rehabilitation more difficult or impossible. What happens is this: the flexible bones yield to the pull of the muscles and are shaped in various positions. As bones develop they contain less organic matter, less cartilage, and become stronger and less flexible. If the flexible bones are held in a certain position long enough they may become permanently fixed in that position. Man's biped position also makes balance more difficult. These and many other anatomical facts have particular meaning for physical education.

Biological Characteristics

Biology is the study of the nature of life in plants and animals. It includes botany, physiology, zoology and other similar divisions. Physiology is the study of the function of living individuals and the relationship of the various parts and system. As in the study of anatomy, physiology discloses principles that have implications for physical education. Plainly, only a few of the many principles can be discussed here. The purpose is merely to indicate how biological knowledge becomes an essential part of philosophy of physical education.

The heart is a muscle and has the same ability as all muscles to become stronger through exercise. A sound and healthy heart, like all muscles, is not injured through judicious exercise. It is always wise not to exercise to the point of complete exhaustion. However, the program of physical education should provide exercises that call for occasional supreme effort for muscles grow in size and strength only when overloaded (the familiar overload principle).

Oxygen cannot be stored in the body; it is used only as it is required by life processes. This indicates that breathing exercises per se are nonessential and are of little or no value. They can prove harmful by disturbing the normal chemical content of the blood. A certain amount of carbon dioxide is needed to stimulate the respiratory center of the brain which automatically controls the respiratory needs of the body. If hyperventilation occurs by voluntary rapid and deep respiration, as in breathing exercises, the normal carbon dioxide content of the blood is reduced to a low point. In a short time the automatic breathing mechanism ceases to function and does not begin until the carbon dioxide content of the blood returns to normal. (2:249) Consequently breathing exercises per se are not recommended as a part of any regular exercise program. Hyperventilation, whether a result of breathing exercises or the artificial administration of oxygen, has little or no value in increasing efficiency or performance (unless there is an oxygen debt) and may at times prove harmful. Some studies indicate drownings may occur if swimmers before diving and swimming under water for distance overventilate their bodies. (5) Another respiratory principle to keep in mind when working with youngsters and organizing their physical education program is that the oxygen needs vary according to the vigorousness of the activity and the differences in individuals.

Reciprocal innervation is a normal phenomenon of muscular action. When nervous impulses stimulate a group of muscles to action, simultaneously other impulses inhibit action in the antagonistic muscles. When the biceps muscle contracts, for example, the triceps relaxes, thus producing a smooth, coordinated movement. If impulses for producing action are sent to both active and antagonistic muscles at the same time, both muscles contract; as a result a state of tenseness occurs and the resultant movement is stiff and uncoordinated. Awkward movement is commonplace in the learning of new motor skills. This principle of reciprocal innervation suggests some techniques that should be applied when teaching or coaching skills in physical education and sports. The first job of instruction is to teach students to relax. Students cannot learn properly when their muscles are tense and stiff. One look at a novice golfer in his uncoordinated efforts at hitting a golf ball indicates the importance of muscle coordination. Physical skill presents a very paradoxical situation. A golfer, for example, must keep his muscles relaxed, yet firm, but not too relaxed or too tense to make a smooth swing. This is a difficult thing to do. To swing a golf club smoothly requires fine coordination between the active and inhibitory nerve impulses to the muscles and a close synchronization of muscle action.

SOCIOLOGICAL FACTORS

Sociology is another field of knowledge which directly affects one's philosophy; it is the scientific study of the nature, origin and development of society. An understanding of such forces as human behavior, social problems, change and adjustment of society, social institutions and group process can have a very interesting and important influence upon one's beliefs and behavior. It is through the study of customs, traditions, mores, activities and folkways that we learn about man, his culture, his personality and the various forms of social living.

Since this book is concerned with philosophy of physical education and physical education is one avenue through which education is achieved, we must relate sociology to education. Educational sociology is simply the application of sociological principles to the field of education. It is concerned with educational problems as they relate to the community, society, educational agencies, the teacher, the pupil, the school and curriculum. The study of sociology overlaps many other fields such as economics, psychology and political science. The attention here, however, is directed toward a very brief overview of the sociological needs of the individual and toward the sociological principles and factors which affect human relations as they apply to physical education.

Sociological Needs

From the very beginning of life, and throughout the long period of early childhood development, the child depends upon his parents for food, clothing, shelter and protection. Even his education and culture come from association with other people, from the customs, traditions, language, and folkways of his environment. At no stage can man live alone. He therefore needs to do certain things if he is to live happily with others in society. He needs to love, share, cooperate, compete, be gregarious, be accepted within the group, and be secure.

LOVE. Regardless of the type of individual — good, bad or indifferent, rich or poor — he needs and wants affection. To receive love and affection he must be willing to give love and affection. Friendships are not made without due respect and consideration for the rights and welfare of others. Love brings happiness to individuals and makes them better members of society. Respect and consideration should be demonstrated to all people in all walks of life. There is no better place to demonstrate this than in the physical and recreational activities of sports and games. The kind of attitude that teachers and coaches display before their students has a great influence on the kind of future citizens they may become.

SHARING. If man cannot live alone, if he cannot live independently from other people, then he must learn to share for otherwise his life would lack fullness and richness. Many of the things we know, and the ideas we have, come from our predecessors; come from the process of living in society; come from sharing the fruits of prosperity or the pains of adversity with our fellow men. We receive a heritage from our ancestors and share in their trials, tribulations, prosperity and joys. We in turn share with our fellowmen and pass on our own thoughts, ideals, and ways of acting to our posterity. Physical education offers a tremendous opportunity for youngsters in the elementary and secondary schools to learn to share humbly the joys of winning and success and to learn to accept reverses and defeats gracefully. Strong habits and attitudes established at this period of life and reinforced in the many activities on the playground and gymnasium may well be carried over into adult life.

COOPERATION. To live successfully and happily in society and to achieve definite goals, cooperation is necessary. Cooperation requires concerted effort toward a desired objective; this necessitates both group thinking and group action. Whether a group objective be good or bad, cooperation is necessary. A group of robbers must coordinate their efforts successfully to achieve their purpose. Whether we use things for the good or the detriment of society depends upon our moral attitude and the direction in which our concerted efforts are channeled.

Cooperation requires not only concerted effort but also careful planning and attention to detail. Cooperation also calls for friendship. understanding and faith and confidence in a mutual undertaking or objective. Cooperation is one of the desirable social traits which can be practiced in athletic games and physical education activities.

COMPETITION. Man has been competitive from the beginning of time. He has struggled against the elements of the weather; fought against the wild beasts of the forest; opposed the enemy in time of war; competed with his adversary in business, politics, and athletic sports; competed with his rival for the hand of a fair lady; and resisted insects, rodents and pestilence. It is natural for man to be competitive. It serves as a strong stimulus to learning. It is, therefore, beneficial and expedient for teachers of physical education and coaches (and all other teachers as well) to capitalize on this natural trait to stimulate desirable learning. Care must be taken, however, not to exploit this trait and overemphasize competition to the detriment of the individual, school or society. It should be remembered that, paradoxical as it may seem, cooperation is an essential aspect of competition.

GREGARIOUSNESS. If man is to establish social unity he must think, act, live and commune with other people. Man cannot develop traits of friendship, love, sharing, and cooperation by living alone. He must be with the group, must learn to adjust, and must learn to be sociable. Man by nature wants to be with others. Physical education throughout its program of activities can and does capitalize on this natural instinct.

ACCEPTANCE. As we have already noted, man is influenced and conditioned by the customs, traditions, folkways, laws, and language of his environment. His success, prosperity and happiness depend upon his acceptance by the members of his society. Thus, if he wants to be a member of the group, he must learn to make certain adjustments and obey its rules, regulations and laws. Selection as a member of a basketball team requires not only the possession of necessary skill but also the willingness to observe the rules of the game. The boy or girl who wishes to be a member of a team must undergo training in motor skill and acquire certain social traits in order to be accepted by the group.

SECURITY. Regardless of the level of advancement, man desires and strives for a degree of security. Security, however, requires the surrender of some freedom. The greater the security, the higher the loss of freedom. Man must not become to complacent with his state of security or he may lose what he has. He must always be striving for it, must conform to group ways of thinking and acting and must be accepted by the group. At the same time he must remember that there is danger in too much conformity.

POLITICAL FACTORS

Political factors are important in influencing one's attitudes and beliefs. Man's way of acting, thinking, and living with others is altered, modified or changed entirely by the way he is governed and by the attitude of the state toward him as an individual. Man has created and lived under, willingly or unwillingly, many different forms of government or social organizations throughout the centuries. Each develops and hands down certain social and educational doctrines. These influence the kind of policies, practices and forms of education. Some of these are anarchism, aristocracy, autocracy, communism, democracy, fascism and monarchy. These represent societies with a wide range of political power and control: (1) no control or absolute freedom, (2) absolute control, and (3) freedom with control. What effect do these forms of government have upon education and physical education?

Absolute Freedom

Anarchism is an example of no control, a lawless condition of society. It is a belief. Anarchists believe that all forms of government are not only unnecessary but are unjust and evil for they restrain the individual and interfere with his liberty. Individuals are supposed to be able and willing to cooperate and work together as free men without direction from a political state. The individual is supposed to be able to control his thoughts, deeds and actions. In his work he is expected to perform in his area of competency, producing as much as he can. He receives his needs in return for his labors. (3:278) Learning, under absolute freedom, would be a voluntary affair. According to these views, parents should be free to decide whether or not their children would go to school and how much education would be provided for them. It is difficult to see how a very effective educational program could be organized and conducted with everything depending upon what each individual feels are his natural duty and responsibility. To live effectively and happily in such a permissive society would be most difficult.

Absolute Control

At the opposite pole are governments possessing absolute control over the affairs of the state and the individual. There are two types of governments in this classification: (1) those which are ruled by "the one," as in autocracy and monarchy or any government having an absolute king or dictator and (2) those which are ruled by "the select few," as in aristocracy, communism, and fascism. It probably makes little difference to educational and physical educational philosophy whether or not the absolute power is directed by "the one" or by "the few"; the end results are likely to be similar.

In the autocratic state political power comes from the ruler. He is all supreme and all wise and knows what is best for his subjects. All decisions are made by him. He directs and the masses follow his bidding. Since he is the ruler he must have the best education available. Since the masses follow his directions it is not necessary nor desirable for them, as far as the ruler is concerned, to have as high an education as he has. A good education might cause people to think. Too much thinking might bring dissatisfaction and subsequent trouble to the ruler. The ruling class thus monopolizes higher forms of education. In this system teachers are puppets directed to inculcate in the masses the doctrines set forth by the ruler. Schools are formal. The method is drill and repetition. The curriculum is fixed. Pupils are taught obedience, discipline, and loyalty. There is no place in this educational system for the development of individual freedom, initiative, and self-expression. With minds throttled and education stereotyped there is little hope for the people to develop a dynamic philosophy of life.

In the instance of the communistic state the political power comes from the dictator of the minority political party; this, however, is supposed to be only a temporary stage. In theory there is no state, just a classless society. The state, however, must stay in power until a classless society is established. The government owns the farm, factories, public utilities, transportation systems and other similar things. The people are not permitted to own property or to make profit on commodities. There is no freedom of speech nor free communication in meeting places. The citizen is subjected to the authority of the state. The curriculum of the schools is infiltrated by the communistic ideology and pupils are taught to accept this philosophy without question. There is no academic freedom in education except within the limits described by the communistic doctrine. (1:129)

Education in the early period of communism was free and included some higher education centered around the children of the proletariate. Later, during World War II, a tuition fee was instituted and the curriculum was designed more for students of the moderately rich, of party officials, and of military leaders. (3:3087) Education, ultimately, is said to be for the members of a classless society, not for the ruling elite, and students will be encouraged to advance to the limits of their capacity. Here, as in an autocracy, however, there is little opportunity for individual freedom of thought and action. Thinking and directing is a priority and duty of the leaders. Everything is approved and dictated by them. This includes the type and kind of education for teachers, the construction of the curriculum, and the method of teaching. Individuality, leadership, creativeness and self-expression are discouraged. This brief description of communism indicates the narrow limits within which citizens may operate and formulate their own ideas and theories of life and education.

In the case of fascism the political power comes from the leader or dictator of the state and/or the one political party. Unlike communism, where eventually it is hoped that the state and leaders will disappear and a classless society will be established, absolute rule by the dictator is to continue forever. (1:130) In fascism the state controls the economy, industries, businesses, the press and actually all of the activities of the citizens. Freedom of speech is prohibited and publications of all kinds are suppressed unless approved by the state. Citizens work and live only for the glory of the state, not for their happiness or welfare. Education, type and place of work, and recreation are dictated by the state. The state is absolute and controls everything. Education for the masses is formal, strict, limited to the needs for serving the state, and is molded by the fascistic ideology. The ruling elite enjoy a more favored position and a more excellent education than the masses. For the general populace there is no opportunity for self-determination, self-expression, choice, or individual freedom. Instead, obedience, servitude, self-sacrifice and loyalty are demanded from them. Schools are essential, for it is through them that the indoctrinated education is disseminated to the people. Under this type of regime the ideas of people are colored, shaped and shaded according to the philosophy of the propaganda handed down from the leaders at the top.

Freedom With Control

Democracy is an example of a government of freedom with control, where the political power comes from "the many." It is a government where the people choose their own officials and these representatives are empowered to act for them. This type of government is radically different from the others described. Democracy unshackles the individual from unjust restraints and servitude as in autocratic and totalitarian societies and gives him greater relief and freedom – but not absolute freedom. He is held morally and socially responsible for his acts. There are checks and balances built in the over-all governmental mechanism. He is assured, for instance, of almost complete freedom of speech, yet he can be sued for libel; he must therefore keep within the bounds of truth and the law or be penalized. There are freedom of the press and the right to criticize as long as these do not jeopardize the welfare and safety of the nation. In a democracy everyone has some opportunity to determine the things that may affect his life, but he cannot do absolutely what he pleases. He must abide by the laws, rules, and regulations of the land. Democracy tries to see that everyone is treated fairly and has an equal chance for liberty, happiness, education, suffrage, work, housing and other necessities and privileges of life. The government receives its existence from the people so is concerned about their welfare. The people do not exist merely for the good of the state as in other forms of social organizations.

In a democracy there is the right to assemble and to express one's ideas, the right for free and equal education, the right to hold a job, the right to attend the church of one's choice and the opportunity to share in decisions concerning one's welfare. These basic qualities of democracy are reflected in education (as well as other phrases of life) and result in definite values such as personal worth, dignity and responsibility of the individual, dignity of labor, initiative, leadership, followership, self-expression and self-determination. Physical education with its creative and natural type of physical activity in sports, games, recreation and dance provides excellent opportunity for boys and girls to practice these basic values.

ECONOMIC FACTORS

Economics, among other things, is concerned with creation, distribution and use of finances, commodities and properties. The type of economy in which man earns his living, the sum of money he makes and saves, the amount of leisure time and education available, accepted and employed wisely, help determine his views on all phases of life, including education and physical education. These economic factors are closely related to both the sociological and political ones already discussed, and all have profound effect upon one's attitudes, beliefs and behavior. In this section are briefly discussed certain economic conditions dealing with the economic needs of man, with the development of economic society and with types of economy.

Economic Needs

The necessities of life are related to and dependent upon biological, political and social factors as well as economic ones. The bare biological necessities of life include food, water, some kind of clothing and shelter. Man strives hard to obtain these necessities either peacefully and cooperatively or by force and aggression if necessary. Many conflicts throughout history have been concerned with the possession of resources which provide these necessities. The nation which controls large areas of natural land and water resources and develops them is powerful politically and economically.

The necessities and luxuries which are available depend upon the type of economy and the wealth of resources. These are related to the amount of production and distribution of commodities. People usually want more than just the bare necessities of life. They desire good jobs, housing, education, leisure, and at least a few luxuries. A given economy creates a definite kind of environment. The individual lives in and is influenced by this environment, and it can be challenging and stimulating or detrimental and depressing. The experiences he has greatly condition his thinking and his philosophy, create attitudes, and form patterns of behavior. Heredity and environment determine almost completely his needs, wealth, leisure, character, ambitions, development and destiny.

Development of Economic Society

In the primitive stages of man, life was crude, individualistic and unorganized. Man lived alone or in very small groups. The main aim of life was survival. He spent most of his time searching for food, protecting himself from the weather, wild animals and unfriendly tribes.

Thousands of years later when the world was more populated, larger groups were formed and nomadic tribes roamed the land. During this pastoral period there was some need for rudimentary organization within the group, especially for leadership in order to provide protection, food, water, and necessary supplies. There was little time for leisure after the necessities of life were procured. As man began to settle down and depend more upon the commodities obtained from tilling the soil, there was a greater need for societal organization. While this agricultural life was not highly developed it was more complex than during either the primitive or pastoral stages of man.

Years later many influences began to bring about a different type of life built on vocation, commerce and education; the Crusades of the eleventh to the fifteenth centuries A.D., the invention of gunpowder, the invention of the printing press, the growth of towns, and the establishment of guilds and schools. With continued growth of the towns, brought about by industrialization and trade, and the rapid movement of people from the country to the cities, came a change in living habits. There were congested housing, unsanitary living and working conditions, less opportunity for physical activity and recreation, long working hours, little or no time for leisure or education. This industrial life created many new problems. In order to protect the physical and mental health of people and to provide satisfactory social, economic, educational and recreational needs, it was necessary for society to become more organized.

Safety laws, first enacted in England in 1802 and later in Germany, France, Italy, Russia and the United States, were the initial positive and definite steps taken to protect the health and safety of employees in their new and artificial environment. (4:2, 3) Throughout the years subsequent laws, rules and regulations have been formulated in many countries between management, unions and employees with the co-operation, assistance or consent of the government. Society in recent years continues to become more complex because of greatly increased population, widespread movements of people from rural areas to the cities or suburbs, and new methods of manufacturing brought about by automation. These innovations have increased the old problems of life and ushered in new ones. Society today must be even better organized and equipped to handle the daily problems of living, working and playing together.

Types of Economy

Types of economy have a direct influence upon the values that man holds, for they determine the amount of wealth and leisure as well as the amount and kind of education in a given society. In tracing the historical development of societies we have noted four types: pastoral, agricultural, commercial and industrial.

In the pastoral period there was no definite kind of economic society. Man had not advanced far from the primitive stage. There were few people in the world, and their wants and needs were supplied through itinerant discovery in nature not through productivity by man. There was little need for education except of a strictly practical kind. Values were limited to survival, brute leadership, aggressiveness and indvidualism. There was no accumulated wealth and no leisure.

Conditions in an agricultural society differ from those in a pastoral one. Man becomes more or less stabilized and is rooted to the soil; he produces something, he has greater need for commodities, for education, wealth and leisure. There is concern for societal organization in order that man may live and work better with his fellowmen. He labors long and hard to produce his own needs and there is hope that he may have some surplus commodities which can be converted into wealth. Education is both practical and academic. Because of the practical nature and physical work required in agrarian pursuits a high level of education was not necessary. Long hours of laborious work left little time or desire for leisure and recreation. Today farming is very scientific and consequently higher education is required. The economy of the farm is dependent, to a large extent, upon the whims of nature. Inclement weather brings bad crops and therefore less income. The amount of available money and leisure time affects the extent and kind of education. The scientific education of the professions and industrial occupations is expensive in time and money. As long as the farm economy is low, difficulties are encountered by young people in preparing themselves educationally to enter other occupations and professions.

Agrarian society creates a type of environment which influences people in various ways. It has a tendency to develop certain characteristics or qualities of personality. The person reared in a farming community is often independent, individualistic, industrious, thrifty, loyal and dependable. The agrarian individual has definite ideas concerning the relationship between the value of physical farm work and the physical education provided in the schools. He is likely to look upon sports, games and physical education activities as unnecessary because he thinks people receive all the physical exercise they need working on the farm. He often fails to see the need for a balanced physical education program, total fitness, and sports, games, and recreational skills.

The commercial economy is founded on both agriculture and trade. The merchant makes his money buying and selling commodities in the market place. His profits from business are more predictable and greater in amount than those of the farmers. He transacts business with financiers, merchants and tradesmen all over the world and comes in contact with highly cultured people. He must have training and experience in business procedures, records, bookkeeping, language, mathematics and law. His profession calls for a more varied and extensive education than the farmer. Also, he has greater wealth and more leisure and can afford the time and money to obtain a formal education. In this economy, therefore, a higher regard for education is found. (1:170)

Industrial economy is based upon science and research and consequently places a greater value upon education than the previous economies discussed. This economy is able to produce, distribute and utilize more commodities than others. There is more wealth and leisure and more opportunity to obtain a highly technical and cultural education. People with more extensive and advanced education need and/or want more commodities and luxuries. This demand creates an energetic market for economic goods, stimulates production and improves the general business economy.

Industrial economy brings many changes in living conditions which affect the health and safety of people. It brings changes not only in work patterns and daily habits but also in the attitudes and personalities of people. As more people from rural communities rush to the cities and urban centers, living areas become crowded, and problems of adequate housing, clean water, disposal of waste and provision for recreation appear. The industrial worker has more leisure time but often is without sufficient knowledge regarding how to use it wisely, or he may have inadequate recreational facilities and equipment which prevent him from participating in certain leisure time activities. The city employee in the office and even the worker in the factory use less strenuous physical labor to do their jobs than the agricultural worker. In order to combat the debilitating effect of sedentary work and the less strenuous work of the factory, a well-balanced program of conditioning and compensating physical exercises and recreational activities is needed for the total well-being of the worker.

Furthermore, there is a difference in the attitude between the worker on the farm who may also in his spare time make commodities in his home, the worker in the small shop who makes certain craft goods for the market, and the worker in a manufacturing plant. In the home and in the small shop, the worker plans and directs the production of the commodity. The old fashioned shoemaker participated in each step from the act of processing the leather to the final completion of the shoe. Participating in the whole operation of making a finished product gives one personal pride and satisfaction in his work. This develops initiative, thriftiness, responsibility, honesty and dependability. Such trades are generally learned by observation and by participation as an apprentice. The regard for formal academic or scientific education is relatively low.

The picture changes, however, when economic goods are made under mass production methods in large manufacturing plants. To set up, organize and manage highly mechanized and automated factories and produce large quantities of goods requires scientific knowledge. This calls for a highly technical and scientific education and management's regard for education is high. The worker, however, places a different value on education and his attitude toward his work is different. His job in the factory is related to the machines which do only a specific part in manufacturing a finished product. The worker needs to know only how to operate his machine. His work is routine, monotonous and boring. It is difficult for him to have the personal pride, initiative, drive and incentive of the worker in the small shop. He is likely to develop a "get by" attitude.

This difference in attitude between the worker in the small shop and the worker in the large industrial plant poses some questions. What shall the schools teach about the value and meaning of work? What kind of attitudes toward work and work habits should be encouraged? Shall schools, on the basis of job analyses, prepare students for selected jobs in industry? If so, this could mean a narrow education, for certain specific jobs require little imagination, initiative and reflective thinking. Or shall the schools provide a broad liberal education? If so, this should give the student an opportunity to think for himself and choose what he would like to do within the range of his ability and training. This education should encourage high personal values and pride and satisfaction in excellent performance. This attitude should permeate all phases of one's life: work, education, business, and recreation. The student who forms the habit of not putting forth the supreme effort, just enough to "get by," will not become the great scholar or the great athletic champion and is likely to carry this same attitude into his life's work with similar disappointing results.

SUMMARY

Facts derived from a study of anatomy and biology contribute knowledge applicable to physical education. A few of these have been mentioned to indicate how this type of knowledge contributes to the thought and practice of physical education. One's personal philosophy of physical education is built partly upon an analysis and application of facts gleaned from these sciences.

Sociology is the study of the origin, nature and development of society – a study of people, their behavior, problems and institutions. The customs, traditions, folkways and all the activities and forces of man's culture tend to influence his way of thinking and acting, his beliefs and philosophy of education and physical education. Sociology combines wtih education to find solutions to problems in the social and educational fields. Education and physical education are areas in which one gains social training and learns social traits which are essential in establishing social unity in society. Physical education activities and sports are exceptional areas where social values are taught and are taught best by persons who possess the right kind of social values and display them through exemplary action. Ideas such as these become a part of one's philosophy of physical education.

Some of the different forms of social organizations under which man lives have been classified as: (1) absolute freedom, as in anarchism, (2) absolute control, as in monarchy (rule by "the one") communism and fascism (rule by "the few"), and (3) freedom with control, as in democracy (rule by "the many"). We have seen that all forms of governments have an influence on the kind, amount and theory of education. Each holds a different view regarding the purpose of the state, of education, of religion and of the rights of the individual. Only in a democracy, however, is found the highest respect for the dignity, worth and rights of the individual; only here is he encouraged and taught to think for himself. These values are mirrored in education and in no discipline can these values be practiced more than in physical education.

Man has basic economic needs and strives hard to satisfy them; in addition, he hopes to obtain more than just the necessities of life. The amount of necessities and the amount and kind of luxuries which are desired depend upon the type of economy, the resources developed, and the values held. The type of economy determines, to a great extent, the amount of leisure and money available for education and recreation. It influences relative values and tends to develop certain characteristics of personality and attitudes toward life.

QUESTIONS FOR REVIEW AND DISCUSSION

1. In building a philosophy of physical education there are many factors operating to influence one's ideas. Cite examples of these

given in this chapter. Can you think of any others? Do they operate at the same time? Are they of the same importance?
2. Name some anatomonical principles discussed in this text. Can you add others? How do they help formulate one's philosophy of physical education?
3. Discuss how biological knowledge forms an essential part of philosophy of physical education.
4. Name and discuss some biological principles which help to shape one's ideas about physical education.
5. Discuss social values which are taught in sports and physical education activities. How do they affect one's philosophy?
6. How do political factors influence philosophy of education and physical education?
7. What effect do various forms of government have upon the content and method of teaching physical education? Compare and discuss.
8. What basic qualities of democracy are reflected in education? What are some of the end values?
9. What are some of the basic economic needs of man? Upon what are they dependent?
10. Name and explain the types of economy. Show how they may affect the amount and kind of education.
11. Describe how different types of economy may influence the development of certain personality characteristics.

Bibliography

Books

1. BRUBACHER, JOHN S. *Modern Philosophies of Education.* New York: McGraw-Hill Book Co., 1950.
2. CARLSON, ANTON J., AND VICTOR JOHNSON. *The Machinery of the Body.* Chicago: The University of Chicago Press, 1948.
3. JONES, J. MORRIS. *The World Book Encyclopedia.* Chicago: The Quarrie Corporation, 1947.
4. STACK, HERBERT J., ELMER B. SIEBRECHT AND J. DUKE ELKOW. *Education For Safe Living.* New York: Prentice-Hall, Inc., 1949.

Journal

5. CRAIG, JR., ALBERT B., "Causes of Loss of Consciousness During Underwater Swimming," *Journal of Applied Physiology* 16:583-86, 1961.

References

1. KRETSCHMER, E. *Physique and Character.* New York: Harcourt Brace Co., 1925.
2. SHELDON, W. H., S. S. STEVENS, AND W. B. TUCKER. *The Varieties of Human Physique.* New York: Harper and Brothers Publishers, 1940.

9 Some Elements of Philosophy of Physical Education

Where do one's ideas about physical education originate? What are some of the elements of a philosophy of physical education? Where do these elements come from? What are their meanings? Philosophy of physical education is determined in part from a study of philosophy, in part from a study of the meanings, purposes, and interpretations of physical education itself as it has developed through the ages, and in part from an analysis of and conclusions drawn from other disciplines upon which it partly depends.

ORIGIN OF IDEAS ABOUT PHYSICAL EDUCATION AND ITS PHILOSOPHY

Ideas come from our experiences, from the people with whom we associate, from our readings and study, from our travels and observations, from the home, the school and the church – in total, from the environment with all its influencing forces – educational, religious, social, economic and political. Although our ideas about physical education and its philosophy are influenced by these forces, these ideas originate as undeveloped and untested concepts. A procedure of processing, validating and refining these ideas and untested concepts must occur before the elements which compose one's philosophy can be identified and formulated. This procedure may be described as developing on two levels: on an elementary or rudimentary level and a higher or more advanced level, with many intermediate stages in between the two.

The elementary level of concept formation may be exemplified as notions, imaginations, conjectures, casual opinion, unconfirmed beliefs and intuitions. This wide range of unverified experiences and explorations creates the basis for a large reservoir of ideas. This elementary level serves as an initial phase which can lead to a higher level where ideas are examined, refined and categorized. The large store of unconfirmed ideas and alleged facts are unsuitable, without certain treatment, for use as data in formulating principles, theories, doctrines and laws which constitute the higher and more refined and reliable concepts of our profession. Untested ideas must first be verified and their validities established before they are employed in making final generalizations. This is accomplished by the processes of reasoning, constructive criticism, reflective and critical thinking, the use of hypothesis, analysis, review, evaluation, interpretation and generalization.

ELEMENTS OF PHILOSOPHY OF PHYSICAL EDUCATION

In processing our store of elementary level concepts by means of scientific methods we arrive at certain elements which have meaning and direction for our profession of physical education. We begin to rely upon these elements, sometimes generalized into terms, to express our thoughts. We speak of principles, aims, objectives, attitudes, appreciations, goals, outcomes, standards, criteria, policies and procedures. This is not an exhaustive list nor are these elements necessarily placed in order of importance. Some do naturally fall in the first rank of importance – principles, aims, and objectives. Principles are particularly fundamental to the formation of aims and objectives and certainly influence the character of the other elements as well. The task at hand is to disclose their origin and then to follow up with a discussion of their purpose, interpretation and application. Principles also are derived from aims and objectives.

ORIGIN OF THE ELEMENTS OF PHILOSOPHY OF PHYSICAL EDUCATION

The general data from which one's professional philosophy is formed comes from one's total experiences in the educational, religious, social, economic, political and physical environment. As has been stated, these concepts should be verified and validated, and all bias and prejudices eliminated before conclusions and generalizations are made.

Some of the specific data which help one to formulate ideas about the principles, aims, and objectives of physical education originate from related areas of study. Some natural contributors, and ones which perhaps contribute the most, are anatomy, physiology, biology, sociology and psychology. Other areas which furnish scientific data from which elements of philosophy can be derived are physics and chemistry. From all of these areas, in addition to the unique contributions which come from physical education itself, come our basic beliefs which are associated with physical education.

PRINCIPLES

Meaning and Interpretation of "Principles"

The word "principle," etymologically speaking, is a term derived from the Latin word *principium,* meaning a beginning, something primary, ultimate or original. Hence, when the word is used in relation to philosophy it carries the connotation of something fundamental. The finality of a "law" is not associated with our use of the word principle. But since the principles of which we speak are more or less uniform and universal they are useful as guides for conduct and/or procedure. When we interpret the original meanings of the word principle (fundamental, truth, uniform, universal, guide) and relate these to philosophy of education and physical education we can arrive at a formulated statement: *a principle is a fundamental truth or cause more or less uniform and universal which serves as a guide for conduct and procedure. A principle is a generalization by means of which unclassified data can be judged and interpreted. It is a guide which is useful in the attainment of an aim or an objective.*

Needs and Purposes

Some professions such as medicine and dentistry are old disciplines and long ago principles were formulated upon which their branches of knowledge were founded. Because of these basic truths they have become respected professions. These serve as firm foundations upon which guiding philosophy is constructed. Physical education in relation to these disciplines is a newcomer but like all other professions it, too, is based on fundamental truths and is rapidly developing scientific facts and accepted statements of action. However, this was not always so in physical education (nor in the history of any profession). During the early history of physical education, every teacher and administrator more or less operated on his own untested ideas with little regard for the opinion of others or of available facts. Continuance of this practice would have lead to confusion and, perhaps, even to the termination of the profession. Statements have been formulated, however, which provide underlying tenets of the profession, indicate direction of action and suggest procedure.

No profession can improve, grow strong and become effective, or even survive long, without valid and reliable policy statements and guides to chart its course. Principles are used for the purpose of giving this direction. Principles are also useful in clearing up many misconceptions and criticisms and assist in freeing a profession from the fetters of unvalidated customs and traditions. By serving as guides, principles help the individual to mold the changing societal environment from which new ideas come. Before a vocation can be called a profession it must be based upon high standards and sound principles. This is the only way dignity, worthiness and respectability can be achieved.

Source and Formulation of Principles

The ingredients from which principles are composed are derived from many sources. Broadly speaking, they come from all reflections and experiences man has in his social environment and from scientific facts concerning the nature of man and the universe. Specifically speaking, sources are expressed in fuller terms. Mental reflections and experiences are philosophic in character and relate to insight and understanding gained from such disciplines as sociology, anthropology, economics, political science, psychology and philosophy. Scientific facts relevant to the nature of man are derived from such studies as anatomy, physiology, biology, kinesiology, physiological-chemistry and physics.

These fields of study supply data from which principles are derived. But how do principles really come about? They do not spring forth by themselves. In any discipline when certain facts, events, causes and results are observed to occur fairly consistently, regularly and universally these data command attention, become noteworthy and begin to take on the character of validity and reliability. These data are analyzed. Are they fundamental truths, or at least worthy "stuff" from which truths can be formed? Can they be confirmed or substantiated? Can accurate judgments be made and relationships shown? Can generalizations be drawn from these data? Can these generalizations be applied? If these conditions, at least the majority of them, can be met and interpreted, then principles can be formulated. They become a part of our basic beliefs and can be used as guidelines for conduct and procedure. While principles are verifiable enough to be used as guides to action they are not as highly verifiable, definite, universal and valid as laws. Some of the fields of study which have firmly established principles and laws are anatomy, physiology, physics and chemistry. It is upon the principles and laws of these and other disciplines that the profession of physical education is partly based. While principles have been formulated in physical education, no laws have been established.

Variability of Principles

Principles can and do change. Some principles are based upon abstract and subjective data. These data are difficult to verify and principles formulated from them are not as firmly established as others based on concrete and objective evidence. Alterations, modifications and changes therefore are likely to occur. Because of differences in social structure, people see things differently and have different needs and desires. This is the reason that a system of physical education molded to the needs of one country cannot usually be transplanted successfully to another country. Other differences occur in the philosophic concepts held by people of different nations such as in regard to social justice, respect for individual worth and brotherhood of man. Furthermore, differences exist between people within one country. For instance, some believe the best form of economy is founded upon deficit spending and welfare programs, while others believe it is based upon individual enterprise. Some people prefer conformity and security with a resultant loss of individual freedom, while others prefer individual initiative and resourcefulness.

Some principles are more stable, and therefore more basic, than others. These data are derived from anatomy, physiology, chemistry and physics. However, there is no guarantee that principles based upon even the highly verifiable and scientific facts of these sciences will remain unchanged. Scientific facts are considered true and reliable. But with the advancement of science and technology, and with the changes which are occurring in the social, political, educational and economic structure of society, new scientific data are disclosed; consequently new truths may be formulated. As these are verified and accepted, changes occur in principles. Whether one accepts all these new data depends upon one's basic belief about truth. Some, such as the idealists and traditionalists, hold that truth is truth, always was and always will be . . . it has only to be discovered . . . it will not change. Others, like the scientists and pragmatists, believe that truth is only tentative, that truth comes from the study of the developing, unfolding and changing realities of life . . . nothing is ever the same . . . truth is relative.

There are, however, some basic principles that are permanent and will never change, unless the biological nature of man himself changes. We refer to some of the principles that are involved in the anatomical-physiological nature of man. We know, for example, that the ankle is a hinge joint and because of the particular arrangement of muscles, tendons and bones forming this joint a forward pointing of the toe is indicated for efficient walking procedure. We know that the vitamin "B" complex cannot be stored in the body for very long, so must be supplied in adequate amounts daily. Carbon dioxide is an important chemical regulator of the respiratory center and is essential to breathing.

We see, therefore, that some principles may be altered, modified or changed depending on the quality and verifiability of data, while others are likely to remain permanent. Change also depends upon source of data, whether philosophic or scientific; upon the accuracy of investigations and their interpretations; upon the kind, quality and amount of new research which uncovers new facts; and upon the altering social patterns and structure of society.

Philosophy teaches us to interpret facts, and shows us when and for what purpose they should be used. Philosophy helps us form suitable attitudes and appreciations and helps us learn right conduct — all of which assists us in the solution of our problems. We obtain scientific knowledge from the sciences but it remains for philosophy to interpret and apply it.

AIMS

Meaning and Interpretation of "Aims"

The simple linguistic analysis of the term "aim" conveys the meaning of "pointing at something" or of "directing one's effort toward attaining something." From an educational point of view the meaning becomes more comprehensive and includes requirements of voluntary action and intentional direction toward a remote situation. An aim may be described as "a relatively remote situation to be attained by voluntary action" (17:8) or as "a foreseen end that gives direction to an activity and motivates behavior." (3:23) Some writers in physical education describe aims in terms of ultimate end, something general and idealistic. (18:80) Some define aims as "a general and high ideal or remote end toward which one is striving." (2:45) Others write that "aims are big general things toward which all education is directed." (13:56) Another states that an aim points out direction, indicates the goal and gives general purpose. (19:324)

Confusion Concerning the Meaning of Aims

All authorities do not agree upon a simple meaning of the word aim. It is sometimes used interchangeably with other terms and, as a result, communication and understanding become difficult and confused. Some educators use aims as goals, aims as ends and aims as objectives. Many do not discriminate between aims and objectives. Others speak only of objectives and eliminate the term aims. Some have suggested the use of several aims, "such as for instance the hygienic, the recreational, the developmental and the educational." (10:72) Sharman suggested that common agreement is needed for the purpose of discussion, and he listed the sequence as aims, objectives and goals. Noting that the terms aims, objectives, goals and even outcomes are used interchangeably, Wayman also stated that this practice is a source of confusion. She discusses them in this sequence: aims, remote objectives, immediate objectives, goals and outcomes. Many writers have, in fact, commented on the indiscriminate and interchangeable use of these terms; apparently they convey different meanings to different people and this sometimes creates misunderstandings.

Is it better for all to agree upon the meaning of these terms and thus eliminate the confusion, or to hold to individual beliefs? What is important? Can the right of the individual to form meanings, flavored by his own store of experience and explorations, be preserved and at the same time build strong structural supports for a philosophy of physical education?

At least a common ground of understanding possibly could be established in the following manner: Individuals could identify and define their terms when speaking or writing. Then the reader, at least, would understand the specific meanings given the terms whether or not he agreed with them. However, it would seem more professional if there could be agreement.

No matter the terms used, greater delineation of the actual physical education ends for which people are striving would strengthen the profession of physical education. Regardless of semantic difficulties it seems necessary to seek agreement on purposes. Toward this end a number of pertinent questions are asked: What are the purposes of aims? From whose viewpoints are aims considered? Do aims change? Are aims attainable? What are some of the aims of physical education?

Purposes of Aims

To attain anything one must have a purpose. To give direction is the purpose of an aim. Knowledge of aim gives a clue to general philosophy and to a person's philosophy of life and of physical education, disclosing the resultant organization, development and execution of the curriculum. (18:82) The end to be attained must be known from at least the "big view." It must also be worthy and educationally sound. If an aim did not have these characteristics the physical educator could not efficiently proceed toward satisfactory ends. Not only must he have an adequate aim but "must have worthwhile objectives and know how to cause them to be achieved." (16:28) Aims, together with objectives, activities and evaluation aid in justifying the program of physical education. (6:7) The main purpose of physical education is to contribute to the maximum growth and development of all the personal qualities of an individual and help him adjust to situations through a program of physical education. (10:73)

Sources of Viewpoints

It is not sufficient to state that the purpose of aims is the attainment of some worthy and satisfactory ends; we must also know from whose veiwpoint they are so considered. It is not likely that administrators, teachers, students and parents will all hold the same views regarding the aims of physical education. Each will determine and evaluate these in light of his own position in life, his needs, desires, duties and responsibilities. The administrator's point of view is intertwined with policies and procedures relative to finance, personnel, facilities and curriculum. The teacher's aims should be concerned with guiding students so that they might grow into useful and wholesome citizens. Pupils are concerned with adjusting to changes brought about by growth and development and with having fun and enjoying life. Parents probably regard physical education as a place for their youngsters to develop physically, mentally, socially, and morally. If questioned, most parents will speak of physical fitness, of sportsmanship and of health. Different viewpoints (if they are indeed different) may or may not be reconciled, but at least they must be understood. To identify the source of the viewpoint opens the door for meaningful discussion.

Do Aims Change?

All knowledge is tentative. The theories, principles, laws and beliefs that we now possess have been formulated from the data that have been revealed previously. To the best of our knowledge *this* now is the truth. It remains valid so long as no new opposing facts are discovered. When new evidence is uncovered old theories are altered or discarded and new ones are established. This is the way advancement occurs. This is the way that certain laws, discoveries and inventions have changed the thoughts of man, his philosophy, his aims and objectives of life, his culture and education, his habits and manner of living.

History abounds with examples of discoveries which have affected man's life: the invention of gunpowder in the thirteenth century, Gutenberg's invention of the printing press in the fifteenth century, Harvey's discovery of the circulation of the blood in the sixteenth century, Galileo's theories of astronomy in the sixteenth century, Newton's laws of gravity and motion in the seventeenth century, the germ theory of disease formulated in the nineteenth century, Edison's invention of the electric light, Einstein's theory of relativity, and the subsequent discovery of atomic energy in the twentieth century.

These discoveries and inventions have advanced knowledge and have left their influence upon the social, economic and political forces of man. These forces in turn have made impressions upon the cultural and educational environment of people. Through the ages, as we have seen, the aim of physical education has changed in accordance with the effect that such influences have had upon this field of study. It will be remembered that to the Greeks the aim of physical education was embodied in the idealistic attainment of beauty, grace, form and the all-around development of mind and body; to the Romans the aim was a practical application of the knowledge of health, exercise, and nutrition for military purposes; to the knights of the feudal period it was partly for the social aspects of gallantry, chivalry and combat; in most countries of modern Europe physical education was formal and precise with the aim of strengthening the body, developing patriotism and preparing for war; in England physical education was directed informally toward sports and games and was more democratic in nature; and in the United States after a transitional period of formal gymnastic exercises, the new physical education program was developed, based upon the learnings gleaned from physiology, anatomy, psychology and sociology, with emphasis on individual needs and interests. It was informal and democratic in nature, with a sports and games as well as a physical fitness aspect.

We see, therefore, that the aims of physical education have been different from one century to another, from country to country, and from one period of time to another. It is not be expected that aims of physical education will become fixed and static.

Are Aims Attainable?

Are aims attainable? Writers do not agree in their answers. Some think they are and others think they are not. The way one answers this question depends upon his way of thinking and outlook upon life. Some people are challenged more by setting aims high above their grasp. Aims to them can be seen but never reached. They serve as incentives to beckon one to strive continuously for higher performances and achievements. People who reason this way believe that the highest thing in life is perfection. Human beings are not perfect and can never achieve perfection. They can achieve only relative perfection in anything, as for example, health. No one can attain perfect health. But some people are healthier than others. Health, therefore, is a relative quality of life, a thing constantly to be sought and never completely achieved.

These people reason further that it is impossible to measure some things with a limited measuring stick. Take height for example – the measuring stick must be greater than the height to be measured. But the question is, how high is height? A similar inquiry is exemplified in the quality of roundess. One may describe the shape of an apple as round, but it is only a degree of roundness. It is not as round as a baseball. A baseball is not as round as a marble. A marble is not as round as a steel ball bearing machined to the nth degree. How round does something have to be to be perfect? How round is round? Roundness must be a relative quality, the same as many other qualities of the physical world and of human life. One's aims, therefore, must be "out of this world," beyond reach, or signify perfection so that one can be guided to the highest achievement which is humanly possible.

To other writers and thinkers, it seems more meaningful to establish aims which are achievable. They think of aims as something remote which will require considerable time and effort to achieve, but something which can finally be attained. As soon as these aims are attained, they set new aims for themselves and start working toward their accomplishment.

So we see different opinions regarding the attainability of aims. One authority believes that if aims are stated in such a way that they can be attained, they cease to be aims and become objectives (2:45), while other writers state that an "aim should be general in character and beyond realization so that it can serve continually as a goal." (20:67) Williams (19:330) believes that when an aim is achieved it becomes an objective; consequently aims are never attained. Wayman (18:82) thinks that neither aims nor objectives can ever be completely achieved because the moment they are accomplished they simply become outcomes. How one interprets aims depends upon his philosophic viewpoint.

What Are Some of the Aims of Physical Education?

As with definitions and interpretations of other philosophic terms, there are about as many different statements concerning the meaning and description of the aims of physical education as there are writers. These statements are not totally different in all respects but neither are they completely the same. What are some of the aims of physical education? From the point of view developed in this discussion, aims are big, general and ultimate things which give direction to the accomplishments of our profession. Within the boundary of this definition must therefore be found the aims of physical education.

If physical education is education through the physical, a logical first aim is movement education. Through movements of all kinds . . . . jumping, throwing, swimming, painting, drawing, dancing . . . .

we gain experience and learn about the spiritual, social, physical and intellectual phases of life. We are concerned with producing an integrated personality. We are concerned that an individual has an opportunity to develop good moral character and proper behavior patterns; to develop social efficiency; to develop a strong, healthy body; and to develop an active, alert mind. All of an individual's potentialities should be developed to their maximum. Above all, the ultimate aim of physical education is to help produce through the physical (through the physical is only one but is an important approach to the total education of the individual) the best individual and most useful citizen possible.

Let us review briefly the thought of several outstanding authorities. Hetherington (4:45) emphasized the need for big muscle activities for health, growth, development and adjustment of the individual, and believed that organization and leadership are necessary to bring about these things. To develop an individual's mental and physical potentialities to the highest degree through wholesome and interesting physical activities in order to produce a good citizen is the aim of physical education as expressed by LaPorte. (8:36) Paramount as an aim in physical education, according to Oberteuffer (11:5), are experiences in natural movements present in play and recreational activities, for these influence the development of the total capacities of an individual. Able leadership and suitable facilities sufficient for bringing about acceptable physical, mental and social activity within the individual express the view of Williams. (19:325)

The aim of physical education is concerned with influencing an individual's experiences to the fullest extent of his capabilities for the purpose of bettering and fulfilling his needs and increasing his social efficiency. (Sharman, 13:65) For others, the aim is centered around the provision of opportunities for boys and girls to learn and to participate in activities taught by competent instructors, which will be interesting and will be conducive to the complete moral, social, mental and physical growth of individuals. (Vannier, Foster, 15:6) The aim also may be concerned with increasing the excellency of life. This is accomplished by offering a supervised program of activities conducted with adequate equipment and facilities which produce as an end result greater social efficiency and higher quality of living for the individual. (Davis, 2:46) In a similar vein, aim is conceived as assisting students to develop their mental, emotional, social, and physical selves to the highest degree possible so that they can achieve greater happiness and render greater service in life. (Hughes, 6:8)

The aim as expressed by others is to assist through maximum effort in developing the total capacities of the individual by creating a favorable environment and producing muscular and associated activities necessary to produce this development. (Nixon, Cozens, 10:73) Wayman (18:85) stresses social efficiency as an ultimate aim of physical education. She believes physical education should provide the individual with the necessary education and skill to make adequate adjustment to society as well as make worthwhile contributions to it. Another description of an aim begins by identifying physical education as a phase of education which is concerned with producing maximum development within the individual by choosing and directing suitable experiences which help him adjust to and live best in a democratic and mutually dependent society. (Kozman, Cassidy, Jackson, 7:108-109)

Many points in these statements are concerned with the means of bringing something about: competent leadership, adequate facilities and appropriate physical, play and recreational activities. These contribute to the maximum development of the whole individual. The main purpose is to produce the most happy, well-adjusted, socially efficient individual and most useful citizen. By studying physical education aims as stated by authorities it can be seen that there is, after all, a fairly general agreement among them. Most of these experts believe that physical education is not an area of activity separated from education but a phase of general education which has the same general aims as education. However, it is recognized that the subject, the methods and approaches used in attaining these aims may differ. While there seem to be as many aims as there are writers in both physical education and education, it has been pointed out (5:50) that in most cases the aims of education can be classified into four general categories: culture, discipline, growth or adjustment and preparation for life. Since physical education and education have similar general aims, this classification should have useful application to physical education.

OBJECTIVES

Meaning and Interpretation of "Objectives"

The common meaning of the term objective, used as a noun, is a point, a condition, a situation, an object or something for which one strives. Inherent in this description is the meaning that one actively engages in a pursuit. When applied to education this term has similar but more distinctive and characteristic connotations. The desirable results or ends for which one strives are knowable, practical, exact, attainable, general and/or specific. Objectives are considered by some writers as steps or signposts toward the attainment of a more general and ideal end, or aim. (19:330) They are related to the aim but not synonymous with it; they are "steps in the approach toward the aim." (10:76) While some authors agree that objectives are exact and concrete and can be analyzed into definite steps, they contend that objectives do not necessarily lead directly and automatically to the aim but are directed toward it and are in agreement with it. Formal, rigid steps leading unswervingly to the aim would not permit, with ease, the acceptance of new ideas and the establishment of new values. (2:152) After all, recognition and utilization of new ideas and values are essential to the growth and improvement of the profession of physical education.

Objectives may be thought of also as precise accounts of exact intentions of arriving at definite ends. They may be expressed as "ends or goals which serve as agents for directing and organizing experiences." (1:60) They are also described as definite expressions of value or statements of direction pointing out the essence of desired ends. (20:171) These few impressions of authors concerning the meaning of objectives are fairly representative of other writers in physical education and are generally accepted by the profession. These are not, however, the only thoughts about the meaning and nature of objectives.

Interchangeability of Terms

While there is quite general agreement about what objectives are, the terms used to describe them are many and frequently are used interchangeably. We often find such terms as outcomes, purposes, objectives, aims and goals used indiscriminately, and sometimes even the terms policies, criteria and standards are used synonymously with them. Sometimes objectives are used as general standards for testing the validity of a program. (2:50) This free use of terms may be somewhat confusing. There are suggestions which may help in clarifying this situation though some believe there is no real basis for distinction among objectives, purposes, and goals since they all apply to the same phase of experience. Instead of attempting to differentiate between terms, statements of accomplishments which are relative such as "general" and "long range" and "specific" and "immediate" may be used to qualify them. This may simplify matters. It should be remembered that some writers discuss objectives from different viewpoints, as from the administrators', teachers' or students' points of view. Unless the point of view is made clear, misunderstanding may occur.

The responsibility for clarifying this confusing situation and creating a better understanding must rest with both the writer and the reader. The writer must clearly define the meaning of the terms as used in his discourse, and the reader must remember that no matter what terms the writer uses he is describing the desirable and achievable ends of education and physical education.

Purposes of Objectives

Objectives of education and physical education have many purposes. They reflect the nature of our society and indicate ways of preparing individuals to live efficiently, effectively, wholesomely and happily within it. They help to explain the process of education and to identify its desired ends. They assist in understanding the effect that the social, political and economic changes of society have upon the construction of the school curriculum. They indicate the values to be attained from the study of the curriculum. They serve as guides in planning a program of physical education and directing the activities in it. Finally, they aid the individual in realizing the real aim of life.

Sources of Objectives

The objectives around which this discussion is centered are those of the general field of health, physical education and recreation, on all levels of education — elementary, secondary and university — and for both sexes. The individuals for whom objectives are considered are the students. The source of objectives therefore must be located in the students themselves. We find out about the nature of objectives by observing and studying the students, by ascertaining their needs, wants, interests, desires and abilities, and determining their capabilities. In order to obtain a true picture of the students' needs and interests we must also study the environment in which they live and the effect of society upon them.

Many things help to determine what the objectives of physical education should be: the basic relationship of physical education objectives to educational objectives; the type of community; the kind of climate; the number and kind of facilities and equipment available; the number and kind of qualified and competent teachers and administrators; the nature and availability of activities; the knowledge that administrators, teachers, counselors, psychologists, sociologists, anthropologists and other professional people have about students; the information that the father, mother, brothers or sisters have about students. All of these factors, conditions, and situations assist in deciding what the objectives of physical education in specific locale should be. Finally, in establishing objectives one must keep in mind that they must be useful, practical and achievable – difficult enough to be challenging but not too simple to be uninteresting. One also must remember that it is not possible, however desirable it may be, to tailor-make objectives for each individual student. Objectives must be set up according to the needs, interests and abilities of the typical student.

Classification of Objectives

To arrange objectives into a definite and satisfactory system of classes or groups is almost an impossibility. Yet many reasons can be cited for at least attempting to do so. We have seen that some misunderstandings occur by using different terms synonymously. Also, a study of the literature reveals descriptions of many kinds, levels, categories and hierarchies of objectives. What do all of these mean? How are they interpreted? How and when are they used and for what purpose? Answers to these and other questions must be sought. We know that a clearer comprehension of objectives will produce a fuller understanding of philosophy of physical education. This is something for which we must strive. It is not the intent here to attempt to set up one grand system of classifying objectives but rather to discuss various approaches to classification. Several classifications have been established by Bookwalter (21:26), Rogers (12:99-103), Wayman (18:81), and Williams (19:331) to mention a few.

1. Objectives may be organized *according to degree of accomplishment* in time, efffort and difficulty as described by the terms "general" and "specific." By "general" is meant something big and encompassing which is difficult to achieve and takes long to attain; in other words, something that is remote – for instance health. Health is a relative quality of life. It is difficult to measure. Everyone has a certain degree of health, but no one has perfect health.

By "specific" we mean something that is more limited in scope, is easier to achieve, requires less time to attain and is less remote. Specific things are more definite, exact and easier to measure. Things "specific" may be described in stages of immediacy as: intermediate, as organic development; immediate, as certain physical changes; very immediate, as desirable body mechanics in running, jumping, throwing, climbing, catching and striking.

2. Objectives may be considered *according to methods of learning*, as technical, associated and concomitant. Technical objectives in a tennis class include learning the fundamental skills of the game such as proper grip of racket, forehand and backhand swing, footwork, service, receiving, and court play. These may also be called the primary

objectives of a tennis class because the main purpose is to teach the game of tennis. This may not be the most important reason for this class but it is the primary reason the particular class was organized. There are other important things that occur in connection with the teaching of skill, the associated and concomitant objectives. The question is not which of these learnings is the most important, for they are all important to the education of the individual, but which one should be emphasized at a particular time. The objectives emphasized during a certain period of time are, at that moment, the most important to the teacher.

What, then, are the associated and concomitant objectives? Taken together they may be called incidental objectives. Associated objectives are those which are closely related to and connected with the learning of technical skills. One learns, for example, about selecting a racket, what kind of wood is best and the type of string that gives the best service and resiliency. One learns about the rules and strategy of the game and comes to realize the necessity for maintaining proper health habits of rest, diet and exercise. These have some determining effect upon the outcome of a contest and upon the success and happiness of the individual.

Concomitant objectives are those which are attendent to or accompany the technical objectives. These involve how one feels and acts toward his opponents, his teammates, officials and spectators during the game. Does he behave fairly, honestly and respectfully? Does he play with confidence, interest and vigor with the purpose of winning the game but not at any cost? Does he accept winning modestly and defeat gracefully? Does he learn to share with and help others? These indicate the type of social and moral attitudes, the quality of appreciations, the kind of ideals and the depth of interest one can attain through a game. They also influence the success and enjoyment inherent in any performance or activity of life.

3. Objectives may be thought of *according to administrative and instructional points of view*. Administrative objectives are those which contribute to the establishment of an environment most adequate, efficient and conducive to learning and all-around growth and development of young people. To accomplish this type of atmosphere calls for serious reflection and careful planning in relation to the type of administrative organization (line, line and staff or functional), school philosophy, policies, facilities, equipment, supplies, finance, personnel and salaries. Instructional objectives are those which are established in accordance with the needs, interests and desires of students, and are reflected in the program, lesson plans and activities.

4. Objectives may be classified *according to product and process objectives.* (9:15-28) Product objectives are outcomes which accrue from individual and group participation in the program of activities (social, physical skills, organic, knowledges and appreciations), adjustment of the individual to the environment, and leadership and followership. Process objectives are concerned with the means of guiding teachers properly in constructing programs to insure the most favorable results to the individual.

5. Objectives may be arranged *according to kinds of personnel or viewpoints of people*: administrator, teacher, student, parent and others. Each person views life differently. This obviously produces varied opinions among people. The difference in purpose, position, rank, occupation and status of individuals affect the kind of objectives they set-up for a particular subject, as for physical education; therefore, we cannot expect people always to agree upon the same objectives. To understand them we must try to place ourselves in their position and see the situation through their "educational eyes."

6. Objectives may be classified *according to certain levels*: philosophical, sociological, biological and pedagogical. (21:26) The philosophical level refers to the aim of physical education and its development, through activity, of the totally integrated individual. The sociological level is concerned with such objectives as worthy use of leisure time, ethical character and health. The biological level includes intermediate objectives related to development: neuromuscular, interpretative-cortical, emotional-impulsive and organic. The pedagogical level involves those immediate objectives allied with habits and skills, knowledges and insights, attitudes and appreciations and physical changes produced by participation in physical activities, stunts and games.

ATTITUDES

Attitude, a derivative of the Latin word *aptitudo,* originally meant a suitable bodily posture for a specific activity or a bodily posture indicating a certain mental state or emotion. By extension through common usage the word now refers to a persistent mental posture or mental state of readiness and feeling, and it is commonly associated with personality. It is through a consistency of response that an individual identifies an attitude. There may or may not be an observable physical reaction to a situation and if there is, it may not be consistent with the mental reaction. Consistency depends to a greater extent upon the strength of the emotion associated with the mental response. (10:131)

What is the relationship between forming attitudes and developing habits and skills? Are attitudes formed first and habits and skills developed afterwards or vice versa? Do teachers first try to change the attitude of students, for instance toward mental health, and then help them develop suitable mental health habits, or is an attempt made first to establish the habits? Some knowledge concerning the answer to these questions may be found in the following example.

Let us assume that we are teaching a golf class. The primary concern of a golf class is to learn the fundamentals of golf. This does not mean, however, that skill is necessarily the most important thing. Attitudes are formed indirectly through the experience of learning to play. One may develop a desirable attitude toward life in general (a long and remote objective); one may learn to play golf without losing his temper (a specific and intermediate objective); one may learn to play five out of nine holes without becoming emotionally tense or upset (a very specific objective). Attitudes are the by-products of primary learnings. Attitudes which can be so formed – such as honesty, fair play, cooperation, respect for the rules and for one's opponent – are just as important, if not more so, in helping an individual develop a well-adjusted personality and become a useful citizen than the skill and physical development received from the activity. Both are important and are necessary to the complete development of the individual. The relationship then between attitudes and habits and skills must be one of interrelationship. To learn a skill well, one must devote his full attention to the task. A favorable attitude is necessary to bring about this quality of attention. Furthermore, favorable attitudes come from participating in pleasurable experiences. Likewise unfavorable attitudes are produced by annoying experiences. We therefore are forming attitudes at the same time we are trying to acquire habits and skills. Before desirable habits and skills can be firmly established in a sport, however, there must first be a favorable disposition established toward that activity.

APPRECIATIONS

Appreciation means the judgment of worth or significance of certain experiences, events and situations. Appreciation involves feelings; it is an inner awareness of value; it results in esteem and enjoyment. These feelings come to us indirectly as by-products from participating in various kinds of activities. Development of skill in bowling, for example, is a primary learning or objective, but the ultimate value of the activity, the enjoyment, fun, sociability are the concomitant results.

Appreciations, like attitudes, are concerned with intrinsic feeling and value. Appreciations are not concerned with the validity of resultant impressions but with the quality of meaningfulness and desirability. It is difficult to evaluate in concrete terms such things as the beauty sensed in effective movement, the development of grace and poise in a dance, the growth in honesty and unselfishness in a team endeavor. Yet appreciations are important by-products of educational experience and play a major role in determining not only an individual's present but future behavior. We have not been able to develop a device adequate to measure the qualities or characteristics of appreciations but the absence of good measuring instruments should not deter us from trying to develop these important by-products of the educational process.

GOALS

Goal is a term used generally to describe something one intends or hopes to accomplish. It involves three essential elements: (1) a starting point, (2) an aroused motive and strong initiative, and (3) a desirable end. This word also is used interchangeably by many speakers and writers with aim, objective, and end result; others use it to indicate either remote and/or immediate achievement. A commonly accepted practice in physical education, however, is to interpret a goal as something which can be attained in the very immediate future. It is something definite, explicit, concrete and capable of being measured. *Goals assist in attaining specific objectives; specific objectives contribute to the realization of remote objectives; and the latter in turn help in attaining the aim.* Goals are concerned with the immediate purposes of daily activity (specific lectures, classes, lesson plans, projects, exhibitions, demonstrations and practice periods).

OUTCOMES

Literally speaking, the term outcome means "result." Academically, outcome refers to a change in the individual's behavior due to participation in learning experiences. Outcomes are what we anticipate will materialize if objectives are attained. However, outcomes and objectives are not always the same thing. The outcome of any learning experience is the actual result of that activity, whereas, the objective is the desired result. For example, in a bowling class the objective might be to attain an average score of 160 by the end of the term, but the actual end result may be 120, which is the outcome. If an average score of 160 is reached, then the objective and the outcome are the same.

A comprehensive and well-planned physical education program will be interested in both long range and immediate outcomes. The long range outcomes may include certain psychological, sociological and philosophical facets of man. The immediate outcomes may be stated as habits, skills, physical changes, attitudes and appreciations. These are more easily observed and measured and more quickly attained than some psychological results. For instance, it is easier and quicker to learn to putt eight out of ten golf balls into the cup than to learn to control one's temper in a highly competitive game.

STANDARDS

The term standard as used in education refers to a predetermined level of performance by which comparisons and judgments can be made. The comparisons may be either quantitative or qualitative, but are usually the former. For example, 11 3/5 seconds is the unit or measure of time required for passing the 100-yard dash in the 15 item test battery for Sigma Delta Psi, the national honorary athletic fraternity for college men. Standards evolve from principles and serve as guides in carrying out principles, in evaluating achievement, in constructing curriculums, in supervising student extracurricular programs, in administering health service programs and other administrative functions. Standards may be established for the individual or the group, but are usually more effective and suitable if established for each individual according to his needs and capacity. Standards therefore should be flexible so that variable needs of different students can be met.

CRITERIA

A criterion is an external basis for judgment, a measure by which comparisons and judgments can be made. The comparisons may be either quantitative or qualitative, but are often the latter. For example, in the case of the 100-yard dash in the Sigma Delta Psi athletic event, the time of 11 3/5 seconds is a standard based on the criterion of performance of students in 200 colleges. Completion of the 15 tests provides a single base or criterion upon which judgment of athletic excellence is determined. Furthermore, criteria represent judgments or validating variables that are used to determine the worth of many things such as leadership, social development, motor development, the goodness of physical education skill tests and the selection of learning experiences.

POLICIES AND PROCEDURES

The term policy as applied to education is thought of as a governing plan or course of action formulated for the purpose of attaining the aims and objectives of a certain assignment. How policies originate and operate may best be described by the following developmental stages. The points emphasized obviously are reflections of the philosophic bent of the writer and would differ from those of a person holding a different philosophic point of view.

Principles are rules of conduct derived from scientific facts (biological and sociological heritage) and from essential elements of philosophy (insights, intuitions, experiences, and understandings).

Needs arise from the environment and the daily activities of children. Needs reflect interests, wants, desires and purposes. Basic beliefs are necessary for discovering, recognizing and understanding needs of children. Needs are screened and interpreted in light of basic beliefs and then are reflected in the program.

Educational Aims and Objectives are set up in relation to individual needs, upon the foundation provided by the basic principles and guided by the prevailing philosophy.

Program is constructed according to the aims and objectives to be attained. The selection of the activities for this program is made according to established and acceptable standards and criteria.

Policies arise from and are conditioned by standards and criteria. Policies come from standards, as standards are derived from principles. Policies are more numerous and more definitive than standards, as standards are more numerous and definitive than principles. (14:200) The purpose of a policy is to guide the administrator in implementing the program and meeting needs. Policies are to administration what aims and objectives are to curriculum.

Procedures put the plan into action while the policies indicate the plan to be followed. Procedures take in such factors of the local situation as availability of time, space, facilities and equipment, and interpret the policies to meet these conditions. Procedures have a similar responsibility in carrying out the fulfillment of policies in administration as objectives do in guiding action to fulfillment in curriculum construction.

SUMMARY

We have seen in the early part of these pages where ideas about physical education and its philosophy come from and something about the process of their refinement and validation which are necessary before final generalizations can be made. We have learned that by processing our store of alleged facts by the scientific method we arrive at certain elements of philosophy: principles, aims, objectives, attitudes, appreciations, goals, outcomes, standards, criteria, policies and procedures. This is not an exhaustive list of elements; others could be added such as ideals, hypotheses, values, knowledges, interests, purposes and attributes, to name a few. We have discussed the origin, meaning and nature of some of the various elements that compose philosophy of physical education. We can begin now to rely upon these elements to express our thoughts in a philosophic manner. What remains to be accomplished is to formulate these elements into a functional philosophy. Experience and wisdom will be of great assistance in this endeavor.

QUESTIONS FOR REVIEW AND DISCUSSION

1. Trace the origin and development of ideas about physical education and its philosophy. How are these ideas refined?
2. Name the elements of philosophy of physical education discussed in this chapter. Can you suggest any others?
3. Which element is basic to all others? Why?
4. Discuss the origin of the elements of philosophy of physical education.
5. What is the meaning of the word principle — in common terms; in philosophical terms?
6. Can principles change? If they can, how do they? State some principles.
7. What are aims, educationally speaking? How are they related to principles, to objectives?
8. Discuss the confusion concerning the meaning of aims in relation to other elements or terms.
9. Do aims change? Are they attainable? Explain.
10. State some aims of physical education. Discuss.
11. What is the meaning of objectives? How may they be interpreted? What are their purposes?
12. How may objectives be classified? Discuss.
13. Describe the following kinds of objectives and give examples of each: general, specific, technical, associated and concomitant.
14. Define and give examples of attitudes.
15. What is the relationship between attitudes and habits? Which are developed first? Discuss.
16. Discuss the meaning of appreciations and give some examples.

17. What are goals? What are the three essential elements of a goal? Give some examples of goals.
18. What are outcomes? Give some examples. Explain the relationship between outcomes and objectives.
19. Define the term standards. Give some examples. How can you justify standards as an element of philosophy?
20. Explain the meaning of criteria. How and for what are criteria used?
21. What are policies and procedures? What are their functions? How are they related?

Bibliography

Books

1. COWELL, CHARLES C., AND HELEN W. HAZELTON. *Curriculum Designs in Physical Education.* New York: Prentice-Hall, Inc., 1955.
2. DAVIS, ELWOOD CRAIG, AND EARL L. WALLIS. *Toward Better Teaching in Physical Education.* Englewood: Prentice-Hall, Inc., 1961.
3. GOOD, CARTER V. *Dictionary of Education.* New York: McGraw-Hill Book Company, Inc., 1959.
4. HETHERINGTON, CLARK. *School Program in Physical Education.* New York: World Book Company, 1922.
5. HOPKINS, L. THOMAS. *Curriculum Principles and Practices.* Chicago: Benjamin H. Sanborn and Company, 1929.
6. HUGHES, WILLIAM LEONARD. *Administration of Health, and Physical Education in Colleges.* New York: A. S. Barnes and Company, 1935.
7. KOZMAN, HILDA C., ROSALIND CASSIDY, AND CHESTER O. JACKSON. *Methods in Physical Education.* Philadelphia: W. B. Saunders Company, 1958.
8. LAPORTE, WILLIAM RALPH. *The Physical Education Curriculum.* Los Angeles: The Caslon Printing Company, 1937.
9. LARSON, LEONARD A., AND LUCILLE F. HILL. *Physical Education in the Elementary School.* New York: Henry Holt and Company, 1957.
10. NIXON, EUGENE W., AND FREDERICK W. COZENS. *An Introduction to Physical Education.* Philadelphia: W. B. Saunders Company, 1952.
11. OBERTEUFFER, DELBERT. *Physical Education.* New York: Harper and Brothers, 1956.
12. ROGERS, FREDERICK RAND. *Educational Objectives of Physical Education.* New York: A. S. Barnes and Company, 1929.
13. SHARMAN, JACKSON R. *Introduction to Physical Education.* New York: A. S. Barnes and Company, 1934.
14. SHEPARD, NATALIE MARIE. *Foundations and Principles of Physical Education.* New York: The Ronald Press Company, 1960.
15. VANNIER, MARYHELEN, AND MILDRED FOSTER. *Teaching Physical Education in Elementary Schools.* Philadelphia: W. B. Saunders Company, 1954.
16. VOLTNER, EDWARD F., AND ARTHUR A. ESSLINGER. *The Organization and Administration of Physical Education.* New York: Appleton-Century-Crofts, Inc., 1938.

17. WARREN, HOWARD C. *Dictionary of Psychology*. Boston: Houghton Mifflin Company, 1934.
18. WAYMAN, AGNES R. *A Modern Philosophy of Physical Education*. Philadelphia: W. B. Saunders Company, 1938.
19. WILLIAMS, JESSE FEIRING. *The Principles of Physical Education*. Philadelphia: W. B. Saunders Company, 1964.
20. WILLIAMS, JESSE FEIRING, AND CLIFFORD L. BROWNELL. *The Administration of Health and Physical Education*. Philadelphia: W. B. Saunders Company, 1940.

Journals

21. BOOKWALTER, KARL W. "The Objectives of Physical Education," *Journal of Health and Physical Education,* 5:26 February, 1934.

17. Warren, Howard C. A Dictionary of Psychology. Boston: Houghton Mifflin Company, 1934.
18. Wayman, Agnes R. A Modern Philosophy of Physical Education. Philadelphia: W. B. Saunders Company, 1938.
19. Williams, Jesse Feiring. The Principles of Physical Education. Philadelphia: W. B. Saunders Company, [illegible].
20. [illegible] The Administration [illegible] Philadelphia: W. B. Saunders Company, [illegible].

Journal

21. [illegible], "The [illegible] of Physical Education," Journal of Health and Physical Education, [illegible]

Part III

Philosophy in Action

A Philosophy of Administration for Physical Education

10

We have learned that philosophy is composed of and is a result of many elements: principles, aims, objectives, attitudes, appreciations, goals, outcomes, standards, criteria, policies and procedures, to name a few. It is more than mere concepts expressed on paper. To be effective philosophy must be dynamic. It must be put to work in an active and practical manner.

Every administrator, whether or not he realizes it, has some kind of a philosophy. He needs a sound working philosophy, one which provides a sturdy foundation upon which to build an effective administrative structure. Let us consider, therefore, what administrative structure is like and of what it is composed by discussing certain basic factors: origin and meaning, functions, scope of duties, theories and types of political organizations, principles, and philosophy of the administrator.

ORIGIN AND MEANING OF ADMINISTRATION

Origin

One might say that administration becomes necessary and is usually initiated at the moment that the instructional and operational duties of teaching become too burdensome, too complicated, too time- and energy-consuming for the simultaneous conduct of efficient and effective instruction. The teacher in a one- or two-room school may be able to manage and direct all of the affairs which revolve around the job of teaching, but in a large school this is not possible. There are many details involved in operating a large school because of big enrollments, expanded facilities, complicated budgets and so forth. Someone is needed to look after the multitudinous details of the school system and to create an environment conducive to good teaching. This kind of work is called administration and the person who performs the duties is the administrator. In a very small school this may be referred to as organization but in a large school, because of many more details and complex affairs, it is more likely to be called administration. The difference between the two terms is one of degree rather than type of activity. (1:270)

Meaning

Administration has many aspects which are similar, related and interrelated: managerial, organizational, educational, business, leadership, guidance and direction. Because of these many aspects administration may mean different things to different people, depending upon what aspect is deemed most important and what needs demand the greatest amount of attention at a particular time. Furthermore, the aspect that is considered the most essential depends upon the training, experience, wisdom and open-mindedness of the administrator. Also, the same person may hold different beliefs at different times depending upon the changing need of the school community and upon his personal aspirations and objectives. Unfortunately some administrators think of their work as something to do for personal gain rather than for the improvement of instruction.

Educationaly speaking, the two main aspects of administration are educational and business. It is difficult to differentiate between the two because of their close relationship and interdependence, operationally speaking. Strictly, however, all the affairs of the school should be conducted for educational purposes. Educational administration is concerned mainly with those aspects relating closely to classroom instruction such as curricula of studies and activities, use of instructional aids, guidance and direction of personnel and students. The main purpose of business administration is to take care of those school affairs that are indirectly related to classroom instruction such as providing materials, facilities, equipment and supplies, and conducting registration and scheduling classes.

Administration applied to physical education is the organizing and directing of all of the affairs of that department which are essential to the efficient and effective operation of the program of studies and activities in accordance with the established aims, objectives and purposes. It must be kept in mind at all times that the main job of administration is to facilitate and improve instruction. Administration should not be permitted to become the all important thing – an end in itself – but a means to an end, namely adequate and efficient instruction. No administrator should exalt or glorify administration for the sake of power, influence or prestige.

As part of the understanding of administration, it is well to know who the administrators are. They are the nonteaching personnel, the superintendents of schools, general supervisors, special supervisors of various school subjects, principals, and business officials. That part of the faculty charged with the teaching responsibility is known as the instructional staff, the teachers. The faculty includes both of these groups of people, those involved in administration and instruction.

GENERAL FUNCTIONS OF ADMINISTRATION

The general function of administration is to accomplish something and to provide order within a basic framework. The task is that of insuring a smooth and continuous operation of school affairs so that teaching and guiding students can proceed most efficiently and effectively. The function of administration is twofold: to preserve the social and educational heritage of the past that has important bearing upon the problems of today, integrating it with the accepted new ideas of the present, and to discover still newer ways to improve methods of teaching, supervision and administration. New ideas, however, should be thoroughly screened, tested and developed before they are put into use. Administration must not be employed to perpetuate a particular ideology or regime, to serve political purposes, to keep officials in office, to achieve power or personal gratification. It should be used to give structure, permanence and stability to the school system in order to insure the best environment possible for the instruction and direction of students.

Furthermore, it is the function of the administration to clear the path for teachers, eliminating unnecessary duties so that they can give their full attention to teaching and counseling students. It should be remembered, however, that some teachers prefer to be involved in some administrative duties, particularly those which relate to establishing policies and procedures. There are some administrators, however, who encourage faculty involvement in administrative affairs to the extent that they tend to overload the teaching staff with too many of these duties. The extra time and energy devoted to excessive committee work decreases the amount of energy left for the primary purpose, teaching, and eventually lowers the quality of instruction. It is the function of the administration to see that the philosophy of the school is established in light of the needs and interests of students, of the sociological, political and economic needs of the community, and upon the psychological and philosophical bases of education. It is the function of the administration to see that this philosophy is integrated with the curriculum, with the concepts of the teachers and the activities of the students.

In general, the functions of administration can be classified into three categories: legislative, executive, and supervisory. The legislative function is related principally to legislation dealing with federal and state laws as well as with regulations of the local school boards. These laws and regulations are handed down through various legislative and educational channels and determine to a great extent the nature of the policies, rules and regulations under which the local school administration must operate. These policies should reflect the fundamental principles, aims and objectives of education. The executive function is concerned with putting the policies, rules and regulations into operation. These apply to all of the departments of the school, including physical education, and relate to authority and direction delegated and assumed by the administrative officials in all school affairs. The concern of the supervisory function is twofold: (1) that of observing and evaluating the effect of the executive policies and regulations and endeavoring to improve their effectiveness and continuity; (2) that of providing leadership to teachers by means of such things as conferences and in-service training for the improvement of instruction.

SCOPE OF ADMINISTRATIVE DUTIES

The general functions of administration consist mainly of planning, organizing, directing, financing and budgeting, staffing, coordinating, reporting and evaluating. These functions are interacting and somewhat overlapping. All are important aspects of administration. Some authorities call these components of administration (2:164), others call them activities. (3:31) Regardless of the terminology they are essential duties performed by the administrator.

Planning

Desired objectives cannot be attained without a plan of procedure. Planning means doing many essential things. It necessitates the collection of pertinent facts and ideas about a situation and employing these to arrive at solutions of problems. It involves anticipating future needs and formulating a definite plan of action and clearing the way for action. Needless to say, the plan should be formulated in accordance with the principles of education and the objectives sought. Planning also involves making decisions on how plans are to be formulated. Will the decisions be made solely by the administrators, by the teachers and students or by the total action of all these groups through democratic processes where administrators working with the teachers and students reach decisions together? The method chosen depends to a great extent upon the administrative philosophy. Making budgets, constructing curricula and providing facilities are examples of some of the usual school problems for which accurate planning is necessary. Planning applied specifically to the physical education department is concerned mainly with three major responsibilities: personnel, facilities and program. Other duties such as those related to salaries, organizing, reporting and evaluating naturally are involved and are interrelated, but the larger part of these responsibilities usually are performed by the top school administrative officers.

Organizing

Organizing is concerned with arranging and systematizing individual but related components into a unified or organic structure for the purpose of achieving efficient and dynamic functioning and attaining the planned objectives. As applied to education and to the special field of physical education it involves many aspects: work, people, authority and responsibility, theories, materials and ideas.

WORK. Work must be assigned. It is necessary to have knowledge of the total task in order to subdivide and arrange it into parts which are then assigned to people.

PEOPLE. People must do the work. The people involved are the board members, superintendents, principals, supervisors, specialists, teachers, and students. The task is to assign persons to the specific jobs which they are capable of performing, assign staff members to certain teaching subjects, classify students into grades, and assign administrators, teachers, students and parents to committees.

AUTHORITY AND RESPONSIBILITY. Authority means power to give commands and the right to act. Authority must be properly designated. Authority of school administrators originally comes from federal and state laws and from regulations and decisions from state and local boards of education. In operation, authority may be both limited and discretionary. Discretionary authority is commonly granted by law and is widely employed in school systems in order that the varying needs of the students and of the school community can be met. Responsibility entails assigning or delegating a task to be done to someone and holding that individual accountable for the results. If results are to be good, authority and responsibility cannot be separated. They must go hand in hand. It would be improper and poor administrative procedure to ask someone to perform a task and not give him authority to do it. We find some administrators operate in this fashion, however, either because they are selfish, wishing to keep all power in their own hands, or do not have the competency called for for their position so do not know how to use their authority.

THEORIES AND TYPES OF POLITICAL ORGANIZATION. The effectiveness of an organization depends upon the theory one holds concerning the use of power and the relationship between authority and responsibility. There are at least three common types of organizations which distribute power, authority and responsibility in different ways: "line," "line and staff" and "functional."

The "line" organization is autocratic in nature. The authority and responsibility are dispensed through a "chain of commands" from the top to the bottom position through very definite channels. Information from the people on the lower level may be passed up the line but they have no part in formulating regulations, procedures or plans. The affairs are conducted much as they would be in any military unit. The advantage of this type of organization is that the authority and responsibility are definitely placed and clear, and discipline can be handled effectively. One disadvantage is that a few people are overloaded with duties and responsibilities, some of which they may not be capable of performing. In addition, this type of organization may cause poor morale because the doers, mainly the teachers and students, have little or no opportunity to voice their opinions about their needs and interests or to share in solving some of the problems that concern them.

The idea of the "line and staff" organization is to retain the advantages of the line but to functionalize it by adding a staff of specialists as an advisory group. This relieves administrators from many of their former duties so that they can give more concerted attention to fewer but more important problems and at the same time receive advice from experts. The authority still proceeds through the "chain of commands" as in the "line" organization from the top down. However, the specialists have authority, if they wish, to give directions to those in charge of the work (teachers), but they do not have authority over the students. Here again, as in the "line" there is not much more, if any, opportunity for the doers (teachers and students) to work with the administration in shaping the school environment. This form of organization is only slightly more functional and democratic than the "line."

The idea of the "functional" type of organization is to operate in a democratic fashion, to continue to provide power for action and to call for cooperation, as in the "line and staff," but to stress cooperation with the staff, teachers and students, and to provide opportunity for all to share in making and enforcing the policies and plans which affect them. It continues to use the staff of specialists where needed, but unlike the "line and staff" makes specialized skills and abilities directly available to the students. The authority of the specialists may, where necessary, be extended to direct the students. The power is unified, resides in and is applied by all members of the organization. Communications flow freely up and down the framework of the organization. There is still one man in control but his power is greatly decreased. He invites all of the people in the organization to cooperate with the administration in forming plans and policies. There are, however, a few weaknesses that may develop if careful attention is not given to all functioning parts of the organization. Action in making decisions tends to be slower when more people are involved. Discipline is more relaxed and may, at times, become weak causing poor morale. "Passing the buck" is easier to do and may frequently be resorted to, since responsibility is more difficult to place. The main concept and strength here is, however, action through democracy.

MATERIALS. Materials, equipment, facilities and supplies must be provided. They must be organized into laboratories, libraries, buildings, gymnasiums and playfields for the development and use of knowledge.

FACTS AND IDEAS. Facts, ideas, principles and knowledge are needed for building a philosophy for action, for making policies and procedures and for constructing curricula.

All of these individual aspects, work, people, authority and responsibility, theories and types of organization, materials and ideas do not make an efficient and effective organization by themselves. They must be arranged and unified into a smoothly operating organic body. This transaction calls for the knowledge of science and philosophy of education as well as "know-how" for applying them.

Directing

Directing is another important duty of the administrator. It means managing and conducting all of the affairs of a school system or of a specific department such as physical education. These affairs may be concerned with materials, supplies, equipment, facilities, budgets, personnel and other similar things in the school environment. Directing is concerned also with the authority, power, decision and action. Authority in a democratic society comes from the people in the form of laws, decisions and regulations, and in a school system is a necessary power in the process of directing. It should be used mainly to give official sanction and standing to decisions and for compulsive purposes only in emergent situations. The best type of authority is the one which proceeds through the democratic process; in this case people respect the administration and its leadership and are motivated to carry out their responsibilities willingly, intelligently and purposefully.

Directing is interrelated with planning and arranging. It must start with planning as future needs are studied and a design of action is formulated. Directing must also include organizing, where the component parts of the organization are arranged into a unified and workable whole so that dynamic action can take place. Directing is not only formulating plans, giving orders and instruction, guiding all the affairs of a school system or a department, and seeing that work is being done but includes follow-up procedures. The latter should not be construed as inspection but rather as evaluation of the outcomes of the work. It is an appraisal and a self-criticism for the purpose of improvement and effectiveness.

We see, therefore, that directing is a complex task of working with materials (libraries, laboratories, facilities, playfields, gymnasiums) with people (teachers, doctors, nurses, specialists, librarians, maintenance staff, parents and students) and with laws, decisions and regulations. This is a task that calls for extremely high qualities in the person who is the administrator. He should be a leader, not a dictator, one who possesses fine personal characteristics, one who has excellent ideas, one who is intelligently trained and one who has the competencies for the job. He should be a person who can use his knowledge, skill, personality and authority wisely in attaining the objectives of his position through the democratic educative process.

Financing and Budgeting

The duties of the administrator include those of financing and budgeting. Efficient administration cannot be conducted without knowledge of and plans for financial economy. This fact was found true by governmental agencies and industries where financial accounting originated many years ago and was later adopted as desirable and standard operating procedure by elementary and secondary schools, colleges and universities and other public organizations.

Finance in the schools is concerned with locating the source of funds, raising and expending them for the affairs of the schools. There are several sources of revenue and funds: property within a certain area in which revenue is raised by local taxation; commodities taxed by the state and earmarked for school expenses; gate receipts and students' fees used to supplement budgets for expenses of certain departments within the high schools or colleges, such as the department of physical education and athletics. Moneys from gate receipts and student fees should become a part of the general school fund and dispersed to physical education and athletics according to need as they are to any other school department, subject or function.

The budget is a formulated financial plan for receipts from all revenue and funds and for all proposed expenditures. It is based upon projected needs in relationship to money available. There are many good reasons for budgeting. A few of them are: (1) the needs of a school or department can be met more efficiently, economically and fairly; (2) expenditures can be kept in line with income; (3) methods of dispersing and amount of funds distributed can be disclosed; (4) the chance of moneys' being mishandled can be reduced; and (5) budgetary needs for the ensuing year can be estimated.

For expediency and over-all efficiency, funds in the high school should be handled by the regular school treasurer if the school system is large and has many detailed and major responsibilities and affairs to conduct, or by the principal if there is no full time treasurer. The duties of the treasurer should include the management of funds related to interscholastic athletics and physical education programs. Indeed, whether in high school or colleges and universities, the most acceptable and desirable arrangement in physical education and athletics is for the treasurer or the business officer of the school to conduct all the financial affairs instead of the athletic director or coach. Financial officers are experts in their field and are trained to handle budgets efficiently; therefore, mismanagement and misuse of funds such as subsidization and proselyting can be better controlled or eliminated. It is conceded that competitive athletics between educational institutions can be and are in many cases fine educational experiences when properly conducted. However, the educational value diminishes with the increase of commercialization.

Staffing

Staffing is an extremely important duty of the administrator. A program stands or falls according to the capabilities and morale of the staff members and the manner in which they are assigned to jobs and supervised. The staff includes all personnel who have something to do with the administration, supervision, instruction, clerical work, maintenance and operation of the school. Staffing is selecting and assigning personnel to the duties and responsibilities of the various school positions which are necessary for the instruction, operation and maintenance of the program. The head school official should know the character and demands of each job and position and the ability of each staff member. The number and nature of all positions depend upon what the administrators and the curriculum committee decide the educational experiences (curricula of studies, programs) of pupils and students shall be. The head school official needs to have competent and well-qualified staff members. How competent they are depends upon how well he is able to select them. He can enhance the proficiency of his job of selecting suitable personnel by giving close scrutiny to such basic qualifications as personality, training, experience and health. (4:120) His obvious objective, of course, is to place the right person in the right job. He should also give due consideration to arranging suitable and equitable teaching and work loads and to providing opportunities for professional growth through conferences, workshops, clinics and in-service training.

Coordinating

We have seen that there are many factors and activities involved in the administrative process including planning, organizing, directing, budgeting, staffing, reporting and evaluating. Each is important in and of itself. But since all are parts of a whole, they cannot exist and operate independently if the entire organization is to function effectively toward a chosen objective. The functions of all parts of a school system or department should be synchronized and unified in a cooperative effort toward the common objective which is learning. This is the meaning of coordination in education or physical education. All parts must work together just like the muscles of the body in swinging a golf club. All muscles have certain duties to perform, but all their functions must be harmonized into a unity of action if the desired end, a smooth and powerful swing, is to be developed. The job of the school administrator is to see that a favorable environment is provided in which the educative process (instruction and educational experiences) can take place effectively. He can do this by harmonizing laws, decisions, rules, regulations, teachers, all staff members, pupils, materials, librarians, counselors, ideas, knowledge, principles and methods.

This is not an easy task and requires, on the administrator's part, much knowledge, experience, ingenuity, personality, administrative know-how and human understanding. He should be constantly studying and evaluating his organization and its processes. He should be critical of its operation and welcome criticism from others. Mending fences when broken is a good way to prevent trouble. This means that the administrator must look for possible weaknesses and reorganize his school system by introducing desirable changes where needed, thereby adding strength to his organization. Changes, however, in one part of the system may and usually do affect the functioning of another part. An outstanding point to remember "is that coordination is rarely, if ever, an entirely separate activity." (3:197) Changes in one part of the administrative process therefore may mean necessary adjustments in other parts.

It is the desire of every administraor to succeed in his job because he knows failure in the performance of his duties means unsatisfactory learning, poor staff relations, ineffective organization, troublesome discipline, financial worries and public criticism. An outstanding democratic principle to keep in mind at all times in order to gain and to hold the interest and cooperation of all with whom we work is that the best results come through the coordinated effort of the group process. When each person has a part and is involved in an enterprise he has a greater interest, desire and will to cooperate. This democratic principle should be a part of every administrator's working philosophy.

Reporting

Reporting is informing people to whom one is responsible regarding all activities that are taking place within a given organization or business. In the administration of a school system, for example, the superintendent keeps the public, the school board, the parents, the principals, the supervisors, the teachers, and the pupils informed, and they in turn keep each other informed. It is essential also that the superintendent himself keep up-to-date on facts and figures and events that are taking place. Running a school is as much a business as any other public business. The administrator therefore must have convenient, accurate and sufficient knowledge about how well his business is going. He must know its strengths and weaknesses.

The administrator must have devices which provide him data and information which he can use to direct and to control his educational business. Thus, he employs many kinds of records, makes inspections and scientific investigations. Information may come from any person up or down in the administrative line. The information may be in the form of daily, weekly, monthly, semester or annual reports. These reports may be concerned with finance, equipment, supplies, attendance, excuses, grades, promotion, health, accidents and injuries.

A good administrator will see that the reports are continuous and accumulative. He will try to get interest and cooperation from all personnel in setting up record cards or forms for reports, in gathering information, in coordinating and processing all data. Finally, it must be remembered that reports are not worth the time and energy expended unless something worthwhile is done with them. They do serve, of course, as a public record and give official and professional status to the school, but they must also be put into use in shaping and reshaping the educational process, the learning, the instruction, the program, the curriculum of the school or department. In all of these reporting activities the physical education director, the athletic director, the physical education teachers and the athletic coaches have a duty and responsibility just as the personnel in any other department requiring them to observe, gather, organize and report data pertinent to their work. They must do their share of the total task of reporting and informing within the school system.

Evaluation

Evaluation is a most important phase and duty of the administrator. Evaluation is not a separate entity but is linked to other elements of the administrative process, particularly planning, directing and reporting. Generally speaking, evaluation is the process by which the worth of something is appraised or judged. This process actually begins with the formulation of objectives, continues through the establishment of procedures by which objectives are to be attained and finally arrives at the analysis and appraisal of the results. After the appraisal, a critical review of procedures in relation to objectives may give further understanding. There should be a continuous process of reviewing objectives, procedures and desired results in relationship with each other. The whole process of stock-taking should be on a continuous basis.

In the school system at least two kinds of evaluation can be made: one to appraise the progress of students in learning, the other to appraise the procedures by which the desired outcomes of the curriculum are to be attained. The former type of evaluation is the appraisal of the results of the educative process and has for its purpose the determination of the quality and quantity of growth and development and performance by students in relation to program objectives. The latter is the appraisal of the results of the administrative process and has for its purpose the assessment of the effectiveness of the administrative procedures of planning and directing by checking the program and the performance of the students in the program. This is a type of a follow-up action in which the outcomes of the administrative process are judged by the employment of certain kinds of instruments by which data are collected for analysis, such as interviews, questionnaires, surveys, check lists and tests. As in other phases of the administrative process, for the best results evaluation should be planned, organized and executed through the democratic process of group thinking and acting and on a cooperative basis by all concerned. Evaluation is the concern of all the administrators, teachers and students in the whole school and is as applicable to the department of physical education and athletics as to any of the other departments in the school system.

PRINCIPLES OF ADMINISTRATION

Sound administration must rest upon fundamental principles. These must be based upon philosophy. They are derived from facts and concepts concerned with the various functions of administration discussed under planning, directing, budgeting, staffing, coordinating, reporting and evaluating. They relate generally to aims, objectives, policies and procedures. They also relate to finances, facilities, personnel, program, educational experiences and appraisals. A brief listing of a few of these principles follows. The good administrator:

1. Uses the principles of democracy in all his transactions and undertakings by seeking to obtain the participation of all persons involved in establishing such things as policies, rules, regulations and curricula.
2. Formulates a sound working philosophy based upon fundamental concepts of education and administrative practices.
3. Provides for adequate collection and analysis of facts concerning the value of the educative and administrative process.
4. Establishes a type of organization which gives adequate control, authority and responsibility for the proper functioning of a school system or a department.
5. Provides suitable, sufficient and safe facilities, equipment and supplies which are needed for the execution of the program.
6. Provides necessary funds to defray expenses for educational purposes and prepares an adequate budget. Finances all aspects of each department of the school equitably from the general school fund.
7. Selects adequate and qualified teachers and other school personnel and assigns them to positions commensurate with their competencies.
8. Always delegates authority with responsibility.
9. Properly defines the duties for which a staff member is responsible and allows him full credit for the work accomplished.

10. Coordinates all parts of the administrative process in an effective harmonizing unit for the purpose of attaining the common objective, the education of students.
11. Devises suitable instruments for evaluation purposes and analysis of results. From these results makes revisions where needed.
12. Keep the public, all school personnel and students properly informed with the facts and events which concern them.
13. Seeks, within his power and capability, to protect the health and to insure the well-being of all students and personnel.
14. Provides equality of opportunity for all students in both the curricular and extracurricular activities of the school.

PHILOSOPHY OF THE ADMINISTRATOR

It is ambiguous and trite to say that every administrator should have a philosophy. It is ambiguous because he has one whether or not he proclaims one. He portrays a philosophy by the manner in which he administers his organization. It may not be a satisfactory one but he has one, however good or bad it may be. A sound philosophy is a necessary foundation for the building of a strong administrative structure. This philosophy should be consistent with a dynamic philosophy of education; it should reflect the purposes of education; it should adhere to the objectives of the curricula and programs; and it should be based upon sound principles of administration. It also should reflect the needs and interests of students, the concerted opinion and valued judgments of the school board, members of the faculty, the parents and other citizens of the community.

An administrator with a sound philosophy displays a proper and intelligent attitude toward his position. Some administrators look upon their position as one with power to use for self-gratification and aggrandizement, as a position through which to build an empire of influence, prestige and affluence. The wiser administrator, while knowing that power is inherent in his position, also knows that it is not a personal power and is to be used only when needed. He never displays it, but uses it judiciously. He brushes aside the temptation for personal glory and considers that the sole purpose of his job is to see that students are adequately educated. He permits nothing to interfere with the attainment of this objective. As an athletic director or coach he does not succumb to the temptation of exploiting athletes for personal gain and glory, but sees that good educational experiences are provided through athletics.

The wise administrator uses the democratic principle of operation in which everyone has an opportunity to participate in the administrative and educative processes of the school system; through which differences of opinion can be disclosed and reconciled by discussion; through which decisions usually are made by the whole group and by the executive alone only when necessary to ameliorate or expedite urgent and critical matters. He refrains from the use of either autocratic or laissez faire methods of control. He knows that successful administration depends upon the interest, willingness and responsibility of the staff members to cooperate. He is aware that these characteristics are motivated by working and sharing together in the planning of the hard work, adversities, successes and joys of building a strong administrative structure for processing the educational enterprise.

QUESTIONS FOR REVIEW AND DISCUSSION

1. Why is it essential that the administrator formulate a sound philosophy of administration?
2. Discuss the origin of administration. When does "administration" become necessary?
3. What is the meaning of administration? What is the difference in meaning between administration and organization?
4. What are the two main aspects of administration? How do you differentiate between the two?
5. Who are the administrators of a high school and of a college? What are their duties?
6. Name and discuss the general functions of administration.
7. Discuss the nature and scope of the duties of the administrator in a secondary school and in a large university. Of a physical education chairman in a secondary school and college.
8. What is the meaning of planning as applied to a physical education department? With what major responsibilities is it concerned? What are other related responsibilities?
9. Discuss the process of organizing as it is related to a department of physical education in a small college. With what other administrative aspects is organizing involved?
10. Discuss the philosophy surrounding the act of subdividing the total task of the school and assigning the staff to these jobs.
11. What is the meaning of authority? Where does it originate? What is the difference between limited and discretionary authority?

12. What is the meaning of responsibility? Discuss its relationship with authority.
13. Discuss the types of political organizations of a school system and their theories of control as related to authority and responsibility. Give advantages and disadvantages of each.
14. Discuss the functions involved in directing. How is directing related to other duties of the administrator, particularly those of planning and organizing?
15. Discuss the responsibilities and problems related to the task of financing and budgeting for an athletic department in a large high school; in a small private college; in a large university.
16. What is the importance of staffing in relation to the instructional program? What are some of the duties involved? Who are the members of the staff? Classify them.
17. Define the meaning and describe the functions of coordinating.
18. Discuss the relation and importance of reporting to sound administration.
19. Give the meaning and importance of evaluating as related to administration. Discuss kinds of evaluations that can be made in a school system.
20. Name and discuss several important principles of administration. From what source are they derived? What functions do they serve?
21. If you were an administrator, what would your philosophy be? Describe.

Bibliography

1. Brownell, Clifford L., and E. Patricia Hagman. *Physical Education – Foundations and Principles.* New York: McGraw-Hill Book Company, Inc., 1951.
2. Cowell, Charles C., and Wellman L. France. *Philosopy and Principles of Physical Education.* Englewood Cliffs: Prentice-Hall, Inc., 1963.
3. Sears, Jesse B. *The Nature of the Administrative Process.* New York: McGraw-Hill Book Company, Inc., 1950.
4. Voltmer, Edward F., and Arthur A. Esslinger. *The Organization and Administration of Physical Education.* New York: Appleton-Century-Crofts, Inc., 1958.

References

1. Bucher, Charles A. *Administration of School Health and Physical Education Programs.* St. Louis: The C. V. Mosby Co., 1958.

2. CAMPBELL, RONALD F., AND RUSSELL T. GREGG. *Administrative Behavior in Education.* New York: Harper and Row Publishers, 1957.
3. FORSYTHE, CHARLES E., AND RAY O. DUNCAN. *Administration of Physical Education.* Englewood Cliffs: Prentice-Hall, Inc., 1951.
4. GRIEDER, CALVIN, TRUMAN M. PIERCE AND EVERETT ROSENSTENGEL. *Public School Administration.* New York: The Ronald Press Co., 1961.
5. GRIFFITHS, DANIEL E. *Human Relations in School Administration.* New York: Appleton-Century-Crofts, Inc., 1956.
6. HANLON, JOHN J. *Principles of Public Health Administration.* St. Louis: The C. V. Mosby Co., 1960.
7. HAVEL, RICHARD C., AND EVERY W. SEYMOUR. *Administration of Health, Physical Education and Recreation for Schools.* New York: The Ronald Press Company, 1961.
8. HOWARD, GLEN, AND EDWARD MASONBRINK. *Administration of Physical Education.* New York: Harper and Row, Publishers, 1963.
9. HUGHES, WILLIAM L., ESTHER FRENCH AND NELSON G. LEHSTEN. *Administration of Physical Education for Schools and Colleges.* New York: The Ronald Press Company, 1962.
10. WILLIAMS, JESSE F., CLIFFORD L. BROWNELL AND ELMON L. VERNIER. *Administration of Health Education and Physical Education.* Philadelphia: W. B. Saunders Company, 1958.

11 A Philosophy of Curriculum Building for Physical Education

In the previous chapter we have seen how philosophy is involved in the process of administering the total school organization. Philosophy is equally basic to curriculum building as it is, indeed, a necessary guide to charting our course in all activities and functions of life. Without this guidance and direction, our efforts probably would be ineffective and wasteful, or at least would be inconsistent. Curriculum, so important to the growth and development of young people, needs to be considered with the greatest amount of appreciation and reflective thinking. The discussion in this chapter is arranged around several essential phases of curriculum construction: meaning of terms, philosophic bases, and the development of the curriculum itself.

MEANING OF TERMS

There is disagreement among educational authorities regarding the use of the term *curriculum*. Some speak of it as the total arrangement and supervision of courses in all studies within a school. Others think of it as restricted to study in a single subject matter area such as history, music or physical education. Traditionally, the curriculum was considered to include only those academic subject matter courses which were planned for the students by teachers and other school officials. More recently, however, broader interpretations are made: all school activities and experiences which are planned for students for the purpose of developing their capabilities and personalities are included as part of the curriculum. This means that the previously so-called "out-of-class or extracurricular activities" such as bands, school plays, assemblies, clubs, intramural sports, recreational games and varsity athletics, as well as academic experiences, are all a part of the total curriculum. The broader interpretation means that the students as well as the teachers and other school authorities have a share in developing the educational activities and experiences at school both in or out of class; participation itself therefore is considered a part of the newer concept. From the viewpoint of the philosophy developed in this book, the term curriculum can be defined as all cooperatively planned, progressively and flexibly arranged and supervised activities both in subject matter courses and related class and school experiences which are planned for the development of the total capabilities and personalities of students.

This definition holds whether speaking collectively about the entire subject matter areas and related school experiences of a high school curriculum or referring to the total study designed for a department or special subject matter area in college. In this light, *courses of study* may be considered as a synonym and used interchangeably with curriculum. However, for the purpose of a clearer understanding, it is often desirable to designate whether we are referring to the curriculum of the entire school or to that of a special departmental or subject matter area. For example, when speaking of professional preparation in the department of physical education which exists within a college or a school of physical education within a university, we would refer to it as the curriculum of that department or that college. It would encompass both the traditional type courses and other related activities and experiences. All required and optionally selected academic courses, motor activity courses, and required instructional activity courses would be included in addition to such things as professional club activities, intramural sports and varsity athletics.

A *program* is a phase of the curriculum including educational experiences and/or courses progressively arranged in learning units, as for example, for any particular grade level in the elementary or secondary school. A subject matter unit is organized and arranged for purposes of instruction into a *course.* A *unit* may be designated as either a measure or subdivision of a program (large unit) or of a course (small unit). There are several kinds of units, as for instance, planned or unplanned experience units, subject matter units or any combination of these. A *lesson plan* is a subdivision of a unit which outlines the important aspects and order of a lesson.

PHILOSOPHIC BASES OF THE CURRICULUM

A sound and meaningful curriculum evolves from a happy combination of many factors. What are some of these?

Attitude of Citizens

The physical education curriculum is affected by the attitude of people in the local school community. Do they believe that their children need to be taught about health, physical education, recreation and safety? Are they in favor of extended public education for everyone – education which is adequate, comprehensive and equitable? Are they willing to provide the necessary moral and financial support and leadership for it? Answers to these and other similar questions depend to a large degree upon their personal experiences and philosophy. These are influenced by the kind and amount of their own education and the character and nature of the community in which they live. The more academically oriented citizens naturally have the greater understanding and appreciation of education. The kind and amount of preparation required for participation in the occupation, business or profession in which they engage also influences their attitude toward education. In general, little formal education is necessary for unskilled jobs and those who are so engaged ordinarily have little regard for education, whereas those involved in business or in the professions place great value on education.

We see, therefore, that people from different types of communities – rural, commercial and industrial – and from different occupations and professions place different values on education and consequently on each of its aspects, including physical education. People from agrarian areas may feel that there is little or no need for school physical education because the members of their families have, of necessity, sufficient exercise during their working hours on the farm; others, however, may well realize that physical education is more than physical work and may desire that their children have organized instructional and recreational experiences. People in shops and offices in the city may see the need for the inclusion of health, physical education and recreation in the curriculum because, unless such experiences are organized, no opportunities would exist for these learnings; thus they may believe that facilities, program, instruction and time should be provided in the school curriculum as a substitute for that which is lacking in their artificial environment. On the other hand, such people – because of misunderstanding of the nature and purpose of physical education, and because nothing in their lives seemingly demands optimum health and physical stamina – may believe that physical activity is merely wasteful play.

Type of Government

Government forms one foundation upon which the curriculum is based. Its philosophy permeates the curriculum and determines whether schools will be public, free and independent and organized without strict governmental control for the welfare of the people as in a republic, or strictly controlled and dictated by the state for the good of the state alone as in communism and fascism. In our form of government, it is the duty and privilege of our schools to prepare boys and girls and young men and women to live happily, successfully and respectfully in a democratic society and to encourage them to maintain that society. The curriculum therefore should emphasize and develop concepts such as respect for dignity and rights of the individual, individual freedom with accompanying responsibility for personal acts, social justice, individual initiative, self-expression, self-control, sharing, cooperation and group action.

Philosophy of Professional Educators

Not only does the curriculum stem from the attitude held toward education in the local community but also from the philosophy of those whose profession is education. Philosophy of education reflects the concepts of society and adheres to and works within the legal jurisdiction of the federal and state laws, rulings and regulations. Basic beliefs regarding education which have been followed by the profession of education in our country for many years were formally stated in 1918 and identified as the "seven cardinal principles of education"; these include health, fundamental processes, vocation, citizenship, worthy home membership, worthy use of leisure and ethical character. (1) In 1938 objectives of education were reinterpreted in light of the changing social conditions and trends of society by the Educational Policy Commission as self-realization, human relationship, economic efficiency and civic responsibility. These objectives of education in American democracy "center around the person himself, his relationship to others in home and community, the creation and use of material wealth, and socio-civic activities." (3:47)

Other Influencing Factors

Many other factors need to be considered before the curriculum is constructed. These include the philosophy of the school board members, the superintendent, and the principal. The needs and interests of students must be served. The school plan, school procedures, and number and kind of personnel involved also must be considered.

DEVELOPING THE PHYSICAL EDUCATION CURRICULUM

Organizing for Curriculum Development

The task of either building a new curriculum or revising one presently in operation calls for a tremendous amount of reflective thinking, planning, organizing and constructing. This is the job of a committee whose members should be interested, qualified and dedicated to the assignment. Who appoints the committee and who are its members? If the results of the curriculum study are to apply to several high schools within a city or school district, the superintendent will appoint the committee; if the study is made for one high school alone, the principal will appoint the committee. A temporary chairman is then appointed from committee members who have been nominated by the person in charge of physical education after this person has enlisted the support, interest, and advice of all teachers of health and physical education and all athletic coaches. If the curriculum study is being made in a college or university, the head of the department or school of health and physical education will appoint the committee and its temporary chairman after he has enlisted the cooperative effort of the members of the faculty and after nominations for committee personnel have been made by the faculty. Such a plan is the result of a belief that all phases of curriculum construction are best accomplished through the group process and should function from the first step in curriculum building, the selection of the committee.

The membership of the high school curriculum committee should include persons from the school community who represent all walks of life as well as representatives from the school and the profession of physical education. Included in this committee should be representatives from specific groups: the parents; medical, dental and business associations; health and physical education teachers; other academic teachers; administrative officials; coaches; and students. All grade levels should be represented. It would also be advisable to include professional curriculum specialists who would act as consultants.

On a college or university level the committee would consist of members who represent the teaching staff of health, physical education, recreation and safety; administrative officials of the department or school; coaches; and students. It would be desirable to include administrative officials of the university but these persons in practice often are members *ex officio,* for the demands of their other duties usually preclude active participation on various departmental committees. Sometimes it is desirable to have representatives from elementary and secondary physical education teachers and coaches drawn from the community and/or state on the curriculum committee. A representative of former professional students may be included. Again it would be advisable to have curriculum and other consulting specialists.

Usually the one who appoints the committee also names its temporary chairman. If this is not done a chairman is elected by the members of the committee at the first official meeting. The temporary chairman organizes the preliminary procedures of the committee, makes assignments and defines duties. If he has the cooperation and confidence of the members he usually is elected by them to continue as chairman. If not, or if the temporary chairman prefers not to act in this capacity for the duration of the study, the committee will choose another chairman.

Determining the Philosophy

The curriculum committee examines basic factors previously mentioned: philosophy, attitudes, values, beliefs, and facts as they affect members of the specific community. It considers the needs, interests and development of children. It reviews what is known about the learning process. It considers physical education in particular since it is for this area that the curriculum is being constructed. The philosophy thus developed by the curriculum committee culminates in a statement of principles, aims and objectives. These indicate the scope and function of the educational experiences (academic, motor, mental, recreational and social) of the physical education curriculum. The curriculum thus becomes philosophy interpreted and put into practice.

PRINCIPLES. We learned in Chapter 9 that part of the source from which principles are derived is a large reservoir of untested and unverified data, ideas and concepts based on personal experiences, explorations, reflections, customs, tradition and culture. This wealth of material must be organized, examined, refined and analyzed scientifically before basic truths can be formulated. This process cannot be conducted by just anyone; it must be accomplished by people who are qualified as a result of education and experience – authorities in the profession.

Principles of physical education also come from the scientific facts of many fields of knowledge such as physiology, anatomy, sociology and psychology. We learned previously that a principle is a fundamental truth or strongly supported belief more or less uniformly and universally accepted which may serve as a guide for conduct and procedure. It is a guide which is useful in the attainment of an aim or an objective. We draw on those which are particularly concerned with the learning process, effective teaching methods, administrative procedures, and the needs and interests of students (mental, social, biological, cultural, growth and development).

AIM. The origin, meaning and nature of an aim were discussed at length in Chapter 9. We learned that, generally speaking, an aim gives direction toward a desired, remote, worthy and educationally sound end. The aim of physical education is the provision of competent leadership, adequate facilities and appropriate physical, play, recreational and related activities and experiences for the purpose of contributing to the maximum development of the whole individual so that he can live a happy, well-adjusted and socially efficient life.

OBJECTIVES. Objectives lead toward and contribute to the fulfillment of an aim. Objectives are more specific, exact and attainable than aims. There are many types of objectives: technical, associated and concomitant (discussed in Chapter 9) and all play an essential part in the teaching-learning process. Objectives may be described in terms of relative degree of magnitude and time in which they can be attained: general, specific, remote, intermediate and immediate. They are determined from a study of the social, mental and physical needs of students, from a study of their natural activities and from a knowledge of their growth and development.

Professional authorities, physical education staff members, members of the curriculum committee, and students help determine objectives. Both those persons involved in the preparation of the curriculum and those participating in it should share in the task of determining objectives — cooperative determination is very important. The nature of the curriculum, methods of instruction, selection of activities and the resultant outcomes are determined by the number and kind of objectives that are formulated. Objectives serve as direct guides in planning a program of physical education and directing activities.

SELECTING ACTIVITIES AND EDUCATIONAL EXPERIENCES

After the committee has been organized, philosophy determined, and the aims and objectives formulated, the next logical problem to consider is the selection of activities and educational experiences which will serve as vehicles through which the objectives can be attained. There are many kinds of motor activities and movement related experiences, but all cannot be included in the program. Some are more important and beneficial and lend themselves better to the achievement of specific objectives than others. Those which are more worthy should receive the greater emphasis in the program. How can we be reasonably sure that the activities selected will be the most valuable and suitable for the attainment of the desired outcomes?

Criteria must be established. With these we can judge relative value and worthiness.

CRITERIA. In order to qualify for a place in the physical education curriculum, activities should meet at least a large majority of the following criteria:

1. Activities should be interesting, enjoyable and stimulating to the individual.
2. Activities should be challenging – not too easy so that boredom results and not too difficult to be discouraging.
3. Activities should be chosen which are within the abilities of the students but they should extend student abilities.
4. Activities should be safe but provide opportunities for adventure.
5. Motor experiences should be conducive to the development of strength and endurance of the individual.
6. Motor activities should be selected which involve the natural and basic activities of the human race: running, jumping, climbing, throwing, catching and striking.
7. Educational experiences should be selected on the basis of their creative self-expressive potentials.
8. Activities should provide opportunities for learning about human relationships.
9. Activities should be useful to the individual and closely related to life situations so that transfer of knowledge and skill can more likely occur.
10. Motor experiences should be selected which will help to develop accuracy, speed and skill.
11. Activities should be selected which will help to develop agility, flexibility, rhythm and poise.
12. Activities should be selected which can contribute to the development of the aesthetic nature of the individual – appreciation of beauty, form, line and color.
13. Educational and motor experiences should provide mental stimulation.
14. Activities should contribute to the physical, mental and emotional well-being of the individual.
15. Activities should promote the development of proper body mechanics and the fundamental movements of the body.
16. Activities should offer opportunities for the development of ethical character and good citizenship.

17. Activities should provide the possibility for many varieties of learning.
18. Activities should provide democratic experiences – group process, cooperation, sharing.
19. Activities should be so selected and arranged that they follow a logical sequence and progress from simple to complex in degree of difficulty.
20. Activities should be selected which can be useful to the young individual as he grows and develops and beneficial to him as a mature adult.
21. Activities should be provided which can be used as preventive, corrective and compensatory exercises.
22. Activities should be selected which will provide opportunities for developing moral and social values.
23. Activities should be selected which satisfy many of the student's own immediate purposes such as for appearance, skills in a sport, self-control and relaxation.
24. Activities should be selected with reference to available and/or acquirable facilities and equipment, to the time allotment within the school schedule; and to the climate and other environmental conditions.

ACTIVITIES. The activities and experiences which come closest to meeting the majority of the foregoing criteria and are therefore desirable for inclusion in a curriculum of health, physical education and recreation are listed following. Since some activities can be classified in more than one category, there is some overlapping. The number and type of activities, the amount of time devoted to each and the degree of difficulty will vary according to the age, maturation, abilities and interests of students and the objectives of the program.

1. Self-testing activities: individual and mass athletic events; tests for agility, strength, speed, accuracy and endurance.
2. Aquatics: Swimming, diving and life saving.
3. Apparatus, tumbling and rebound tumbling.
4. Games and relays: activities of low organization which serve as lead-ups to the major dual and team sports.
5. Individual and dual activities: tennis, fencing, archery, golf, handball, squash, badminton, skating, and riding.
6. Team sports: football, basketball, baseball, track and field, volleyball, speedball, field hockey, and field ball.
7. Rhythmic activities and dancing: fundamental rhythmic activities, modern, social or ballroom, folk, and square dance.

8. Social-recreational activities: dramas, plays, concerts, play days, mixers, skits and musical comedies.
9. Conditioning and reconditionig activities: special physical conditioning, adapted, preventive, developmental and rehabilitative.
10. Outdoor educational activities: school camping correlated with the biological sciences, arts and crafts, astronomy, geology, and health.
11. Outdoor recreational activities: camping, hunting, fishing, mountain climbing, skiing, sailing, canoeing and scuba diving.

Philosophy and Method

We organize and interpret knowledge in accordance with our philosophy. As we consider the problem of curriculum construction, we find that method ranks high in our deliberations because we are searching for effective ways of guiding students. What is the meaning and importance of method? What are the bases of method? What are the various kinds of methods? What factors determine choice of methods?

THE MEANING AND IMPORTANCE OF METHOD. In ordinary usage, method carries the connotation of something logically arranged in progressive stages or steps. It is a specific and orderly procedure employed in accomplishing something. Academically, it refers to a specific arrangement (logical, natural, psychological and/or orderly) of procedures and learning experiences. It describes a way of guiding students toward the attainment of prescribed and desired objectives. The use of good methods enables the teacher to present materials and learning experiences effectively, creates a favorable climate conducive to learning, tends to prevent wasteful practices and accomplishes results in an efficient manner. Methods provide means of bringing about changes in the habits, knowledges, attitudes and behavior of students. It is tremendously important that the proper method or methods be chosen so that results will be the desired ones. Teachers must have more than knowledge to do their work – they must also know how to apply principles of good teaching. While it is essential for teachers to be adequately prepared and have a full understanding of the subjects they teach, it is also important for them to know how to present their material wisely and to organize educational experiences in the most effective way. The controversy over which is more important, method or content, is an old one which persists today. Both are essential to good teaching. Methods without content are useless, and content without method is ineffective. The question is: Where should the emphasis be placed?

BASES OF METHOD. Methods evolve from knowledge and their choice from philosophy. Methods of physical education come from our knowledge of growth and development, anatomy, physiology, sociology, psychology, education, health and hygiene. We must know all we can about the nature of young people. We must know how and in what respects they differ from one another. We must know how and in what respects they are fundamentally like other individuals. We must be acquainted with and understand the philosophy and policies of the specific school in which teaching is to occur. We must know the kind and content of the program to be taught. The successful teacher is the one who builds his methods upon sound and scientific foundations, upon a deep knowledge of the subject, and who chooses methods which reflect sound and consistent philosophy.

Types of Methods. There are many different ways of guiding students toward desired objectives, of presenting teaching materials effectively and of controlling educational experiences. The wide choice may, at times, be somewhat confusing to the new teacher. It will be an advantage to him, however, to know about and to understand the use of a large variety of methods. He must learn how to choose the right method or methods in accordance with the nature of the material to be taught, the needs of the students, his own philosophy and that of the school community.

There are so many different kinds of methods that it is difficult even to classify them. By analyzing what we use methods for, however, we can classify them according to function and perhaps make them a little more comprehensible to the beginning teacher: methods of motivating students, methods of organizing and arranging classes and class procedures, methods of measuring and testing outcomes of activities, methods of grading results of experience, methods of guiding and controlling behavior and methods of presenting learning materials. It is recognized that these functions may occur separately, together, sequentially, and in some cases continuously (as in evaluating results, guiding behavior and presenting material). Since "presenting material" involves or/and encompasses most all of these functions or is concerned with them, methods relating to this subject are chosen for further development following.

Lecture. A formal and verbal presentation of subject content by the teacher without interruption by students is called the "lecture method." The speaker customarily divides his presentation into three parts: (1) the introduction, where he tells the students what he is going to say, (2) the analysis of the topic or the body of the lecture, where he tells the students the important content of his message, (3) the conclusion, where he brings his lecture to a close with a climax and then summarizes all the important points. Some teachers use this method very skillfully but many do not. Only a very small percentage of the students may get all of the important points from this method alone and many of their questions may be unanswered.

DISCUSSION. This type of method includes questions, answers, and discussion. Both the instructor and students ask and answer questions. There are two types of arrangements: (1) the informational, in which the teacher gives written or oral information to the students and a question and answer session follows. This is similar to an informal lecture method; (2) the developmental, where the class session begins with students asking questions and this is followed by information and discussion by the teacher. Other forms of discussion methods include the panel and forum. The panel is an informal presentation given by several speakers, followed by group discussion. The forum is a formal type of presentation given by several speakers, followed by group discussion. Students usually obtain more information from the discussion than from the lecture method and are customarily more interested but this is still not an ideal method in all respects.

DEMONSTRATION. The instructor shows by practical example some activity, operation or process which involves the use of apparatus, objects or materials when he employs the demonstration method. All kinds of auditory and visual aids may be used here including video tapes and closed-circuit teaching.

GROUP PERFORMANCES. The instructor demonstrates and explains an activity to students. They participate, attempting to perform according to instructions. The instructor then corrects errors, and perhaps demonstrates and explains again. By the combined use of group performance, demonstration and lecture methods a very high percentage of students get all of the important points of instruction.

PROBLEM SOLVING. After sensing a problem the student tries to learn an activity, such as learning to swing a golf club, by trial and error, experimentation and analyzation of his mistakes. This serves as a laboratory experience for him. In an academic situation this would be related to a project or a research problem where the student plans his work, locates the problem, gathers the data, establishes the hypothesis, analyzes and interprets the data. It should not be assumed that the student receives no guidance when this method is properly employed. In no sense is it a "throw out the ball and bat" method of learning.

DRAMATIZATION. Some materials can well be presented through various forms of acting, sociodrama, skits, role playing and brainstorming.

TUTORIAL. In ideal situations one student or a small group of students is guided by one instructor through private lessons, conferences, reading and writing assignments and special examinations. Particular attention is given to the development of the whole student, his total abilities and interests. This method is not remedial in character and is not concerned only with slow students or those having learning difficulty; neither is it restricted to the exceptionally able. It is, however, particularly beneficial for both.

TEAM TEACHING. This method employs a number of teachers in presenting those materials in which each is a specialist. In some respects it is similar to methods used in coaching a sport. In football, there often are instructors for the backfield, the line, the ends. This approach may be used in minor sports classes where skills of several carry-over sports, such as golf, tennis, badminton and archery, are taught in one course. Each instructor teaches only the activities in which he is most proficient. This, it is thought, is more likely to provide a higher quality of instruction than that which would be possible if all were taught by one instructor.

OTHER METHODS. Many other approaches can be employed in presenting material and guiding the educational experiences of students. In many respects they are either similar or are used as adjuncts to or in relation with the methods just described.

Determining Methods

Which method should the teacher choose? Before making this decision there are several points to consider. It is extremely helpful especially to the beginning teacher to have an opportunity to explore all methods of instruction. Part of this experience comes from study of general and special methods in teacher preparatory courses. Other knowledge is gained through observation and actual teaching experiences. The teacher will discover that there is value in each of these methods. He will learn, too, that there is no one best method which will guarantee desirable changes in students. The method that produces good results one time may not create the same results at another time. It is also possible that more than one method might be needed to bring about desired results.

Some of the factors which help to determine which method to use are: (1) the nature of what is to be taught, the character, needs, interests and kinds of experiences of students, the plan of curriculum organization employed by the school (as Dalton unit plan, Gary platoon plan and others), (2) the philosophy held by the teacher and the school administrator. The veteran teacher is also assisted in determining his method or methods by his practical experience, personal observation and intuition. When all of these factors are expressed through his own personality, certain methods (supposedly the most satisfactory for the particular teacher) emerge. The best method or methods are the ones that bring about the best results, the hoped for objectives, the desired changes in students' awareness, habits, skills, knowledge and behavior.

Evaluating the Curriculum

As we have seen in Chapter 10, at least two kinds of evaluation can be made in any school system: one an appraisal of the results of the educative process and the other an appraisal of the results of the administrative process. A complete and satisfactory appraisal of one cannot be made without due consideration of the other since they are dependent upon each other and the latter exists only for the former. The appraisal of the educative process is concerned with evaluating the total progress students make, and the appraisal of the administrative process is concerned with judging the effectiveness of the procedures used in making this progress possible.

Evaluation is the process by which the value of something can be judged in relation to a set of criteria. The criteria in this case are formulated from the principles and objectives of physical education upon which the curriculum is established. Evaluation is a comprehensive process including all the various aspects of learning, grading, measuring, testing, diagnosing, observing and judging. The purposes are to ascertain the changes that occur in students in relation to desired outcomes; to determine the amount and quality of this achievement in terms of attitudes, total fitness, motor and mental skills, ethical character and personality development; to uncover weaknesses and defects by diagnostic means; to counsel, instruct and advise students and to help them make corrections; to inform and praise them for their accomplishments and successes; to motivate and assist teachers to improve their teaching procedures and to encourage them to establish and maintain a harmonious relationship with students.

Since evaluation of the curriculum is accomplished by finding out what changes have occurred, tools or instruments are needed to determine these changes. Some of these are standardized tests and examinations, individual accumulative records, observational appraisals, questionnaires, interviews and surveys. The final steps in the evaluation process are the analysis of the data collected by these instruments, the appraisal of the results and a critical review of these in relation to the objectives. These steps not only assist in gaining understanding but also indicate where improvements need to be made. To keep the curriculum dynamic, evaluations must be continuous. Evaluations in themselves are not effective until the results are put into action and this may sometimes, and usually does, mean revision of the curriculum. Most curriculums are the result of continuous revisions. Some educators, however, seem to be too anxious to make changes on the assumption that change itself is always good. Once a revision is made, ample opportunity should be given for it to be tested before another plan of action is substituted.

Implementing the Curriculum

When we critically study and reflect on some topic, we arrive at certain convictions and beliefs. When we examine the historical, cultural and scientific bases of physical education we learn that there are many factors which influence our thinking and these help us form certain philosophic concepts about it. When these are inspected, logically analyzed and tempered by experience, we arrive at a personal philosophy concerning this subject. This philosophy permeates all of our ways of doing things, the various aspects of the education process, the selection of activities for the curriculum, the methods of teaching and the way the curriculum itself is administered. There are other things also which help us plan and execute the curriculum intelligently and progressively. These are concerned with such procedures and practices as school plans (Gary, Batavia, New Cambridge and others), scheduling of classes, time allotment, academic credit, requirements for graduation, classification and ability grouping of students, classes for the handicapped and for mentally retarded pupils, selection of teachers and administrative personnel, and the provision of supplies, equipment and facilities. The decisions we make relative to these procedures for implementing the curriculum reflect our philosophy and influence the outcomes of the curriculum. The purpose of the curriculum is to provide complete, well-rounded, unified and continuous educational experiences for students so that they can have an opportunity for successful growth and development. The job of the administration is to see that the curriculum is executed effectively. The problems of both must be worked out together. Curriculum and administration are interrelated and interdependent. In both, philosophy plays a basic role.

Revising the Curriculum

To find out about the quality, effectiveness and adaptability of the curriculum (once it is fashioned according to needs and objectives) it must be put into action. When weaknesses show up, when methods fail to produce good results and when more effective methods of teaching or new techniques of presenting materials are found, alterations or modifications should be considered. Other things also influence revision of the curriculum: changing conditions in the social, political, economic and educational climate and environment of the community, the acceptance of a different philosophy, and advances in knowledge.

Evaluation of all these factors may lead to revision of the curriculum. Revision should not be made, however, until the curriculum has been re-examined and it is apparent that changes are really necessary and that conditions will be immeasurably improved thereby. When revisions are made they must be based on results of study and evaluation and not on untried proposals or popular fads. Changes too hastily and thoughtlessly made weaken the effectiveness of the educational experiences of students. Revisions must be made only on the bases of sound facts and good judgment and then be given an opportunity to prove their worthiness before being discarded in favor of another change.

SUMMARY

We have seen that philosophy is essential both in curriculum building and in its administration. In an attempt to bring greater clarification and understanding to curriculum construction, the meaning of certain terms was considered. Many factors were found important to the development of the curriculum: first is the setting of the stage and organizing and planning for it. Next, is the determination of the philosophy and the subsequent formulation of principles, aims, and objectives. Activities and educational experiences for the program were suggested and criteria for their selection proposed. The basic relationship between philosophy and methods to all of these procedures was noted. Finally consideration was given to evaluation, implementation and revision of the curriculum.

QUESTIONS FOR REVIEW AND DISCUSSION

1. Explain the meaning and relationship among the following terms: curriculum, course of study, program, course, unit and lesson plan.
2. Discuss the philosophic bases of curriculum construction.
3. Discuss the influence of community attitude on the physical education curriculum.
4. Discuss the effect that the philosophy of the local and national social government has upon the kind of a curriculum which is developed.
5. How does the philosophy of the professional educators influence the form, style and content of the curriculum?
6. How does the kind of school plan influence the design of the curriculum?

7. Describe procedures for organizing efforts for curriculum development.
8. Discuss factors which aid in determining the philosophy of the curriculum.
9. How can we be reasonably sure that the activities and educational experiences selected for the physical education curriculum will be the most valuable and suitable for the attainment of the desired outcomes?
10. Describe physical education activities and experiences which meet each of the criteria mentioned in question nine.
11. Describe the relationship between philosophy and method.
12. Discuss bases of method.
13. Discuss relative values of different types of methods.
14. Is there a one best method? Explain your answer fully.
15. Describe factors which help to determine which method or methods to use.
16. Discuss the importance of evaluating the curriculum; how often this should be done?
17. What role does philosophy play in curriculum building and curriculum management?
18. When and how often should revisions of curriculum be made?
19. How are revisions made? Upon what are they based?
20. Discuss the validity of the statement, "Since revisions are necessary for the improvement of the curriculum all changes are good."

Bibliography

1. Commission on the Reorganization of Secondary Education, *Cardinal Principles of Secondary Education.* U. S. Bureau of Education Bulletin, Number 35. Washington, D. C.: Government Printing Office, 1918.
2. Cubberly, Ellwood P. *Public Education in the United States.* Boston: Houghton Mifflin Co., 1947, Pp. 521-534.
3. Educational Policies Commission, *The Purposes of Education in American Democracy.* Washington, D. C.: National Education Association, 1938.

Additional References

1. Kowitz, Gerald T., and Henry Hausdorff, "Research to Improve Instruction," *Phi Delta Kappan,* 45:464-466, June, 1964.
2. Shaplin, Judson T., and Henry F. Olds, Jr. *Team Teaching.* New York: Harper and Row, 1964.
3. Beggs III, David W. *Team Teaching – Bold New Venture.* Indianapolis: Unified College Press, 1964.

Part IV

Establishing a System of Values

Values in Physical Education

12

The purposes of this book have been to aid the student and teacher of physical education to arrive at a greater understanding of the philosophic foundations upon which the profession is based by studying the meaning and significance of the various positions of classical philosophy and by interpreting these theories in physical education. In adddition the purposes have been to provide a large store of fundamental knowledge through the study of the social, educational and cultural heritage of the race, through a study of the various factors influencing one's philosophy of physical education and through a study of the elements composing the philosophy of physical education — all of which help the individual to formulate his own personal professional philosophy. One's philosophy cannot be said to be completely formulated or definitely synthesized until he has fully declared and adequately established his own system of values. Setting up a value structure may be said to be the culminating phase of philosophizing. In essence, philosophy is really a study of values. Most decisions in life are determined on the question of values — the rating and significance given to certain things by different people. A greater understanding of values can be obtained and a system of values established by studying their meaning, importance, source, nature, kinds and classification.

THE MEANING OF VALUES

It is impossible to know the full meaning of value(s) until all its characteristics have been analyzed and interpreted; namely, the source, nature and the kinds and classifications. In essence, this is the mission of axiology, which is the scientific study of the general theory of value. As a starting point, however, until all these phases can be explored and developed, we may begin by giving a broad over-all description of value. Value means different things to different people; sometimes different things to the same person at different times and under different circumstances. It is therefore very difficult, if not impossible, to be definite and decisive or to classify all viewpoints under one heading or one nomenclature. To some philosophers and educators, value expresses at least in part a sense of feeling (3:181); a personal and social meaning (1:21); subjective appreciation (12:288); a measure of worth or excellence (5:576); a want determined by choice (7:15); a satisfaction of a human need (11:295); or an object in which someone has taken an interest. (8:874) Montaigne declared that the value we place in things depends upon our own attitudes. (8:878)

Values may be expressed as intrinsic, extrinsic, contributive, instrumental, individual, social, subjective and objective. These terms and others will be discussed later in this chapter. In order to have a valuing transaction or to conduct a valuing process there must be someone to do the valuing and an object or thing to be valued. Without going into any specific category and giving only a general definition at this time, one may express value as the preferred worth, appreciation, feeling and desire that an individual has for an object or thing in and of itself in comparison with some other object or thing. The term value is an important aspect of philosophy; in fact, one of the main tasks of philosophy is to determine the meanings and values of things and to organize them into an adequate system, order or scale of qualitative worth. (11:106)

THE IMPORTANCE OF VALUE

Values are an important aspect of one's philosophy. They shape and color one's philosophy by influencing the way he thinks, acts and deports himself in his personal and professional life. They influence the kind of parent, neighbor, physician, lawyer, statesman, teacher, administrator, student or business person one is.

To teachers, administrators and other school officials, values are important in helping in the selection of many things: (1) worthwhile objectives arranged from immediate to remote and learning experiences arranged from simple to complex, with both objectives and learning experiences organized according to the needs, wants, interests and ability of students; (2) academic and motor activities for the physical education program relative to number and kind, the place of importance (great, moderate or little emphasis) in the program and the provision or personal, social, moral as well as physical fitness values; (3) equipment and facilities which are adequate, durable, safe and commensurate with the need of the program of activities; (4) qualified personnel who have both desirable personal characteristics and academic competencies to teach and conduct the program; (5) various teaching methods and techniques as formal, informal, direct, indirect, progressive, conservative, lecture, conferences, demonstrations, projects, problem solving and others suitable to the type of activities presented and the nature of the students; (6) the type of administrative organization — line, line and staff or functional — which is adequate, efficient, productive and which will bring about the attainment of the desired objectives of the program: the well-integrated individual who will make the most useful, finest and happiest member of society. Values are essential in determining policies and standards by which the administrative staff can carry out the complete educational process.

Individuals are continuously confronted with the problem of making choices in both personal and professional life. The value we place (for whatever reason(s)) on certain things determines our choices. The environment in which we live, and to a certain degree the physical and mental characteristics we have inherited, influence our reasons for these choices. It is the responsibility of the teachers, in fact of all the school personnel as well as every adult in the community, to help youngsters by precepts and exemplary behavior (especially the latter) develop the right values in order that they can establish a fine personal value system upon which to build their lives. Values are important because they do influence behavior; they are important because they help us to interpret conditions, situations and events in life. It is essential that we continuously re-examine our value system critically and reflectively, in the light of new educational and scientific advancements and in the face of changing situations of our times, if we are to be prepared as individuals (teachers, students, and business and professional people) to meet and solve the new problems of life and to be reasonably happy, useful and successful citizens.

SOURCES AND NATURE OF VALUES

Men have been studying and theorizing about values since the dawn of Western Civilization. They have discussed values and the theory of values freely and have given them an important position in their pronouncements, oral and written. Values have always been an integral part of philosophy and of education throughout the ages. Plato in his theory of Forms or Ideas, which was later developed by Aristotle, initiated the theory of values. Subsequently, throughout history other great philosophers and educators such as Benedict Spinoza, Immanuel Kant, Georg Wilhelm Friedrich Hegel, R. H. Lotze, W. R. Sorley, R. B. Perry, J. Laird, T. H. Green, John Dewey and many others have contributed different but important concepts to the general theory of value. (10:32)

Values come from few or many sources depending upon the philosophic position(s) one holds and the way one classifies the various kinds of values.

An idealist would say that the major values, such as beauty, goodness and truth, come from the Supreme Being or God and that they are permanent, universal and unchanging. Values are intrinsic and found in the nature of things. They emphasize the subjective side of things. Values must be sought. A realist, on the other hand, believes values come from Nature and appear to him through his senses. He views things objectively for the most part, yet he believes as does the idealist in the concepts of the good life and believes that they can be passed on to posterity. A pragmatist would say that values are derived from the experiences an individual has within a society, from the things he observes and participates in, from those things which come from his interests and needs and from the continuous adjustment he makes to his ever-changing environment. He believes values may change with every changing condition and situation and in different periods of time. Some values come from the needs that individuals have in plain everyday living. These are, for the most part, biophysical, psychological, sociological, economic, educational and religious.

Biophysical needs are those concerned with food, rest, sleep, relaxation and exercise. These are necessary for growth and maintenance of body and mind, for health, and for supply of energy for learning, mental and motor skills.

Psychological needs are those related to man's wants, desires, ambitions, interests, emotions, feelings, attitudes and convictions. Man needs recognition for the things he does; he needs to feel he is important and is successful; he needs to feel that he belongs somewhere and to something; he needs to be creative and to have opportunity for self-expression. These things are of value to him; they are intrinsic and they cannot be purchased.

Sociological needs are those concerned with all forms of human relationships, with the customs, traditions, folklore and mores of one's society. Society sets up its own values which influences the individual's standard of values. These values may differ from community to community. What is acceptable in one community may not be acceptable in another. Man, however, lives generally by what Kant called the "law of categorical imperative" – that is, man lives by moral laws and has a duty to refrain from doing something he would not want someone else to do for such action might jeopardize society. The major values set up by society therefore are those of enduring quality such as honesty, fair play, respect for individual rights, unselfishness, equality of man and brotherly love. Men, however, interpret these values differently when applied to themselves and this sometimes causes disagreements, conflicts and wars.

Economic needs are those related to temporal things, those things which have monetary value and can be purchased. The values placed on these needs are considered by some authorities as instrumental and secondary. They are not the permanent or real values in life. In practice, however, many people place great importance on them. They labor under the conception that money and the possession of worldly goods can bring them happiness. This, many scholars think, is the main root of most of the evils of society today: expendable values have been accepted instead of the enduring ones.

Religious needs are those concerned with spiritual guidance and direction. Most people recognize there is some power greater than themselves, whatever they may call it: Nature, Universe, Idea, Mind, Spirit, Supreme Being or God. Man has need to place his faith in something outside of self, to have some ultimate aim and worthy ideals for which to strive; he has need for some power to guide him through alternate periods of trials and tribulations and joys and happiness in life. It has been demonstrated many times throughout history that man can endure better the rigorous vicissitudes of life if he has strong convictions and great faith. This power is of great value to him.

KINDS AND CLASSIFICATION OF VALUES

We have learned something about the sources and nature of values. We know that they come from needs that individuals have in everyday living in the community in their homes, schools, churches, businesses, occupations, professions and organizations. We know that values are dependent upon and vary according to one's interests, attitudes, wants, desires, prejudices, biases and preferences. We know that values change or vary according to time and place, from person to person, and with changing conditions. Since values come from so many different individuals, from so many phases of life and are affected by so many changing situations it is evident that they would exist in a large variety of types, in great numbers and in different degrees of rank. The fact that many people have different ideas about the meaning, nature and number of values indicates the complexity of value concepts. Because of this complexity, values practically defy comprehensive classification. About the only consensus which exists among authorities concerning values is that certain groups are identifiable. Regardless of the difficulty of classification, it is deemed helpful to the physical education student and teacher from the standpoint of further clarification and use of values to consider the possible kinds, grouping and/or classifications.

What are the kinds of values people live with and the choices they make in everyday living? Values resolve themselves into choices we make in the kind of food we eat, the type of physical exercise we participate in, the mental and physical relaxation we take, whether we rest, work, study or go to a show tonight, whether we choose to be happy or sad today when we awake, whether we develop the habit of negative or positive thinking; the choice we make concerning jobs, professions, friends, religious faiths, political beliefs, art, and music; the choices we make between wealth and fame or service to mankind; and whether we accept honesty and integrity or greed, selfishnesses and exploitations as a way of life. The following is a list of headings under which these and many other values could be grouped: biological, physiological, sociological, psychological, intellectual, spiritual, cultural, economic, moral, philosophical, democratic and personal. It is found, however, that many values can be categorized under more than one heading as for example recreation, which could easily be classified under biological, physiological, psychological and moral to name a few. There is no exact or definite identification. This inability to classify recreation as a value does not in any way detract from any of its worthwhileness. Instead, the fact that it has a broad meaning with many characteristics and can be identified with several categories indicates potential of great usefulness. We see, then, that values are of many kinds and range from the simple, practical, expendable and immediate ones through the intermediate to the more complex, ultimate and enduring ones.

Values Classified According to Essentials of Human Living

Many attempts have been made to group or classify values. A few are mentioned for extension of our discussion. Kilpatrick recognized four basic-value assumptions: (1) "The Living of People is the Primary Value." Within this is the basis for everything; (2) "The Good Life is the Inclusive Aim." Life has meaning only if it is a good life; (3)

"Morality is a Social Necessity." We live together in a world community where our acts affect all others. We have a moral obligation to live a high quality of life; (4) "Democracy is the Chosen Way of Life." The great concern here is respect for "liberty, equality and regard for the common good." (7:420-421) As has been stated previously, other writers over the years have stressed basic values of beauty, truth and goodness, and still others have added social justice, brotherhood of man and respect for individual personality to the list.

Everett, in discussing human values lists eight different kinds: economic, bodily, recreation, association, character, aesthetic, intellectual and religious. (6:182) He hastens to say, however, that these values are not entirely separate and unrelated, but overlap and interpenetrate each other. There are no fixed boundaries. Parker lists nine major classifications: self-preservation or health, comfort, ambition, workmanship, love, knowledge, play, art and religion. (9:47) Horne suggests a similar list: health, character, social justice, skill, art, love, knowledge, philosophy and religion. (13:190) We see that there are some similarities, some duplications and some differences. Differences are caused by different views, beliefs and convictions and the different amount and kind of emphasis placed on certain aspects of human living.

Values Classified According to Certain Identifiable Characteristics and Qualities

Perhaps the values most frequently mentioned can be classified as intrinsic and extrinsic. Intrinsic values, sometimes called mediate, are those which are considered by an individual to have worth within themselves — those which do not lead to anything else or depend upon other things for worthiness, but are ends in themselves. These are the permanent, unchanging values we seek as ends in life. They are underlying values of goodness upon which existence of society depends. Moral and spiritual values, for example, are some of the important, if not the most important, ends of life and should not be usurped by power, prestige, fame, wealth and influence. Moral and spiritual values play an important part in education, in physical education and the daily life of every individual. This has been aptly emphasized by the Educational Policies Commission in the booklet entitled, *Moral and Spiritual Values in the Public Schools*, in which are discussed ten essential values of life: human personality — the basic value, moral responsibility, institutions as the servants of men, common consent, devotion to truth, respect for excellence, moral equality, brotherhood, the pursuit of happiness and spiritual enrichment. (4:17-29)

Intrinsic values, furthermore, are concerned with ideals, inspirations, aspirations, imaginations and the feelings one has toward something, some condition or object; for example, the feeling of awe, wonderment and appreciation one has as he observes the skillful technique of musicians in a famous symphony orchestra and hears the varying strains of beautiful musical harmony; or the satisfaction one experiences as a counselor when helping a youngster surmount some of his personal and academic problems and in aiding him to adjust to difficult life situations; or the thrill one experiences as he watches the highly competitive performance of two skilled football teams. In these instances, a person finds value in the skill, grace and precision of the performance of the musicians and football players and finds value in the satisfaction of knowing he has helped a student in living a successful and happy life.

Extrinsic values are those which lead to something else and are a means of attaining other good things or bringing about certain consequences. Since they are means toward attaining other things, they are also called instrumental. For the most part, these values lie in the practical affairs of everyday living. They are things we see and use in the physical world: clothes, automobiles, airplanes, books, money, power, strength, facts, and records. A boy, for example, finds a job to make money in order to finance his way through college. This job is instrumental in helping him obtain an education. It is valued as a means to some other value. Some authorities feel that all values are basically intrinsic because even in using things as means to other things individuals experience intrinsic value. Others feel that all values are extrinsic because it is impossible, they say, to have a feeling of enjoyment or satisfaction which does not lead to something else. (2:20) There is a possibility, therefore, that there is no purely intrinsic or extrinsic value and that intrinsic value may easily change to extrinsic or vice versa. A job, for instance, may be valued at present as a good thing in itself (intrinsic), but later it may be used as a means to become a physician, a lawyer, minister, physical education teacher or coach (extrinsic).

Others classify values as subjective and objective. Subjective values relate to a person's feeling and awarenes. They pertain to the mind and those experiences which are satisfying and interesting to the individual. These are values that the individual places in an object or thing because interest in it brings about a satisfying state of affairs. The object is not of value outside of the interest in it. (11:300) Thus the experience of playing tennis or observing a beautiful sunset may be a subjective value to a person who is interested in them and finds them satisfying. Another individual may not experience the same response. But he might place value in some other experience such as playing a musical instrument or dancing. Some experiences may be not only unsatisfying and uninteresting to an individual, they may be actually annoying and distasteful or bad. In this case, they would not be values. We see, therefore, that subjective values may vary from person to person. One of our jobs as physical education leaders is to convince laymen, professional people and students of the purposes and benefits of physical education, and thus to inject value into physical and recreational activities.

Objective values are those which exist in the world whether or not they are observed. They do not depend upon the imagination, desires, hopes and fears of the individual. They are real and have only to be discovered. Objects, things and experiences seem to have value for the individual; therefore, he takes an interest in them. There is something present in objects such as color, shape and size that is not completely dependent upon judgment. Things in nature such as sunsets, rainbows and flowers are beautiful. Beauty resides in them and exists for everyone to see. The act of judging is not beautiful, but the forms, colors, and sizes that make up the scene are. Beauty is always beauty. It has only to be discovered. It, like goodness and truth, can exist alike in the minds of people, except for differences in individuals resulting from different social and cultural heritage. (11:301-302) When beauty is considered to exist only in the object, it has objective value. When it is considered to exist only in the mind, it has subjective value. In the actual process of evaluation, however, there is considerable relationship and interaction between these two types of values.

Some classify values as individual, social, absolute and relative. (2:18-24). Individual values are those which are more closely associated with and held by the individual and depend upon his interests and preferences; for example, one person may prefer to play golf rather than tennis; another may prefer a quiet type of recreational activity such as checker playing or watching television rather than a physical activity such as badminton. Individual values have a tendency to be instrumental and subjective in character and, when speaking of motor activities, are concerned with such factors as body physique, neuromuscular skill, physical fitness, rhythm and balance.

Social values are those associated with and held by the group. They are concerned with such factors as respect for the rights and property of others, honesty, integrity, trust in dealing with people and loyalty to the group. Social values have a tendency to be objective and intrinsic in character.

Absolute values are those which are unlimited, unchanging, universal and self-contained such as beauty, goodness and truth. Some believe that all values come from the Supreme Being, God; others from Nature (Rousseau), from energy (Spencer), or from pleasure and happiness (Epicurus).

Relative values are those which change or are limited because of changing conditions, time, place and situations and differences of personal opinion. If we say that physical education is good for everyone and should be required of all students, we are assuming it to be an absolute value. If we say, however, that physical education is a question of personal preference, we are assuming it to be a relative value. Concerning the question of exercise, the first problem to solve is whether or not exercise is good for all individuals. After the answer to this problem is obtained, the next question to decide is how much exercise an individual should have for happiness and well-being. Positive answers are not available but perhaps it should be noted that some psychologists list muscular exercise as one of the basic human needs.

FORMING VALUES

How are values established? In the first place, to have a valuing transaction, there must be someone to do the valuing and an object or thing to be valued. We have already seen that value has something to do with preferred worth, appreciation and feeling which an individual has for an object or thing. We have seen that values come from needs, wants, desires, attitudes, interests, biases and prejudices. These are influenced by factors of heredity and environment and by one's associates, parents, teachers, peer group and so on. Satisfying and annoying experiences, failures and success, awards and punishments, poverty and wealth, good and bad people all influence the value we place in and on objects and things. Life is composed of struggles and conflicts. Man must strive for the things he wants and out of this striving he learns to make choices, to reflect, to reason, and to evaluate. From this process of evaluation, values are formed.

All values are not formed incidentally or accidentally through the process of maturing. Much too often their formation is left to chance and many times proper values are not formed. Values influence behavior and are too important to be left entirely to chance. As teachers and coaches of physical education and athletic sports we have the great responsibility of arranging and conducting our programs in such a way that the experiences students have under our tutelage will demonstrate and illustrate the enduring and essential values of human living. It is our duty to help them see and place value in their activities and experiences, to know the meanings of values and how they can be applied in their daily lives. The best way to help students form values is by setting a good example. Students learn a great deal and derive many lasting impressions from watching and imitating their teachers and other adults. This is a better way of influencing the formation of values than by precept. Both, however, are needed and serve important purposes at the appropriate time and situation.

A SYSTEM OF VALUES

As an individual matures and forms values about many conditions, situations, objects, things and experiences in life, he eventually possesses a large store and many kinds of values. Some values form around other similar but larger and more central values thus composing a group of values. Gradually these various groups of values become polarized around a still larger and more central value until a semblance of a system or a structure of values is established. This system of values is formulated through the process of criticising, analyzing, comparing, reflective thinking, reasoning and observing value concepts. Thus a person slowly and eventually establishes a personal value system by which he will live, be guided and directed in all of his activities and experiences and this will influence his behavior for better or for worse. We hope for the better. The essential thing is for the teacher, parent and other adults to help youngsters early in life to make wise choices and to establish a structure of values which can serve as a basis of judgment as well as of action in guiding, motivating and propelling him, within his capabilities and potentialities, toward the goal of becoming the best integrated individual and most useful citizen possible. He must, however, continuously re-examine his system of values in respect to the changing conditions of time, place, situation and new scientific knowledge in order to live the most effective, efficient and abundant life. He must also remember, however, that there are enduring values such as goodness, honesty, truth, integrity, love, and unselfishness which are not affected by time, place, or situation. They are permanent and everlasting. The establishment of a personal system of values is the finalizing act in the process of formulating one's philosophy of life, of education and physical education. Philosophy is the critical study, examination and evaluation of value.

QUESTIONS FOR REVIEW AND DISCUSSION

1. What is the meaning of value(s)? Discuss what different authorities believe to be the central theme of value.

2. How important are values in relation to shaping and formulating one's philosophy?
3. How can teachers, administrators and other school officials help students in selecting values?
4. What are some of the things, in connection with the school environment, which values help to select and to determine?
5. Name and discuss the sources of value. Are there few or many? Upon what does the number of sources depend?
6. From what source would each of the following philosophers say values come: an idealist, a realist, a pragmatist and a naturalist?
7. Values, among other things, come from needs which individuals have in daily living. How can these needs be classified? Explain each classification.
8. Name all of the kinds of values of human living you can think of.
9. Name and discuss how some authorities classify human values. Discuss their similarities and differences. Why do you think these occur?
10. Explain and discuss the meaning of the following terms in relation to values: intrinsic, extrinsic, subjective, individual, social, absolute and relative.
11. How are values established? Are they formed incidentally, accidentally, concomitantly, purposefully or by chance?
12. What is a system of values? How is it formed? Of what value is it?
13. What is the finalizing act in the formation of one's philosophy?
14. What is philosophy? What does it mean to you? Have you reexamined your philosophy recently in light of changing conditions of time, place or situations? Have you noticed any changes or modifications in your philosophy?

Bibliography

1. American Association for Health, Physical Education and Recreation, "Values in Sports." Washington, D. C.: National Education Association, 1963.
2. DAVIS, ELWOOD CRAIG, AND GENE A. LOGAN. *Biophysical Values of Muscular Activity*. Dubuque: Wm. C. Brown Company Publishers, 1961.
3. DAVIS, ELWOOD CRAIG, AND EARL L. WALLIS. *Toward Better Teaching in Physical Education*. Englewood Cliffs: Prentice-Hall, Inc., 1961.
4. Educational Policies Commission, "Moral and Spiritual Values in Public Schools." Washington, D. C.: National Education Association, 1951.
5. ENGLISH, HORACE B., AND AVA C. ENGLISH. *A Comprehensive Dictionary of Psychological and Psychoanalytical Terms*. New York: Longmans, Green and Company, 1961.

6. EVERETT, WALTER G. *Moral Values.* New York: Henry Holt and Company, 1918.
7. KILPATRICK, WILLIAM H. *Philosophy of Education.* New York: The Macmillan Company, 1951.
8. MAGILL, FRANK N. *Masterpieces of World Philosophies in Summary Form.* New York: Salem Press, Inc., 1961. Volume II.
9. PARKER, DEWITT. *Human Values.* New York: Harper and Brothers, 1931.
10. RUNES, DAGOBERT D. *Dictionary of Philosophy.* Paterson: Littlefield, Adams and Company, 1962.
11. TITUS, HAROLD H. *Living Issues in Philosophy.* New York: American Book Company, 1946.
12. WARREN, HOWARD C. *Dictionary of Psychology.* Boston: Houghton Mifflin Company, 1934.
13. ZEIGLER, EARLE F. *Philosophical Foundations for Physical, Health and Recreation Education.* Englewood Cliffs: Prentice-Hall, Inc., 1964.

INDEX